THE WORKS OF JOHN MILTON

THE WORKS OF
JOHN MILTON

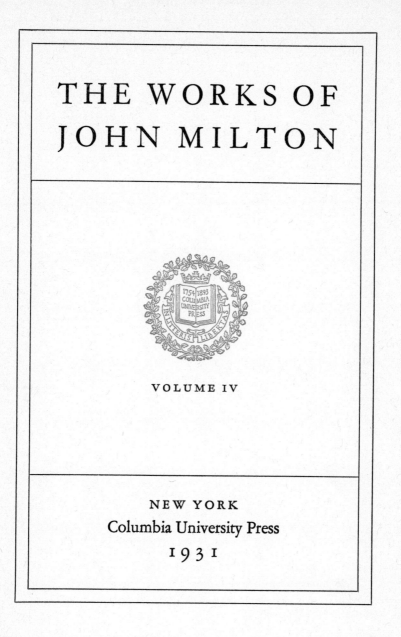

VOLUME IV

NEW YORK

Columbia University Press

1931

PRINTED IN THE UNITED STATES OF AMERICA
BY THE PRINTING HOUSE OF WILLIAM EDWIN RUDGE, INC.
MOUNT VERNON, NEW YORK

CONTENTS

ILLUSTRATIONS

THE JUDGEMENT OF MARTIN BUCER,
CONCERNING DIVORCE

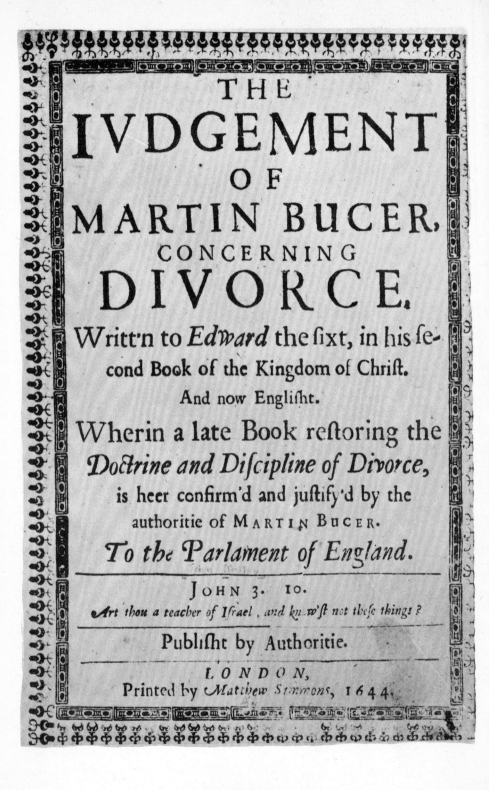

THE
IVDGEMENT
OF
MARTIN BUCER,
CONCERNING
DIVORCE.

Writt'n to *Edward* the sixt, in his second Book of the Kingdom of Christ.
And now Englisht.

Wherin a late Book restoring the *Doctrine and Discipline of Divorce,* is heer confirm'd and justify'd by the authoritie of MARTIN BUCER.

To the Parlament of England.

JOHN 3. 10.
Art thou a teacher of Israel, and kn.w'st not these things?

Publisht by Authoritie.

LONDON,
Printed by *Matthew Simmons,* 1644.

Testimonies of the high approbation

Which learned men have given of *Martin Bucer*.

Simon Grynæus, 1533.

AMONG all the *Germans,* I give the palm to *Bucer* for excellence in the Scriptures. *Melanchton* in human learning is wondrous fluent; but greater knowl-
5 edge in the Scripture I attribute to *Bucer,* and speak it un-fainedly.

John Calvin, 1539.

Martin Bucer a most faithfull Doctor of the Church of Christ, besides his rare learning, & copious knowledge of
10 many things, besides his cleernes of wit, much reading, and other many and various vertues, wherein he is almost by none now living excell'd, hath few equalls, and excells most, hath this praise peculiar to himself, that none in this age hath us'd exacter diligence in the exposition of Scripture.

15   *And a little beneath.*

Bucer is more large then to be read by over-busied men, and too high to be easily understood by unattentive men, and of a low capacitie.

Sir John Cheek, Tutor to K. Edw. the sixth. 1551.

20 Wee have lost our Master, then whom the world scarce held a greater, whether we consider his knowledge of true Religion, or his integrity and innocence of life, or his inces-

sant study of holy things, or his matchless labour of promoting piety, or his authority and amplitude of teaching, or what ever els was praise-worthy and glorious in him. *Script. Anglicana, pag.* 864.

5   *John Sturmius of Strasborrow.*

No man can be ignorant what a great and constant opinion and estimation of *Bucer* there is in *Italy, France,* and *England.* Whence the saying of *Quintilian* hath oft come to my minde, that he hath well profited in Eloquence whom *Cicero*
10 pleases. The same say I of *Bucer,* that he hath made no small progress in Divinitie, whom *Bucer* pleases; for in his Volumes, which he wrote very many, there is the plain impression to be discern'd of many great vertues, of diligence, of charitie, of truth, of acutenes, of judgment, of learning.
15 Wherin he hath a certain proper kind of writing, wherby he doth not only teach the Reader, but affects him with the sweetness of his sentences, and with the manner of his arguing, which is so teaching, and so logical, that it may be perceiv'd how learnedly he separates probable reasons from
20 necessary, how forcibly he confirms what he has to prove how suttly he refutes, not with sharpnes, but with truth.

Theodore Beza on the portraiture of M. Bucer.

This is that countnance of *Bucer,* the mirror of mildnes, temper'd with gravitie; to whom the Citie of *Strasburgh*
25 owes the reformation of her Church. Whose singular learning, and eminent zeal, joyn'd with excellent wisdom, both

his learned books, and public disputations in the general diets
of the Empire, shall witness to all ages. Him the *German*
persecution drove into *England;* where honourably entertain'd by *Edward* the sixt, he was for two years chief pro-
5 fessor of Divinity in *Cambridge,* with greatest frequency and
applause of all learned and pious men untill his death. 1551.
Bezæ Icones.

Mr. *Fox book of Martyrs, Vol.* 3. *p.* 763.

Bucer what by writing, but chiefly by reading and preach-
10 ing openly, wherin being painfull in the Word of GOD, he
never spar'd himself, nor regarded his health, brought all
men into such an admiration of him, that neither his friends
could sufficiently praise him, nor his enemies in any point
find fault with his singular life, & sincere doctrine. A most
15 certain tok'n wherof may be his sumptuous burial at *Cambridge,* solemniz'd with so great an assistance of all the Universitie, that it was not possible to devise more to the setting
out and amplifying of the same.

Dr. *Pern the Popish Vicechancelour of Cambridge*
20   *his adversary.*

Cardinal *Pool* about the fourth year of Queen *Mary,* intending to reduce the Universitie of *Cambridge* to Popery
again, thought no way so effectuall, as to cause the bones of
Martin Bucer and *Paulus Fagius,* which had been foure years
25 in the grave, to be tak'n up and burnt openly with thir Books,
as knowing that those two worthy men had bin of greatest

moment to the reformation of that place from Popery, and
had left such powerfull seeds of thir doctrine behind them, as
would never die, unless the men themselvs were diggd up,
and openly condemn'd for heretics by the Universitie it self.
5 This was put in execution, and Doctor *Pern* Vicechancelor
appointed to preach against *Bucer.* Who among other things
laid to his charge the opinions which he held of the marriage
of Priests, of divorcement, and of usury. But immediatly
after his Sermon, or somwhat before, as the Book of Martyrs
10 for a truth relates, *Vol.* 3. *p.* 770. the said Doctor *Pern*
smiting himself on the breast, and in manner weeping, wisht
with all his heart, that God would grant his soul might then
presently depart, and remain with *Bucers;* for he knew his
life was such, that if any mans soul were worthy of heaven,
15 he thought *Bucers* in special, to be most worthy, *Histor. de
Combust. Buceri, & Fagii.*

Acworth the Universitie Orator.

Soon after, that Queen *Elizabeth* came to the crown, this
condemnation of *Bucer* and *Fagius* by the Cardinal and his
20 Doctors, was solemnly repeal'd by the Universitie; and the
memory of those two famous men celebrated in an Oration
by *Acworth* the Universitie Orator, which is yet extant in the
Book of Martyrs, *Vol.* 3. *p.* 773. and in Latin. *Scripta
Anglic. p.* 936.
25 *Nicolas Carre,* a learned man, *Walter Haddon* Maister of
the Requests to Queen *Elizabeth, Matthew Parker,* afterwards Primate of *England,* with other eminent men, in their

funeral Orations and Sermons expresse abundantly how great a man *Martin Bucer* was, what an incredible losse *England* sustain'd in his death; and that with him dy'd the hope of a perfet reformation for that age. *Ibid.*

5   *Iacobus Verheiden of Grave, in his Elogies*
                    of famous Divines.

Though the name of *Martin Luther* be famous, yet thou *Martin Bucer,* for piety, learning, labour, care, vigilance, and writing, art not to be held inferior to *Luther. Bucer* was a
10 singular instrument of God, so was *Luther.* By the death of this most learned and most faithfull man, the Church of Christ sustaind a heavy losse; as *Calvin* witnesseth; and they who are studious of *Calvin,* are not ignorant how much he ascribes to *Bucer;* for thus he writes in a Letter to *Viretus:*
15 What a manifold losse befell the Church of God in the death of *Bucer,* as oft as I call to minde, I feel my heart almost rent asunder.

Peter Martyr, Epist. to Conradus Hubertus.

He is dead, who hath overcome in many battells of the
20 Lord. God lent us for a time this our Father, and our Teacher, never enough prais'd. Death hath divided me from a most unanimous friend, one truly according to mine own heart. My minde is overprest with grief, in so much that I have not power to write more. I bid thee in Christ farewell, and wish
25 thou maist be able to beare the losse of *Bucer,* better then I can beare it.

Testimonies giv'n by learned men to Paulus Fagius,
who held the same opinion with Martin Bucer
concerning Divorce.

    Paulus Fagius born in the *Palatinate*, became most skilfull *Bezæ*
5 in the Hebrew tongue. Beeing call'd to the Ministery at *Icones.*
Isna, he publisht many ancient and profitable Hebrew Books,
being aided in the expenses by a Senator of that Citie, as
Origen somtime was by a certain rich man call'd *Ambrosius.*
At length invited to *Strasburgh,* he there famously discharg'd
10 the office of a Teacher; until the same persecution drove him
and *Bucer* into *England,* where he was preferr'd to a Professors place in *Cambridge,* and soon after died.

    Melchior Adamus writes his life among the famous *Ger-*
man Divines.

15   *Sleidan* and *Thuanus* mention him with honour in their
History. And *Verheiden* in his *Elogies.*

To the Parlament.

THE Book which among other great and high points of reformation, contains as a principall part thereof, this treatise here presented, Supreme Court of Parlament, was by the famous *Author* Martin Bucer, dedicated to Edward *the sixt: whose incomparable youth doubtless had brought forth to the Church of England such a glorious manhood, had his life reacht it, as would have left in the affairs of religion, nothing without an excellent pattern for us now to follow. But since the secret purpose of divine appointment hath reserv'd no lesse perhaps then the just half of such a sacred work to be accomplisht in this age, and principally, as we trust, by your successful wisdom and authority, religious Lords and Commons, what wonder if I seek no other, to whose exactest judgement, and revieu I may commend these last and worthiest labours of this renowned teacher: whom living, all the pious nobility of those reforming times, your truest and best imitated ancestors, reverenc't and admir'd. Nor was he wanting to a recompence as great as was himself; when both at many times before, and especially among his last sighs and prayers testifying his dear and fatherly affection to the Church and Realm of England, he sincerely wisht in the hearing of many devout men,* that what he had in this his last book written to King *Edward* concerning discipline, might have place in this Kingdom. His hope was then that no calamity, no confusion, or

*Nicol. Car.
de obit
Buceri.

deformity would happen to the Common-wealth; but
otherwise he fear'd, lest in the midst of all this ardency
to know God, yet by the neglect of discipline, our good
endeavours would not succeed. *These remarkable words*
5 *of so godly and so eminent a man at his death, as they are*
related by a sufficient and well known witnes, who heard
them and inserted by Thuanus *into his grave and serious*
history, so ought they to be chiefly consider'd by that nation
for whose sake they were utter'd, and more especially by
10 *that general Counsel which represents the body of that*
nation. If therfore the book, or this part therof, for neces-
sary causes, be now reviv'd and recommended to the use of
this undisciplin'd age, it hence appears that these reasons
have not err'd in the choyce of a fit patronage, for a dis-
15 *course of such importance. But why the whole tractat is*
not heer brought entire, but this matter of divorcement se-
lected in particular, to prevent the full speed of some mis-
interpreter, I hasten to disclose. First, it will be soon man-
ifest to them who know what wise men should know, that
20 *the constitution and reformation of a common-wealth, if*
Ezra *and* Nehemiah *did not mis-reform; is, like a build-*
ing, to begin orderly from the foundation therof, which is
mariage and the family, to set right first what ever is amisse
therein. How can there els grow up a race of warrantable
25 *men, while the house and home that breeds them, is troubl'd*
and disquieted under a bondage not of Gods constraining
with a natureles constraint (if his most righteous judge-
ments may be our rule) but laid upon us imperiously in

*the worst and weakest ages of knowledge, by a canonicall
tyranny of stupid and malicious Monks: who having
rashly vow'd themselves to a single life, which they could
not undergoe, invented new fetters to throw on matrimony,*
5 *that the world thereby waxing more dissolute, they also in
a general loosnes might sin with more favor. Next, there
being yet among many, such a strange iniquity and perversnes against all necessary divorce, while they will needs
expound the words of our Saviour not duly by comparing*
10 *other places, as they must doe in the resolving of a hunder'd
other Scriptures, but by persisting deafely in the abrupt
and Papistical way of a literal apprehension against the
direct* analogy *of sense, reason, law and Gospel, it therfore
may well seem more then time to apply the sound and holy*
15 *persuasions of this Apostolic man, to that part in us,
which is not yet fully dispossest of an error as absurd, as
most that we deplore in our blindest adversaries; and to
let his autority and unanswerable reasons be vulgarly
known, that either his name, or the force of his doctrine*
20 *may work a wholsom effect. Lastly, I find it cleer to be the
authors intention that this point of divorcement should be
held and receav'd as a most necessary and prime part of
discipline in every Christian government. And therfore
having reduc't his model of reformation to 14. heads,*
25 *he bestows almost as much time about this one point of
divorce, as about all the rest; which also was the judgement of his heirs and learned friends in Germany, best
acquainted with his meaning; who first publishing this*

his book by Oporinus *at* Basil *(a Citie for learning and
constancie in the true faith, honorable among the first)
added a special note in the title,* that there the reader
should finde the doctrine of Divorce handl'd so solidly,
5 and so fully, as scars the like in any Writer of that age:
*and with this particular commendation they doubted not
to dedicate the book, as a most profitable & exquisit discours, to* Christian *the 3ᵈ, a worthy & pious King of*
Denmark, *as the author himself had done before to our*
10 Edward *the sixt. Yet did not* Bucer *in that volume only
declare what his constant opinion was herein, but also in
his comment upon* Matthew, *written at* Strasburgh *divers
years before, he treats distinctly and copiously the same
argument in three severall places; touches it also upon the*
15 7. *to the* Romans, *& promises the same solution more
largely upon the* 1. *to the* Corinthians, *omitting no occasion
to weed out this last and deepest mischief of the Canon law
sown into the opinions of modern men against the lawes
and practice both of Gods chosen people, and the best*
20 *primitive times. Wherin his faithfulnes and powerful evidence prevail'd so farre with all the Church of* Strasburgh,
*that they publisht this doctrine of divorce, as an article of
their confession, after they had taught so eight and twenty
years, through all those times, when that Citie flourisht,*
25 *and excell'd most, both in religion, lerning, and good goverment, under those first restorers of the Gospel there,* Zellius, Hedio, Capito, Fagius, *and those who incomparably
then govern'd the Common-wealth,* Farrerus *and* Sturmius.

*If therefore God in the former age found out a servant, and
by whom he had converted and reform'd many a citie, by
him thought good to restore the most needfull doctrine of
divorce from rigorous and harmfull mistakes on the right
5 hand, it can be no strange thing if in this age he stirre up
by whatsoever means whom it pleases him, to take in hand
& maintain the same assertion. Certainly if it be in mans
discerning to sever providence from chance, I could allege
many instances, wherin there would appear cause to es-
10 teem of me no other then a passive instrument under some
power and counsel higher and better then can be human,
working to a general good in the whole cours of this matter.
For that I ow no light, or leading receav'd from any man
in the discovery of this truth, what time I first undertook it
15 in the* doctrine and discipline of divorce, *and had only
the infallible grounds of Scripture to be my guide, he who
tries the inmost heart, and saw with what severe industry
and examination of my self, I set down every period, will
be my witnes. When I had almost finisht the first edition,
20 I chanc't to read in the notes of* Hugo Grotius *upon the 5.
of Matth. whom I strait understood inclining to reasonable terms in this controversie: and somthing he whisper'd
rather then disputed about the law of charity, and the true
end of wedlock. Glad therfore of such an able assistant,
25 how ever at much distance, I resolv'd at length to put off
into this wild and calumnious world. For God, it seems,
intended to prove me, whether I durst alone take up a
rightful cause against a world of disesteem, & found I*

*durst. My name I did not publish, as not willing it should
sway the reader either for me or against me. But when I
was told, that the stile, which what it ailes to be so soon
distinguishable, I cannot tell, was known by most men,*
5 *and that some of the Clergie began to inveigh and exclaim
on what I was credibly inform'd they had not read, I took
it then for my proper season both to shew them a name
that could easily contemn such an indiscreet kind of censure, and to reinforce the question with a more accurat*
10 *diligence: that if any of them would be so good as to leav
rayling, and to let us hear so much of his lerning and
Christian wisdom, as will be strictly demanded of him in
his answering to this probleme, care was had he should not
spend his preparations against a nameles pamphlet. By*
15 *this time I had lernt that* Paulus Fagius, *one of the chief
Divines in Germany, sent for by* Frederic *the* Palatine,
*to reforme his dominion; and after that invited hither in
King* Edwards *dayes to be Professor of Divinity in Cambridge, was of the same opinion touching divorce, which*
20 *these men so lavishly traduc't in me. What I found, I inserted where fittest place was, thinking sure they would
respect so grave an author, at lest to the moderating of their
odious inferences. And having now perfected a second edition, I referr'd the judging therof to your high and impartial*
25 *sentence, honour'd Lords and Commons. For I was confident, if any thing generous, any thing noble, and above
the multitude, were left yet in the spirit of England, it
could be no where sooner found, and no where sooner under-*

stood, then in that house of justice and true liberty where
ye sit in counsel. Nor doth the event hitherto, for some
reasons which I shall not heer deliver, faile me of what
I conceiv'd so highly. Nevertheless being farre otherwise
5 *dealt with by some, of whose profession and supposed*
knowledge I had better hope, and esteem'd the deviser of a
new and pernicious paradox, I felt no difference within
me from that peace & firmnes of minde, which is of neerest
kin to patience and contentment: both for that I knew I
10 *had divulg'd a truth linkt inseparably with the most funda-*
mental rules of Christianity, to stand or fall together, and
was not un-inform'd that divers lerned and judicious men
testify'd their daily approbation of the book. Yet at length
it hath pleas'd God, who had already giv'n me satisfaction
15 *in my self, to afford me now a means wherby I may be*
fully justify'd also in the eyes of men. When the book had
bin now the second time set forth wel-nigh three months, as
I best remember, I then first came to hear that Martin
Bucer *had writt'n much concerning divorce: whom ear-*
20 *nestly turning over, I soon perceav'd, but not without*
amazement, in the same opinion, confirm'd with the same
reasons which in that publisht book without the help or im-
itation of any precedent Writer, *I had labour'd out, and*
laid together. Not but that there is some difference in the
25 *handling, in the order, and the number of arguments, but*
still agreeing in the same conclusion. So as I may justly
gratulat mine own mind, with due acknowledgement of
assistance from above, which led me, not as a lerner, but

*as a collateral teacher, to a sympathy of judgement with
no lesse a man then* Martin Bucer. *And he, if our things
heer below arrive him where he is, does not repent him to
see that point of knowledge which he first, and with an*
5 *uncheckt freedom preacht to those more knowing times of
England, now found so necessary, though what he admonisht were lost out of our memory, yet that God doth now
again create the same doctrin in another unwritt'n table,
and raises it up immediatly out of his pure oracle to the*
10 *convincement of a pervers age, eager in the reformation of
names and ceremonies, but in realities as traditional and
as ignorant as their forefathers. I would ask now the fore-
most of my profound accusers, whether they dare affirm
that to be licentious, new and dangerous, which* Martin
15 Bucer *so often, and so urgently avoucht to be most lawfull,
most necessary, and most Christian, without the lest blem-
ish to his good name, among all the worthy men of that age,
and since, who testifie so highly of him? If they dare, they
must then set up an arrogance of their own against all those*
20 *Churches and Saints who honour'd him without this exception: If they dare not, how can they now make that licentious doctrin in another, which was never blam'd, or confuted in* Bucer, *or in* Fagius? *The truth is, there will be
due to them for this their unadvised rashnes, the best dona-*
25 *tive that can be giv'n them, I mean, a round reproof; now
that where they thought to be most Magisterial, they have
display'd their own want, both of reading, and of judgement. First, to be so unacquainted in the writings of* Bucer,

which are so obvious and so usefull in their own faculty;
next, to be so caught in a prejudicating weaknes, as to
condemn that for lewd, which (whether they knew or not)
these elect servants of Christ commended for lawfull; and
5 for new, that which was taught by these almost the first and
greatest authors of reformation, who were never taxt for so
teaching; and dedicated without scruple to a royall pair of
the first reforming Kings in Christendom, and confest in
the public confession of a most orthodoxall Church &
10 state in Germany. This is also another fault which I must
tell them; that they have stood now almost this whole year
clamouring a farre off, while the book hath bin twice printed,
twice bought up, & never once vouchsaft a friendly conference with the author, who would be glad and thankfull
15 to be shewn an error, either by privat dispute, or public
answer, and could retract, as well as wise men before him;
might also be worth the gaining, as one who heertofore,
hath done good service to the Church by their own confession. Or if he be obstinat, their confutation would have
20 render'd him without excuse, and reclam'd others of no
mean parts who incline to his opinion. But now their work
is more then doubl'd; and how they will hold up their heads
against the sudden aspect of these two great and reverend
Saints whom they have defam'd, how they will make good
25 the censuring of that for a novelty of licence, which Bucer
constantly taught to be a pure and holy law of Christs kingdom, let them advise. For against these my adversaries,
who before the examining of a propounded truth in a fit

*time of reformation, have had the conscience to oppose
naught els but their blind reproaches and surmises, that a
single innocence might not be opprest and overborn by a
crew of mouths for the restoring of a law and doctrin falsely*
5 *and unlernedly reputed new and scandalous, God, that I
may ever magnifie and record this his goodnes, hath unexpectedly rais'd up as it were from the dead, more then one
famous light of the first reformation to bear witnes with
me, and to doe me honour in that very thing, wherin these*
10 *men thought to have blotted me: And hath giv'n them the
proof of a capacity which they despis'd, running equal,
and authentic with some of thir chiefest masters unthought
of, and in a point of sagest moment. However, if we know
at all, when to ascribe the occurrences of this life to the work*
15 *of a special providence, as nothing is more usual in the
talk of good men, what can be more like to a special providence of God, then in the first reformation of England, that
this question of divorce, as a main thing to be restor'd to
just freedom, was writt'n, and seriously commended to*
20 Edward *the sixt, by a man call'd from another Countrey
to be the instructer of our nation, and now in this present
renewing of the Church and Common-wealth, which we
pray may be more lasting, that the same question should
be again treated and presented to this Parlament, by one*
25 *enabl'd to use the same reasons without the lest sight or
knowledge of what was done before. It were no trespas,
Lords and Commons, though something of lesse note were
attributed to the ordering of a heavnly power; this question*

therfore of such prime concernment both to Christian and civil welfare, in such an extraordinary manner, not recover'd, but plainly twise born to these latter ages, as from a divine hand I tender to your acceptance, and most con-
5 *siderate thoughts. Think not that God rais'd up in vain a man of greatest autority in the Church to tell a trivial and licentious tale in the eares of that good Prince, and to bequeath it as his last will and testament, nay rather as the testament and royall law of Christ to this Nation, or that*
10 *it should of it self after so many yeares, as it were in a new feild where it was never sow'n, grow up again as a vitious plant in the minde of another, who had spoke honestest things to the Nation; though he knew not that what his youth then reason'd without a pattern, had bin heard al-*
15 *ready, and well allow'd from the gravity and worth of* Martin Bucer: *till meeting with the envy of men ignorant in thir own undertak'n calling, God directed him to the forgott'n Writings of this faithfull Evangelist, to be his defence and warrant against the gross imputation of broach-*
20 *ing licence. Ye are now in the glorious way to high vertu, and matchless deeds, trusted with a most inestimable trust, the asserting of our just liberties. Ye have a nation that expects now, and from mighty suffrings aspires to be the example of all Christendom to a perfetest reforming. Dare*
25 *to be as great, as ample, and as eminent in the fair progress of your noble designes, as the full and goodly stature of truth and excellence it self: as unlimited by petty presidents and copies, as your unquestionable calling from*

heaven givs ye power to be. What are all our public im-
munities and privileges worth, and how shall it be judg'd
that we fight for them with minds worthy to enjoy them, if
wee suffer our selvs in the mean while not to understand the
5 *most important freedom that God and Nature hath givn us*
in the family; which no wise Nation ever wanted, till the
Popery and superstition of some former ages attempted to
remove and alter divine and most prudent Laws for human
and most imprudent Canons; wherby good men in the best
10 *portion of thir lives, and in that ordinance of God which*
entitles them from the beginning to most just and requisite
contentments, are compell'd to civil indignities, which by
the law of Moses *bad men were not compell'd to. Be not*
bound about, and straitn'd in the spatious wisdom of your
15 *free Spirits, by the scanty and unadequat and inconsistent*
principles of such as condemn others for adhering to tra-
ditions, and are themselvs the prostrate worshippers of
Custom; and of such a tradition as they can deduce from
no antiquitie, but from the rudest, and thickest barbarism
20 *of Antichristian times. But why doe I anticipate the more*
acceptable, and prevailing voice of lerned Bucer *himself,*
the pastor of Nations? And O that I could set him living
before ye in that doctoral chair, where once the lernedest of
England *thought it no disparagement to sit at his feet! He*
25 *would be such a pilot, and such a father to ye, as ye would*
soon find the difference of his hand and skill upon the helm
of reformation. Nor doe I forget that faithfull associate of
his labours, Paulus Fagius; *for these thir great names and*

merits, how pretious so ever, God hath now joyn'd with me
necessarily, in the good or evil report of this doctrin which
I leav with you. It was writt'n to a religious King of this
land; writt'n earnestly, as a main matter wherin this king-
5 *dom needed a reform, if it purpos'd to be the kingdom of*
Christ: Writt'n by him who if any since the daies of Luther,
merits to be counted the Apostle *of our Church; whose un-*
wearied pains and watching for our sakes, as they spent
him quickly heer among us, so did they, during the short-
10 *nes of his life, incredibly promote the Gospel throughout*
this Realm. The autority, the lerning, the godlines of this
man consulted with, is able to out-ballance all that the
lightnes of a vulgar opposition can bring to counterpoise.
I leav him also as my complete suretie and testimonial, if
15 *Truth be not the best witnes to it self, that what I formerly*
presented to your reading on this subject, was good, and
just, and honest, not licentious. Not that I have now more
confidence by the addition of these great Authors to my
party; for what I wrote was not my opinion, but my knowl-
20 *edge; evn then when I could trace no footstep in the way I*
went: nor that I think to win upon your apprehensions
with numbers and with names, rather then with reasons,
yet certainly the worst of my detracters will not except against
so good a baile of my integritie and judgement, as now ap-
25 *peares for me. They must els put in the fame of* Bucer *and*
of Fagius, *as my accomplices and confederats into the same*
endightment; they must dig up the good name of these prime
worthies (if thir names could be ever buried) they must dig

*them up and brand them as the Papists did thir bodies;
and those thir pure unblamable spirits, which live not only
in heaven, but in thir writings, they must attaint with new
attaintures which no Protestant ever before aspers't them*
5 *with. Or if perhaps wee may obtain to get our appeach-
ment new drawn a Writ of Error, not of Libertinism, that
those two principal leaders of reformation may not come
now to be su'd in a bill of licence, to the scandal of our
Church, the brief result will be, that for the error, if thir*
10 *own works be not thought sufficient to defend them, there
livs yet who will be ready, in a fair and christianly dis-
cussive way, to debate and sift this matter to the utmost
ounce of lerning and religion, in him that shall lay it as
an error, either upon Martin Bucer, or any other of his*
15 *opinion. If this be not anough to qualifie my traducers,
and that they think it more for the wisdom of thir virulence,
not to recant the injuries they have bespoke me, I shall not
for much more disturbance then they can bring me, inter-
mitt the prosecution of those thoughts which may render*
20 *me best serviceable, either to this age, or if it so happ'n, to
posteritie; following the fair path which your illustrious
exploits, Honourd Lords and Commons, against the brest
of tyrany have open'd; and depending so on your happy
successes in the hopes that I have conceiv'd either of my*
25 *self, or of the Nation, as must needs conclude me one who
most affectionately wishes and awaits the prosperous issue
of your noble and valorous counsels.*

JOHN MILTON.

THE
JUDGEMENT OF
MARTIN BUCER
Touching Divorce.

Taken out of the second Book entitl'd

Of the kingdom of Christ writt'n by

Martin Bucer to *Edward* the 6th K. of *England*.

CHAP. XV.

The 7th Law of the sanctifying and ordering of mariage.

BESIDES these things, Christ our King, and his Churches require from your sacred Majesty, that you would take upon you the just care of mariages. For it is unspeakable, how many good consciences are heerby entangl'd, afflicted, and in danger, because there are no just laws, no speedy way constituted, according to Gods Word, touching this holy society and fountain of mankind. For seeing matrimony is a civil thing, men, that they may rightly contract, inviolably keep, and not without extreme necessitie dissolv mariage, are not only to be taught by the doctrine and discipline of the Church, but also are to be acquitted, aided,

That the ordering of mariage belongs to the civil power.

5

10

and compell'd by laws and judicature of the Common-wealth.
Which thing pious Emperours acknowledging, and therin
framing themselvs to the law of Nations, gave laws both of
contracting and preserving, and also where an unhappy need
5 requir'd, of divorcing mariages. As may be seen in the Code
of *Justinian* the 5 Book, from the beginning through 24
titles. And in the Authentic of *Justinian* the 22, and some
others.

But the Antichrists of *Rome,* to get the imperial power into
10 thir own hands, first by fraudulent persuasion, afterwards by
force drew to themselvs the whole autority of determining
and judging as well in matrimonial causes, as in most other
matters. Therfore it hath bin long beleiv'd, that the care and
government therof doth not belong to the civil Magistrate.
15 Yet where the Gospel of Christ is receav'd, the laws of Antichrist should be rejected. If therfore Kings and Governours
take not this care, by the power of law and justice to provide
that mariages be piously contracted, religiously kept, and
lawfully dissolv'd, if need require, who sees not what con-
20 fusion and trouble is brought upon this holy society; and
what a rack is prepar'd, evn for many of the best consciences,
while they have no certain laws to follow, no justice to im-
plore, if any intolerable thing happen. And how much it concerns the honour and safety of the Common-wealth, that
25 mariages, according to the will of Christ, be made, maintain'd, and not without just cause dissolv'd, who understands
not? for unlesse that first and holiest society of man and
woman be purely constituted, that houshold discipline may

The P.
have i
vaded
fraud
force t
orderi
mariag

be upheld by them according to Gods law, how can wee expect a race of good men. Let your Majesty therfore know
that this is your duty, and in the first place, to reassume to
your self the just ordering of matrimony, and by firm laws to
5 establish and defend the religion of this first and divine
societie among men, as all wise law-givers of old, and Christian Emperours have carefully don.

The two next Chapters because they cheifly treat about the
degrees of Consanguinity and affinity I omit; only setting
10 *down a passage or two concerning the judicial laws of Moses,*
how fit they be for Christians to imitate rather then any other.

CHAP. XVII. toward the end.

I CONFESSE that wee beeing free in Christ are not
bound to the civil Laws of *Moses* in every circumstance,
15 yet seeing no laws can be more honest, just, and wholsom, then those which God himself gave, who is eternal wisdom & goodnes, I see not why Christians, in things which no
lesse appertain to them, ought not to follow the laws of God,
rather then of any men. Wee are not to use circumcision, sac-
20 rifice, and those bodily washings prescrib'd to the *Jews;* yet
by these things wee may rightly learn, with what purity and
devotion both Baptism and the Lords Supper should be administerd and receav'd. How much more is it our duty to
observ diligently what the Lord hath commanded, and taught
25 by the examples of his people concerning mariage; wherof
wee have the use no lesse then they.

And because this same worthy Author hath another pas-
sage to this purpose in his Comment upon Matthew, Chap.
5. 19. I heer insert it from p. 46.

Since wee have need of civil laws and the power of punish-
5 ing, it will be wisest not to contemn those giv'n by *Moses;* but
seriously rather to consider what the meaning of God was in
them, what he cheifly requir'd, and how much it might be
to the good of every Nation, if they would borrow thence thir
manner of governing the Common-wealth; yet freely all
10 things and with the Spirit of Christ. For what *Solon,* or
Plato, or *Aristotle,* what Lawyers or *Cæsars* could make better
laws then God? And it is no light argument, that many Magistrates at this day doe not anough acknowledge the kingdom
of Christ, though they would seem most Christian, in that
15 they govern thir States by laws so divers from those of *Moses.*

The 18 *Chap. I only mention as determining a thing not*
heer in question, that mariage without consent of parents
ought not to be held good; yet with this qualification fit to
be known.
20 That if parents admit not the honest desires of thir children, but shall persist to abuse the power they have over
them, they are to be mollifi'd by admonitions, entreaties, and
persuasions, first of thir freinds and kindred, next of the
Church-Elders. Whom if still the hard parents refuse to hear,
25 then ought the Magistrate to interpose his power: lest any by
the evil minde of thir parents be detain'd from mariage
longer then is meet, or forc't to an unworthy match: in

which case the *Roman* laws also provided. *C. de nupt. l.* 11. 13. 26.

CHAP. XIX.

Whether it may be permitted to revoke the

5   *promise of mariage.*

HEER ariseth another question concerning Contracts, when they ought to be unchangeable; for religious Emperours decree'd that the contract was not indissoluble, until the spouse were brought home, and the solemnities perform'd. They thought it a thing unworthy of divine and human equitie, and the due consideration of mans infirmitie in deliberating and determining, when space is giv'n to renounce other contracts of much lesse moment, which are not yet confirm'd before the Magistrate, to deny that to the most waighty contract of marriage, which requires the greatest care and consultation. Yet lest such a covenant should be brok'n for no just cause, and to the injury of that person to whom mariage was promis'd, they decreed a fine, that he who deni'd mariage to whom he had promis'd, and for some cause not approv'd by the Judges, should pay the double of that pledge which was giv'n at making sure, or as much as the Judge should pronounce might satisfie the dammage or the hinderance of either partie. It beeing most certain that ofttimes after contract, just and honest causes of departing from promise, come to be known and found out, it cannot be other then the duty of pious Princes, to give men

the same liberty of unpromising in these cases, as pious Emperours granted: especially where there is only a promise, and not carnal knowledge. And as there is no true mariage between them, who agree not in true consent of mind, so it will
5 be the part of godly Magistrates to procure that no matrimony be among thir Subjects, but what is knit with love and consent. And though your Majesty be not bound to the imperial laws, yet it is the duty of a Christian King to embrace and follow what ever he knows to be any where piously and
10 justly constituted, and to be honest, just and well-pleasing to his people. But why in Gods law and the examples of his Saints nothing heerof is read, no marvell, seeing his ancient people had power, yea a precept, that who so could not bend his mind to the true love of his wife, should give her a bill of
15 divorce, and send her from him, though after carnal knowledge and long dwelling together. This is anough to authorize a godly Prince in that indulgence which he gives to the changing of a Contract; both because it is certainly the invention of Antichrist, that the promise of mariage *de præsenti* as they
20 call it, should be indissoluble, and because it should be a Princes care that matrimony be so joyn'd, as God ordain'd; which is, that every one should love his wife with such a love as *Adam* exprest to *Eve:* So as wee may hope that they who marry may become one flesh, and one also in the Lord.

25   CHAP. XX.

Concerns only the celebration of mariage.

CHAP. XXI.

The means of preserving mariage holy and pure.

NOW since there ought not to be lesse care that mariage be religiously kept, then that it be piously and deliberately contracted, it will be meet that to
5 every Church be ordan'd certain grave and godly men, who may have this care upon them, to observ whether the husband bear himself wisely toward the wife, loving, & inciting her to all piety and the other duties of this life; and whether the wife
10 be subject to her husband, and study to be truly a meet help to him, as first to all godlines, so to every other use of life. And if they shal find each to other failing of their duty, or the one long absent from the other without just and urgent cause, or giving suspicion of irreligious and impure life, or of living in
15 manifest wickednes, let it be admonisht them in time. And if thir autority be contemn'd, let the names of such contemners be brought to the Magistrate, who may use punishment to compell such violaters of mariage, to thir duty, that they may abstain from all probable suspicion of transgressing;
20 and if they admit of suspected company, the Magistrate is to forbid them; whom they not therin obeying, are to be punisht as adulterers, according to the law of *Justinian, Authent.* 117. For if holy wedlock the Fountain and Seminary of good subjects, be not vigilantly preserv'd from all blots and disturb-
25 ances, what can be hop'd, as I said before, of the springing up of good men, and a right reformation of the Commonwealth. We know it is not anough for Christians to abstain

from foul deeds, but from the appearance and suspicion therof.

CHAP. XXII.

Of lawfull divorce, what the ancient Churches have thought.

5 NOW we shall speak about that dissolving of matrimony which may be approv'd in the sight of God, if any greevous necessity require. In which thing the Roman Antichrists have knit many a pernicious entanglement to distressed consciences: for that they might 10 heer also exalt themselvs above God, as if they would be wiser and chaster then God himself is, for no cause, honest, or necessary, will they permit a finall divorce, in the mean while whordoms and adulteries, and worse things then these, not only tolerating in themselvs and others, but cherishing, 15 and throwing men headlong into these evils. For although they also dis-joyn married persons from board and bed, that is, from all conjugall society and communion, and this not only for adultery, but for ill usage, and matrimoniall duties deni'd, yet they forbid those thus parted, to joyn in wedlock 20 with others, but, as I said before, any dishonest associating they permit. And they pronounce the bond of mariage to remain between those whom they have thus separat. As if the bond of mariage, God so teaching and pronouncing, were not such a league as bindes the maried couple to all society of life, 25 and communion in divine & humane things; and so associated keeps them. Somthing indeed out of the latter Fathers they may pretend for this thir tyranny, especially out of *Austine* and some others, who were much tak'n with a pre-

posterous admiration of single life; yet though these Fathers,
from the words of Christ not rightly understood, taught that
it was unlawfull to marry again, while the former wife liv'd,
whatever cause ther had bin either of desertion or divorce,
5 yet if we mark the custom of the Church, and the common
judgement which both in their times and afterward prevail'd,
we shall perceave that neither these Fathers did ever cast out
of the Church any one for marying after a divorce, approv'd
by the Imperiall laws.

10   Nor only the first Christian Emperours, but the later also,
ev'n to *Justinian,* and after him, did grant for certain causes
approv'd by Judges, to make a true divorse; which made and
confirm'd by law, it might be lawfull to marry again: which
if it could not have bin done without displeasing Christ and
15 his Church, surely it would not have been granted by Christian Emperours, nor had the Fathers then winkt at those
doings in the Emperours. Hence ye may see that *Jerom* also,
though zealous of single life more then anough, and such a
condemner of second mariage though after the death of either
20 party, yet forc't by plain equity, defended *Fabiola,* a noble
Matron of Rome, who having refus'd her husband for just
causes, was married to another. For that the sending of a
divorce to her husband was not blame-worthy, he affirms, because the man was hainously vitious, and that if an adulterous
25 wife may be discarded, an adulterous husband is not to be
kept. But that she maried again, while yet her husband was
alive, he defends in that the Apostle hath said, *It is better
to mary then to burn,* and that yong widows should mary,

for such was *Fabiola,* and could not remain in widowhood.

But some one will object that *Jerom* there addes, *Neither did she know the vigor of the Gospel, wherin all cause of marying is debarr'd from women, while thir husbands live,* 5 *and again, while she avoided many wounds of Satan, she re-ceav'd one ere she was aware.* But let the equall Reader minde also what went before; *Because,* saith he soon after the beginning, *there is a rock and storm of slanderers oppos'd against her, I will not praise her converted, unlesse I first absolve her* 10 *guilty.* For why does he call them slanderers who accus'd *Fabiola* of marying again, if he did not judge it a matter of Christian equity and charity, to passe by and pardon that fact, though in his own opinion he held it a fault. And what can this mean? *I will not praise her, unlesse I first absolv her.* 15 For how could he absolv her but by proving that *Fabiola* neither in rejecting her vitious husband, nor in marying another, had committed such a sin, as could be justly condemn'd. Nay, he proves both by evident reason, and cleer testimonies of Scripture, that she avoided sin.

20   This also is hence understood, that *Jerom* by the vigor of the Gospel, meant that height and perfection of our Saviours precept, which might be remitted to those that burn; for he addes, *But if she be accus'd in that she remain'd not unmarried, I shall confesse the fault, so I may relate the necessity.* 25 If then he acknowledg'd a necessity, as he did, because she was young, and could not live in Widowhood, certainly he could not impute her second mariage to her much blame: but when he excuses her out of the word of God, does he not

openly declare his thoughts, that the second mariage of
Fabiola was permitted her by the holy Ghost himself for the
necessity which she suffer'd, and to shun the danger of fornication, though she went somwhat aside from the vigor of the
5 Gospel. But if any urge that *Fabiola* did public penance for
her second mariage, which was not impos'd but for great
faults. 'Tis answer'd, she was not enjoyn'd to this pennance,
but did it of her own accord, *and not till after her second husbands death.* As in the time of *Cyprian* we read that many
10 were wont to doe voluntary penance for small faults, which
were not liable to excommunication.

CHAP. XXIII.

*That Mariage was granted by the ancient Fathers, ev'n after
the vow of single life.*
15 *I omit his testimonies out of Cyprian, Gelasius, Epiphanius,
contented only to relate what he thence
collects to the present purpose.*

SOME will say perhaps, wherfore all this concerning
mariage after vow of single life, when as the question
20 was of mariage after divorse? For this reason, that
they whom it so much moves, because some of the Fathers
thought mariage after any kind of divorce, to be condemn'd
of our Saviour, may see that this conclusion follows not. The
Fathers thought all mariage after divorce to be forbidd'n of
25 our Saviour, therfore they thought such mariage was not to
be tolerated in a Christian. For the same Fathers judg'd it
forbidd'n to marry after vow; yet such mariages they neither
dissolv'd nor excommunicated. For these words of our Sa-

viour, and of the holy Ghost, stood in their way; *All cannot receav this saying, but they to whom it is giv'n. Every one hath his proper gift from God, one after this manner, another after that. It is better to marry then to burn. I will that* 5 *younger Widows marry,* and the like.

So there are many Canons, and Laws extant, wherby Priests, if they maried, were remov'd from their office, yet is it not read that their mariage was dissolv'd, as the Papists now-a-dayes doe, or that they were excommunicated, nay ex- 10 pressly they might communicate as Lay men. If the consideration of human infirmitie, and those testimonies of divine Scripture which grant mariage to every one that wants it, persuaded those Fathers to bear themselvs so humanly toward them who had maried with breach of vow to God, as 15 they beleev'd, and with divorce of that mariage wherin they were in a manner joyn'd to God, who doubts, but that the same Fathers held the like humanitie was to be afforded to those who after divorce & faith broken with men, as they thought, enter'd into second mariage: for among such are 20 also found no lesse weak, and no lesse burning.

CHAP. XXIV.

Who of the ancient Fathers have granted marriage after divorce.

THIS is cleer both by what hath bin said, and by that 25 which *Origen* relates of certain Bishops in his time, *Homil. 7.* in Matth. *I know some,* saith he, *which are over Churches, who without Scripture have permitted the*

wife to mary while her former husband liv'd. And did this
against Scripture which saith, The wife is bound to her hus-
band so long as he lives, and she shall be call'd an adulteresse,
if, her husband living, she take another man, yet did they not
5 *permit this without cause, perhaps for the infirmitie of such*
as had not continence, they permitted evill to avoid worse.
Ye see *Origen* and the Doctors of his age, not without all
cause, permitted women after divorce to marry, though their
former husbands were living: yet writes that they permitted
10 against Scripture. But what cause could they have to doe so,
unlesse they thought our Saviour in his precepts of divorce,
had so forbid'n, as willing to remit such perfection to his
weaker ones, cast into danger of worse faults.

The same thought *Leo,* Bishop of *Rome, Ep.* 85. to the
15 African Bishops of *Mauritania Cæsariensis,* wherin complaining of a certain Priest, who divorcing his wife, or being divorc't by her, as other copies have it, had maried another,
neither dissolvs the matrimony, nor excommunicates him,
only unpreists him. The fathers therfore as wee see, did not
20 simply and wholly condemn mariage after divorce.

But as for me, this remitting of our Saviours precepts,
which these ancients allow to the infirm in marrying after
vow and divorce, I can in no ways admit; for what so ever
plainly consents not with the commandment, cannot, I am
25 certain, be permitted, or suffer'd in any Christian: for heav'n
and earth shall passe away, but not a tittle from the commands of God among them who expect life eternal. Let us
therfore consider, and waigh the words of our Lord concern-

ing mariage, and divorce, which he pronounc't both by himself, and by his Apostle, and let us compare them with other
Oracles of God; for whatsoever is contrary to these, I shall
not persuade the least tolerating therof. But if it can be taught
5 to agree with the Word of God, yea to be commanded that
most men may have permission giv'n them to divorce and
marry again, I must preferre the autority of Gods Word before the opinion of Fathers and Doctors, as they themselvs
teach.

10   CHAP. XXV.

*The words of our Lord, and of the holy Ghost by the Apostle
Paul concerning Divorce are explain'd.*

BUT the words of our Lord and of the holy Ghost, out of
which *Austin,* and some others of the Fathers think it
15   concluded that our Saviour forbids mariage after any
divorce are these, *Mat.* 5. 31, 32. *It hath bin said &c.* And
Mat. 19. 7. *They say unto him, why did Moses then command, &c.* And *Mark* the 10th, and *Luke* the 16. *Rom.* 7.
1, 2, 3. 1 *Cor.* 7. 10, 11. Hence therfore they conclude that
20 all mariage after divorce is call'd adultery; which to commit
beeing no ways to be tolerated in any Christian, they think it
follows that second mariage is in no case to be permitted
either to the divorcer or to the divorsed.

But that it may be more fully and plainly perceav'd, what   The 1.
25 force is in this kind of reasoning, it will be the best cours to   that C

lay down certain grounds wherof no Christian can doubt the
truth. First it is a wickednes to suspect that our Saviour
branded that for adultery, which himself in his own Law,
which he came to fulfill, and not to dissolv, did not only per-
5 mit, but also command; for by him the only Mediator was
the whole law of God giv'n. But that by this law of God mariage was permitted after any divorce is certain by *Deut.* 24. 1.

could not
condemn
of adultery
that which
he once com-
manded.

CHAP. XXVI.

That God in his law did not only grant, but also command
10   *divorce to certain men.*

DEUT. 24. 1. *When a man hath taken a wife, &c.*
But in *Mala.* 2. 15, 16. is read the Lords command
to put her away whom a man hates, in these words.
Take heed to your spirit, and let none deal injuriously against
15 *the wife of his youth. If he hate, let him put away, saith the*
Lord God of Israel. And he shall hide thy violence with his
garment, that maries her divorc't by thee, *saith the Lord of*
hosts; But *take heed to your spirit, and doe no injury.* By
these testimonies of the divine law, wee see that the Lord did
20 not only permit, but also expresly and earnestly commanded
his people, by whom he would that all holiness and faith of
mariage covnant should be observ'd, that he who could not
induce his minde to love his wife with a true conjugal love,
might dismisse her that shee might marry to another.

CHAP. XXVII.

That what the Lord permitted and commanded to his ancient people concerning divorce, belongs also to Christians.

NOW what the Lord permitted to his first-borne people, that certainly he could not forbid to his own among the Gentils, whom he made coheires and into one body with his people, nor could he ever permit, much lesse command ought that was not good for them, at least so us'd, as he commanded. For beeing God, he is not chang'd as man. Which thing who seriously considers, how can he imagine that God would make that wicked to them that beleeve, and serv him under grace, which he granted and commanded to them that serv'd him under the Law. When as the same causes require the same permission. And who that knows but humane matters, and loves the truth, will deny that many mariages hang as ill together now, as ever they did among the Jews? So that such mariages are liker to torments then true mariages. As therfore the Lord doth always succour and help the oppressed, so he would ever have it provided for injur'd husbands and wives, that under pretence of the mariage-bond, they be not sold to perpetual vexations, instead of the loving and comfortable mariage-duties. And lastly, as God doth always detest hypocrisie, and fraud, so neither doth he approve, that among his people, that should be counted mariage, wherin none of those duties remain, wherby the league of wedlock is chiefly preserv'd. What inconsiderat neglect then of Gods law is this, that I

may not call it worse, to hold that Christ our Lord would not
grant the same remedies both of divorce and second mariage
to the weak, or to the evil, if they will needs have it so, but
especially to the innocent and wronged, when as the same
5 urgent causes remain, as before; when the discipline of the
church and Magistrate hath tri'd what may be tri'd.

CHAP. XXVIII.

That our Lord Christ intended not to make new Laws
of mariage and divorce, or of any civil matters.

10 IT is agreed by all who determine of the Kingdom, and   The second
offices of Christ by the holy Scriptures, as all godly men   Axiom.
ought to doe, that our Saviour upon earth took not on
him either to give new laws in civil affairs, or to change the
old. But it is certain that matrimony and divorce are civil
15 things. Which the Christian Emperours knowing, gave conjugal laws; and reserv'd the administration of them to thir
own Courts; which no true ancient Bishop ever condemn'd.
Our Saviour came to preach repentance, and remission;
seeing therfore those who put away thir wives without any
20 just cause, were not toucht with conscience of the sin,
through misunderstanding of the law, he recall'd them to a
right interpretation, and taught that the woman in the beginning was so joyn'd to the man, that there should be a perpetual union both in body and spirit: where this is not, the
25 matrimony is already broke, before there be yet any divorce
made or second mariage.

CHAP. XXIX.

That it is wicked to strain the words of Christ beyond thir
purpose. This is his third Axiom, wherof there
needs no explication heer.

CHAP. XXX.

5

That all places of Scripture about the same thing are to   Axic
be joyn'd, and compar'd, to avoid Contradictions.

This he demonstrates at large out of sundry places in the
Gospel; and principally by that precept against swearing,   Mat.
10 *which compar'd with many places of the Law and Prophets,*
is a flat contradiction of them all, if we follow superstitiously
the letter. Then having repeated briefly his foure Axioms, he
thus proceeds.

THESE things thus preadmonisht, let us enquire
what the undoubted meaning is of our Saviours
words; and enquire according to the rule which is
observ'd by all learned and good men in their expositions;
that praying first to God, who is the only opener of our
hearts, wee may first with fear and reverence consider well
20 the words of our Saviour touching this question. Next, that
wee may compare them with all other places of Scripture,
treating of this matter, to see how they consent with our
Saviours words, and those of his Apostle.

CHAP. XXXI.

This Chapter disputes against Austin and the Papists, who deny second mariage, ev'n to them who divorce in case of adultery, which because it is not controverted among true
5 *Protestants, but that the innocent person is easily allow'd to marry, I spare the translating.*

CHAP. XXXII.

That a manifest adulteresse ought to be divorc't, and cannot lawfully be retain'd in mariage by any true Christian.

10   *This though he prove sufficiently, yet I let passe, because this question was not handl'd in the Doctrine and discipline of divorce; to which book I bring so much of this Treatise as runs parallel.*

CHAP. XXXIII.

15   *That adultery is to be punisht by death.*

This Chapter also I omitt for the reason last alleg'd.

CHAP. XXXIV.

That it is lawfull for a wife to leav an adulterer, and to marry another husband.

20   *This is generally granted, and therfore excuses me the writing out.*

CHAP. XXXV.

Places in the Writings of the Apostle Paul touching divorce explain'd.

5 L ET us consider the answers of the Lord giv'n by the Apostle severally. Concerning the first which is *Rom.* 7. 1. *Know yee not brethren, for I speak to them that know the law, &c.* Ver. 2. *The woman is bound by the law to her husband so long as he liveth.* Heer it is certain that the holy Ghost had no purpose to determine ought of mariage,
10 or divorce, but only to bring an example from the common and ordinary law of wedlock, to shew that as no covnant holds either party beeing dead, so now that wee are not bound to the law, but to Christ our Lord, seeing that through him wee are dead to sin, and to the law; and so joyn'd to
15 Christ that wee may bring forth fruit in him from a willing godlines, and not by the compulsion of law, wherby our sins are more excited, and become more violent. What therfore the holy Spirit heer speaks of matrimony, cannot be extended beyond the general rule.
20   Besides it is manifest, that the Apostle did allege the law of wedlock, as it was deliver'd to the *Jews;* for, saith he, I speak to them that know the law. They knew no law of God but that by *Moses,* which plainly grants divorce for several reasons. It cannot therfore be said that the Apostle cited this
25 generall example out of the law, to abolish the several exceptions of that law, which God himself granted by giving autority to divorce.

Next when the Apostle brings an example out of Gods law concerning man and wife, it must be necessary that wee understand such for man and wife, as are so indeed according to the same law of God; that is, who are so dispos'd as that they are both willing and able to perform the necessary duties of mariage; not those who under a false title of mariage, keep themselves mutually bound to injuries and disgraces; for such twain are nothing lesse then lawfull man and wife.

The like answer is to be giv'n to all the other places both of the Gospel and the Apostle, that what ever exception may be prov'd out of Gods law, be not excluded from those places. For the Spirit of God doth not condemn things formerly granted, and allow'd, where there is like cause and reason. Hence *Ambrose* upon that place, 1 *Cor.* 7. 15. *A brother or a sister is not under bondage in such cases;* thus expounds; *The reverence of mariage is not due to him who abhors the author of mariage; nor is that mariage ratify'd which is without devotion to God: he sins not therfore who is put away for Gods cause, though he joyn himself to another. For the dishonor of the Creator dissolves the right of matrimony to him who is deserted, that he be not accus'd, though marrying to another. The faith of wedlock is not to be kept with him who departs, that he might not hear the God of Christians to be the author of wedlock. For if Ezra caus'd the mis-beleeving wives and husbands to be divorc't, that God might be appeas'd, and not offended, though they took others of thir own faith, how much more shall it be free, if the mis-beleever*

depart, to marry one of our own Religion. For this is not to
be counted matrimony which is against the law of God.

Two things are heer to be observ'd toward the following
discourse, which truth it self, and the force of Gods word
5 hath drawn from this holy man. For those words are very
large, *Matrimony is not ratify'd without devotion to God.*
And *the dishonour of the Creator dissolvs the right of mat-*
rimony. For devotion is farre off, and dishonor is done to
God by all who persist in any wickednes and hainous crime.

10   CHAP. XXXVI.

That although it seem in the Gospel, as if our Saviour
granted divorce only for adultery, yet in very
deed he granted it for other causes also.

N OW is to be dealt with this question, Whether it
15   be lawful to divorce and marry again for other
            causes besides adultery, since our Saviour ex-
prest that only. To this question, if we retain our principles
already laid, and must acknowledge it to be a cursed blasphemy, if we say that the words of God doe contradict one
20 another, of necessity we must confesse that our Lord did
grant divorce, and mariage after that for other causes besides
adultery, notwithstanding what he said in *Matthew.* For first,
they who consider but only that place, 1 *Cor.* 7. which treats
of beleevers and misbeleevers matcht together, must of force
25 confesse, that our Lord granted just divorce, and second
mariage in the cause of desertion, which is other then the
cause of fornication. And if there be one other cause found

lawfull, then is it most true that divorce was granted not
only for fornication.

Next, it cannot be doubted, as I shew'd before, by them to
whom it is giv'n to know God and his judgements out of his
5 own word, but that, what means of peace and safety God
ever granted and ordain'd to his elected people, the same he
grants and ordains to men of all ages who have equally need
of the same remedies. And who, that is but a knowing man,
dares say there be not husbands and wives now to be found in
10 such a hardnesse of heart, that they will not perform either
conjugal affection, or any requisit duty therof, though it be
most deserv'd at thir hands.

Neither can any one deferre to confesse, but that God
whose property it is to judge the cause of them that suffer in-
15 jury, hath provided for innocent and honest persons wedded,
how they might free themselvs by lawfull means of divorce,
from the bondage and iniquity of those who are falsly term'd
thir husbands or thir wives. This is cleer out of Deut. 24. 1.
Malach. 2. Matth. 19. 1 Cor. 7. and out of those principles
20 which the Scripture every where teaches, That God changes
not his minde, dissents not from himself, is no accepter of
persons; but allows the same remedies to all men opprest with
the same necessities and infirmities; yea, requires that wee
should use them. This he will easily perceave, who considers
25 these things in the Spirit of the Lord.

Lastly, it is most certain, that the Lord hath commanded
us to obey the civil laws every one of his own Common-
wealth, if they be not against the laws of God.

CHAP. XXXVII.

For what causes divorce is permitted by the civil Law
ex l. consensu Codic. de repudiis.

5

IT is also manifest that the law of *Theodosius* and *Valentinian,* which begins *Consensu, &c.* touching divorce, and many other decrees of pious Emperours agreeing heerwith, are not contrary to the word of God. And therfore may be recall'd into use by any Christian Prince or Commonwealth, nay ought to be with due respect had to every nation.

10 For whatsoever is equall and just, that in every thing is to be sought and us'd by Christians. Hence it is plain that divorce is granted by divine approbation, both to husbands and to wives, if either party can convict the other of these following offences before the Magistrate.

15   If the husband can prove the wife to be an adulteresse, a witch, a murdresse, to have bought or sold to slavery any one free born, to have violated sepulchers, committed sacrilege, favor'd theevs and robbers, desirous of feasting with strangers, the husband not knowing, or not willing, if she

20 lodge forth without a just and probable cause, or frequent theaters and sights, he forbidding, if she be privie with those that plot against the State, or if she deale falsly, or offer blows. And if the wife can prove her husband guilty of any those fore-named crimes, and frequent the company of lewd

25 women in her sight; or if he beat her, she had the like liberty to quit herselfe; with this difference, that the man after di-

vorce might forthwith marry again; the woman not till a
year after, lest she might chance to have conceav'd.

CHAP. XXXVIII.

An exposition of those places wherein God declares the
5   *nature of holy wedlock.*

NOW to the end it may be seen that this agrees
with the divine law, the first institution of mariage is to be consider'd, and those texts in which
God establisht the joyning of male and female, and describ'd
10 the duties of them both. When God had determin'd to make
woman, and give her as a wife to man, he spake thus, *Gen.*
2. 18. *It is not good for man to be alone, I will make him a*
help meet for him. And Adam said, but in the Spirit of God,
v. 23. 24. *This is now bone of my bone, and flesh of my*
15 *flesh. Therfore shall a man leav his father and mother, and*
shall cleav to his wife, and they shall be one flesh.

To this first institution did Christ recall his own; when
answering the Pharises, he condemn'd the license of unlawfull divorce. He taught therfore by his example, that we, ac-
20 cording to this first institution, and what God hath spok'n
therof, ought to determin what kind of covnant mariage is,
how to be kept, and how farre; and lastly, for what causes to
be dissolv'd. To which decrees of God these also are to be
joyn'd, which the holy Ghost hath taught by his Apostle,
25 that neither the husband nor the wife *hath power of their*
own body, but mutually each of eithers. That *the husband*
shall love the wife as his own body, yea as Christ loves his

Church, and that the wife ought to be subject to her hus-
band, as the Church is to Christ.

By these things the nature of holy wedlock is certainly
known; whereof if only one be wanting in both or either
5 party, and that either by obstinate malevolence, or too deep
inbred weaknes of minde, or lastly, through incurable impotence of body, it cannot then be said that the covnant of
matrimony holds good between such; if we mean that covnant which God instituted and call'd Mariage, and that
10 wherof only it must be understood that our Saviour said,
Those whom God hath joyn'd, let no man separate.

And hence is concluded, that matrimony requires continuall cohabitation and living together, unlesse the calling
of God be otherwise evident; which union if the parties
15 themselves dis-joyn either by mutuall consent, or one against
the others will depart, the marriage is then brok'n. Wherein
the Papists, as in other things oppose themselvs against
God; while they separate for many causes from bed and
board, & yet will have the bond of matrimony remain, as if
20 this covnant could be other then the conjunction and communion not only of bed & board, but of all other loving and
helpfull duties. This we may see in these words; *I will make*
him a help meet for him; bone of his bones, and flesh of his
flesh; for this cause shall he leav father and mother, and
25 *cleav to his wife, and they twain shall be one flesh.* By which
words who discerns not, that God requires of them both so
to live together, and to be united not only in body but in
mind also, with such an affection as none may be dearer and

more ardent among all the relations of mankind, nor of
more efficacy to the mutual offices of love, and loyalty. They
must communicate and consent in all things both divine and
human, which have any moment to well and happy living.
5 The wife must honour and obey her husband, as the Church
honours and obeys Christ her head. The husband must love
and cherish his wife, as Christ his Church. Thus they must
be to each other, if they will be true man and wife in the
sight of God, whom certainly the Churches ought to follow
10 in thir judgement. Now the proper and ultimate end of mariage is not copulation, or children, for then there was not
true matrimony between *Joseph* and *Mary* the mother of
Christ, nor between many holy persons more; but the full
and proper and main end of mariage, is the communicating
15 of all duties, both divine and humane, each to other, with
utmost benevolence and affection.

CHAP. XXXIX.

The properties of a true and Christian mariage, more
distinctly repeated.

20 BY which definition wee may know that God esteems
and reckons upon these foure necessary properties to
be in every true mariage. 1. That they should live
· together, unlesse the calling of God require otherwise for a
time. 2. That they should love one another to the height of
25 dearnes, and that in the Lord, and in the communion of true
Religion. 3. That the husband beare himself as the head and
preserver of his wife, instructing her to all godlines and in-

tegritie of life; that the wife also be to her husband a help, according to her place, especially furdering him in the true worship of God, and next in all the occasions of civil life. And 4. That they defraud not each other of conjugal benevo-
5 lence, as the Apostle commands, 1 *Cor.* 7. Hence it follows according to the sentence of God, which all Christians ought to be rul'd by, that between those who either through obstinacy, or helples inabilitie, cannot or will not perform these repeated duties, between those there can be no true matri-
10 mony, nor ought they to be counted man and wife.

CHAP. XL.

Whether those crimes recited Chap. 37 *out of the civil law dissolv matrimony in Gods account.*

NOW if a husband or wife be found guilty of any
15 those crimes, which by the law *consensu* are made causes of divorce, tis manifest that such a man cannot be the head, and preserver of his wife, nor such a woman be a meet help to her husband, as the divine law in true wedlock requires; for these faults are punisht either by
20 death, or deportation, or extream infamy, which are directly opposite to the covnant of mariage. If they deserve death, as adultery and the like, doubtles God would not that any should live in wedlock with them whom he would not have to live at all. Or if it be not death, but the incurring of no-
25 torious infamy, certain it is neither just, nor expedient, nor meet, that an honest man should be coupl'd with an infamous woman, nor an honest matron with an infamous man.

The wise Roman Princes had so great regard to the equal
honour of either wedded person, that they counted those
mariages of no force which were made between the one of
good repute, and the other of evill note. How much more
5 will all honest regard of Christian expedience and comlines
beseem & concern those who are set free and dignify'd in
Christ, then it could the Roman Senate, or thir sons, for whom
that law was provided.

And this all godly men will soon apprehend, that he who
10 ought to be the head and preserver not only of his wife, but
also of his children and family, as Christ is of his Church,
had need be one of honest name: so likewise the wife which
is to be the meet help of an honest and good man, the mother
of an honest off-spring and family, the glory of the man, ev'n
15 as the man is the glory of Christ, should not be tainted with
ignominy; as neither of them can avoid to be, having bin
justly appeacht of those forenamed crimes; and therfore cannot be worthy to hold thir place in a Christian family: yea
they themselvs turn out themselvs and dissolv that holy cov-
20 nant. And they who are true brethren and sisters in the Lord,
are no more in bondage to such violaters of mariage.

But heer the Patrons of wickednes and dissolvers of Christian discipline will object, that it is the part of man and wife
to bear one anothers crosse, whether in calamitie, or infamy,
25 that they might gain each other, if not to a good name, yet to
repentance and amendment. But they who thus object, seek
the impunity of wickednes, and the favour of wicked men,
not the duties of true charity; which preferrs public honesty

before private interest; and had rather the remedies of wholsom punishment appointed by God should be in use, then
that by remisness the licence of evil doing should encrease.
For if they who by committing such offences, have made
5 void the holy knott of mariage, be capable of repentance,
they will be sooner mov'd when due punishment is executed
on them, then when it is remitted.

Wee must ever beware, lest, in contriving what will be
best for the souls health of delinquents, wee make our selvs
10 wiser and discreeter then God. He that religiously waighs his
oracles concerning mariage, cannot doubt that they who
have committed the foresaid transgressions, have lost the
right of matrimony, and are unworthy to hold thir dignity
in an honest and Christian family.

15   But if any husband or wife see such signes of repentance
in thir transgressor, as that they doubt not to regain them by
continuing with them, and partaking of thir miseries and
attaintures, they may be left to thir own hopes, and thir own
mind, saving ever the right of Church and Common-wealth,
20 that it receav no scandal by the neglect of due severity, and
thir children no harm by this invitation to licence, and want
of good education.

From all these considerations, if they be thought on, as in
the presence of God, and out of his Word, any one may per-
25 ceav, who desires to determine of these things by the Scripture, that those causes of lawfull divorce, which the most religious Emperours *Theodosius* and *Valentinian* set forth in
the forecited place, are according to the law of God, and the

prime institution of mariage. *And were still more and more straitn'd, as the Church and State of the Empire still more and more corrupted and degenerated.* Therfore pious Princes & Common-wealths both may and ought establish them
5 again, if they have a mind to restore the honour, sanctitie, and religion of holy wedlock to thir people, and dis-intangle many consciences from a miserable and perilous condition, to a chaste and honest life.

To those recited causes wherfore a wife might send a di-
10 vorce to her husband, *Justinian* added foure more, *Constit.* 117. And foure more, for which a man might put away his wife. Three other causes were added in the *Code de repudiis l. Jubemus.* All which causes are so cleerly contrary to the first intent of mariage, that they plainly dissolv it. *I set them*
15 *not down beeing easie to be found in the body of the civil Law.*

It was permitted also by Christian Emperours, that they who would divorce by mutuall consent, might without impediment. *Or if there were any difficulty at all in it, the law*
20 *expresses the reason, that it was only in favour of the children, so that if there were none, the law of those godly Emperours made no other difficulty of a divorce by consent.* Or if any were minded without consent of the other to divorce, and without those causes which have bin nam'd, the Chris-
25 tian Emperours laid no other punishment upon them, then that the husband wrongfully divorcing his wife should give back her dowry, and the use of that which was call'd *Donatio propter nuptias;* or if there were no dowry nor no

donation, that he should then give her the fourth part of his goods. The like penalty was inflicted on the wife departing without just cause. But that they who were once maried should be compell'd to remain so ever against thir wills, was
5 not exacted. Wherin those pious Princes follow'd the law of God in *Deut.* 24. 1. and his expresse charge by the Profet *Malachy* to dismisse from him the wife whom he hates. For God never meant in mariage to give to man a perpetuall torment, instead of a meet help. Neither can God approve that
10 to the violation of this holy league (which is violated as soon as true affection ceases and is lost,) should be added murder, which is already committed by either of them who resolvedly hates the other, as I shew'd out of 1 *John* 15. *Who so hateth his brother is a murderer.*

15   CHAP. XLI.

Whether the husband or wife deserted may marry to another.

THE wives desertion of her husband the Christian Emperours plainly decreed to be a just cause of divorce, when as they granted him the right therof, if
20 she had but lain out one night against his will without probable cause. But of the man deserting his wife they did not so determine: Yet if we look into the Word of God, wee shall find, that he who though but for a year without just cause
25 forsakes his wife, and neither provides for her maintenance, nor signifies his purpose of returning, and good will towards

her, when as he may, hath forfeited his right in her so forsak'n. For the Spirit of God speaks plainly, that both man
and wife hath such power over one anothers person, as that
they cannot deprive each other of living together, but by con-
5 sent and for a time.

Hither may be added that the holy Spirit grants desertion
to be a cause of divorce, in those answers giv'n to the *Corin-*
thians concerning a brother or sister deserted by a mis-beleever. *If he depart, let him depart, a brother or a sister is not*
10 *under bondage in such cases.* In which words, who sees not
that the holy Ghost openly pronounc't, that the party without cause deserted, is not bound for anothers wilfull desertion, to abstain from mariage, if he have need therof.

But some will say, that this is spok'n of a mis-beleever de-
15 parting. But I beseech yee, doth not he reject the faith of
Christ in his deeds, who rashly breaks the holy covnant of
wedlock instituted by God? And besides this, the holy Spirit
does not make the mis-beleeving of him who departs, but the
departing of him who mis-beleevs to be the just cause of free-
20 dom to the brother or sister.

Since therfore it will be agreed among Christians, that
they who depart from wedlock without just cause, doe not
only deny the faith of matrimony, but of Christ also, what
ever they professe with thir mouths, it is but reason to con-
25 clude, that the party deserted is not bound in case of caus-
lesse desertion, but that he may lawfully seek another consort, if it be needfull to him toward a pure and blameles
conversation.

CHAP. XLII.

That impotence of body, leprosie, madnes, &c. are just
causes of divorce.

5 O F this, because it was not disputed in the doctrine
and discipline of divorce, him that would know
furder I commend to the Latin original.

CHAP. XLIII.

That to grant divorce for all the causes which have
bin hitherto brought, disagrees not from
10 *the words of Christ naming only*
the cause of adultery.

N OW wee must see how these things can stand with
the words of our Saviour, who seems directly to
forbid all divorce except it be for adultery. To
15 the understanding wherof, wee must ever remember this:
That in the words of our Saviour there can be no contrarietie.
That his words and answers are not to be stretcht beyond the
question propos'd. That our Saviour did not there purpose to
treat of all the causes for which it might be lawfull to divorce
20 and marry again; *for then that in the Corinthians of marry-*
ing again without guilt of adultery could not be added. That
it is not good for that man to be alone who hath not the special gift from above. That it is good for every such one to be
married, that he may shun fornication.
25   With regard to these principles let us see what our Lord

answered to the tempting Pharises about divorce, and second
mariage, and how farre his answer doth extend.

First, No man who is not very contentious, will deny that
the Pharises askt our Lord whether it were lawfull to put
5 away such a wife, as was truly, and according to Gods law,
to be counted a wife; that is, such a one as would dwell with
her husband, and both would & could perform the necessary
duties of wedlock tolerably. But shee who will not dwell
with her husband, is not put away by him, but goes of her
10 self: and shee who denies to be a meet help, or to be so, hath
made her self unfit by open misdemeanours, or through incurable impotencies cannot be able, is not by the law of God
to be esteem'd a wife; as hath bin shewn both from the first
institution, and other places of Scripture. Neither certainly
15 would the Pharises propound a question concerning such an
unconjugall wife; *for thir depravation of the law had brought
them to that passe, as to think a man had right to put away
his wife for any cause, though never so slight.* Since therfore
it is manifest that Christ answer'd the Pharises concerning a
20 fit and meet wife according to the law of God, whom he forbid to divorce for any cause but fornication. Who sees not
that it is a wickednes so to wrest and extend that answer of
his, as if it forbad to divorce her who hath already forsak'n,
or hath lost the place and dignitie of a wife by deserved in-
25 famy, *or hath undertak'n to be that which she hath not naturall ability to be.*

This truth is so powerfull that it hath mov'd the Papists to
grant their kind of divorce for other causes besides adultery,

as for ill usage, and the not performing of conjugal dutie; and to separate from bed and board for these causes, which is as much divorce, as they grant for adultery.

But some perhaps will object, that though it be yeilded, that our Lord granted divorce not only for adultery, yet it is not certain that he permitted mariage after divorce, unlesse for that only cause. I answer, first, that the sentence of divorce, and second mariage, is one and the same. So that when the right of divorce is evinc't to belong not only to the cause of fornication, the power of second mariage is also prov'd to be not limited to that cause only; and that most evidently, when as the holy Ghost, 1 *Cor.* 7. so frees the deserted party from bondage, as that he may not only send a just divorce in case of desertion, but may seek another mariage.

Lastly, Seeing God will not that any should live in danger of fornication and utter ruine for the default of another, and hath commanded the husband to send away with a bill of divorce her whom he could not love, it is impossible that the charge of adultery should belong to him who for lawfull causes divorces and marries, or to her who marries after she hath bin unjustly rejected, or to him who receavs her without all fraud to the former wedlock. For this were a horrid blasphemy against God, so to interpret his words, as to make him dissent from himself; for who sees not a flat contradiction in this, to enthrall blameles men and women to miseries and injuries, under a false and soothing title of mariage, and yet to declare by his Apostle that a brother or sister is not

under bondage in such cases. No lesse doe these two things
conflict with themselvs, to enforce the innocent and faultles to endure the pain and misery of anothers perversnes, or
els to live in unavoidable temptation; and to affirm elswhere
5 that he lays on no man the burden of another mans sin, nor
doth constrain any man to the endangering of his soul.

CHAP. XLIV.

*That to those also who are justly divorc't, second mariage
ought to be permitted.*

10   *This although it be well prov'd, yet because it concerns
only the offendor, I leav him to search out his own charter
himself in the Author.*

CHAP. XLV.

*That some persons are so ordain'd to mariage, as that they
15   cannot obtain the gift of continence, no not by
earnest prayer, and that therin every one is
to be left to his own judgement, and
conscience, and not to have a burden laid upon him by any other.*

20   ## CHAP. XLVI.

*The words of the Apostle concerning the praise of
single life unfolded.*

These two Chapters not so immediatly debating the right
of divorce, I chose rather not to insert.

CHAP. XLVII.
The Conclusion of this Treatise.

THESE things, most renowned King, I have brought together, both to explain for what causes the un-happy, but sometimes most necessary help of divorce ought to be granted, according to Gods Word, by Princes and Rulers: as also to explain how the words of Christ doe consent with such a grant. I have bin large indeed both in handling those Oracles of God, and in laying down those certain principles, which he who will know what the mind of God is in this matter, must ever think on, and remember. But if wee consider what mist and obscuritie hath bin powrd out by Antichrist upon this question, and how deep this per-nicious contempt of wedlock, and admiration of single life, ev'n in those who are not call'd therto, hath sunk into many mens persuasions, I fear lest all that hath bin said, be hardly anough to persuade such that they would cease at length to make themselvs wiser & holier then God himself, in beeing so severe to grant lawfull mariage, and so easie to connive at all, not only whordoms, but deflowrings, and adulteries. When as among the people of God, no whordom was to be tolerated.

Our Lord Jesus Christ, who came to destroy the works of Satan, send down his Spirit upon all Christians, and princi-pally upon Christian Governours both in Church and Com-mon-wealth (for of the cleer judgement of your royall Maj-esty I nothing doubt, revolving the Scripture so often as yee doe) that they may acknowledge how much they provoke

the anger of God against us, when as all kind of unchastity
is tolerated, fornications and adulteries winkt at: But holy
and honourable wedlock is oft withheld by the meer persuasion of Antichrist, from such as without this remedy, cannot
5 preserve themselves from damnation! For none who hath
but a spark of honesty will deny that Princes and States
ought to use diligence toward the maintaining of pure and
honest life among all men, without which all justice, all fear
of God, and true religion decayes.

10   And who knows not that chastity and purenes of life, can
never be restor'd, or continu'd in the Common-wealth, unlesse it be first establisht in private houses, from whence the
whole breed of men is to come forth. To effect this, no wise
man can doubt that it is necessary for Princes and Magis-
15 trates first with severity to punish whordom and adultery;
next to see that mariages be lawfully contracted, and in the
Lord, then that they be faithfully kept; and lastly, when that
unhappines urges, that they be lawfully dissolv'd, and other
mariage granted, according as the law of God, and of nature,
20 and the Constitutions of pious Princes have decreed; as I have
shewn both by evident autorities of Scripture, together with
the writings of the ancient Fathers, and other testimonies.
Only the Lord grant that we may learn to preferre his ever
just and saving Word, before the Comments of Antichrist,
25 too deeply rooted in many, and the false and blasphemous
exposition of our Saviours words. *Amen.*

The End.

A Post-Script.

THUS farre *Martin Bucer;* Whom where I might without injury to either part of the cause, I deny not to have *epitomiz'd:* in the rest observing a well-warranted rule, not to give an Inventory of so many words, but to
5 weigh thir force. I could have added that eloquent and right Christian discours, writt'n by *Erasmus* on this Argument, not disagreeing in effect from *Bucer.* But this, I hope, will be anough to excuse me with the meer *Englishman,* to be no forger of new and loose opinions. Others may read him in his
10 own phrase on the first to the *Corinthians,* and ease me who never could delight in long citations, much lesse in whole traductions; Whether it be natural disposition or education in me, or that my mother bore me a speaker of what God made mine own, and not a translator. There be others also
15 whom I could reck'n up, of no mean account in the Church (and *Peter Martyr* among the first) who are more then half our own in this controversy. But this is a providence not to be slighted, that as *Bucer* wrote this tractat of divorce in *England* and for *England,* so *Erasmus* professes he begun heer
20 among us the same subject, especially out of compassion, for the need he saw this Nation had of some charitable redresse heerin; and seriously exhorts others to use thir best industry in the cleering of this point, wherin custom hath a greater sway then verity. That therfore which came into the minde
25 of these two admired strangers to doe for *England,* and in a touch of highest prudence which they took to be not yet re-

cover'd from monastic superstition, if I a native am found to
have don for mine own Country, altogether sutably and con-
formly to their so large and cleer understanding, yet without
the lest help of theirs, I suppose that hence-forward among
5 conscionable and judicious persons, it will no more be thought
to my discredit, or at all to this Nations dishonor. And if these
thir books, the one shall be printed often, with best allowance in most religious Cities, the other with express autority
of *Leo* the tenth a Pope, shall for the propagating of truth be
10 publisht and republisht, though against the receav'd opinion
of that Church, and mine containing but the same thing, shall
in a time of reformation, a time of free speaking, free writing,
not find a permission to the Presse, I referre me to wisest men,
whether truth be suffer'd to be truth, or liberty to be liberty
15 now among us, and be not again in danger of new fetters and
captivity after all our hopes and labours lost: and whether
learning be not (which our enemies too profetically fear'd)
in the way to be trodd'n down again by ignorance. Wherof
while time is, out of the faith owing to God and my Country,
20 I bid this Kingdom beware: and doubt not but God who
hath dignify'd this Parlament already to so many glorious
degrees, will also give them (which is a singular blessing) to
inform themselvs rightly in the midst of an unprincipl'd age;
and to prevent this working mystery of ignorance and eccle-
25 siastical thraldom, which under new shapes and disguises
begins afresh to grow upon us.

The End.

TETRACHORDON

EXPOSITIONS UPON THE FOURE CHIEF PLACES
IN SCRIPTURE, WHICH TREAT OF MARIAGE, OR
NULLITIES IN MARIAGE

Tetrachordon:
EXPOSITIONS
UPON

The foure chief places in Scripture,
which treat of Mariage, or nullities in Mariage.

On

Gen. 1. 27. 28. compar'd and explain'd by Gen. 2.
Deut. 24. 1. 2.   (18. 23. 24.
Matth. 5. 31. 32. with Matth. 19. from the 3ᵈ. v. to
1 Cor. 7. from the 10ᵗʰ to the 16ᵗʰ.   (the 11ᵗʰ.

Wherin the Doctrine and Discipline of Divorce, as was
lately publish'd, is confirm'd by explanation of Scripture, by testimony of ancient Fathers, of civill lawes
in the Primitive Church, of famousest
Reformed Divines,

And lastly, by an intended Act of the Parlament and
Church of England in the last yeare of
E D V V A R D the sixth.

By the former Author J. M.

Milton

Σκαιοῖσι καινὰ προσφέρων σοφὰ

Δόξεις ἀχρεῖος, κ'ου σοφὸς πεφυκέναι·

Τῶν δ'αὖ δοκούντων εἰδέναι τι ποικίλον,

Κρείσσων νομισθεὶς ἐν πόλει, λυπρὸς φανῆ. *Euripid. Medea.*

LONDON:
Printed in the yeare 1645.

To the PARLAMENT.

THAT which I knew to be the part of a good Magistrate, aiming at true liberty through the right information of religious and civil life, and that which I saw, and was partaker, of your Vows and solemne Cov'-
5 nants, Parlament of England, your actions also manifestly tending to exalt the truth, and to depresse the tyranny of error, and ill custome, with more constancy and prowesse then ever yet any, since that Parlament which put the first Scepter of this Kingdom into his hand whom God and
10 extraordinary vertue made thir Monarch, were the causes that mov'd me, one else not placing much in the eminence of a dedication, to present your high notice with a Discourse, conscious to it self of nothing more then of diligence, and firm affection to the publick good. And that ye took it
15 so as wise and impartial men, obtaining so great power and dignitie, are wont to accept, in matters both doubtfull and important, what they think offer'd them well meant, and from a rational ability, I had no lesse then to perswade me. And on that perswasion am return'd, as to a
20 famous and free Port, my self also bound by more then a maritime Law, to expose as freely what fraughtage I conceave to bring of no trifles. For although it be generally known, how and by whom ye have been instigated to a hard censure of that former book entitl'd, The Doctrine, and
25 Discipline of Divorce, an opinion held by some of the best among reformed Writers without scandal or confutement, though now thought new and dangerous by some of our

severe Gnostics, *whose little reading, and lesse meditating
holds ever with hardest obstinacy that which it took up with
easiest credulity, I do not find yet that ought, for the fur-
ious incitements which have been us'd, hath issu'd by your*
5 *appointment, that might give the least interruption or disrepute either to the Author, or to the Book. Which he who
will be better advis'd then to call your neglect, or connivence
at a thing imagin'd so perilous, can attribute it to nothing
more justly, then to the deep and quiet streame of your di-*
10 *rect and calme deliberations; that gave not way either to
the fervent rashnesse, or the immaterial gravity of those
who ceas'd not to exasperate without cause. For which uprightnesse and incorrupt refusall of what ye were incens'd
to, Lords and Commons, (though it were don to justice, not*
15 *to me, and was a peculiar demonstration how farre your
waies are different from the rash vulgar) besides those al-
legiances of oath and duty, which are my public debt to
your public labours, I have yet a store of gratitude laid up,
which cannot be exhausted; and such thanks perhaps they*
20 *may live to be, as shall more then whisper to the next ages.
Yet that the Author may be known to ground himself upon
his own innocence, and the merit of his cause, not upon
the favour of a diversion, or a delay to any just censure,
but wishes rather he might see those his detracters at any*
25 *fair meeting, as learned debatements are privileg'd with a
due freedome under equall Moderators, I shall here briefly
single one of them (because he hath oblig'd me to it) who I
perswade me having scarse read the book, nor knowing him*

who writ it, or at least faining the latter, hath not forborn
to scandalize him, unconferr'd with, unadmonisht, un-
dealt with by any Pastorly or brotherly convincement, in
the most open and invective manner, and at the most bitter
5 *opportunity that drift or set designe could have invented.*
And this, when as the Canon Law, though commonly most
favouring the boldnesse of their Priests, punishes the nam-
ing or traducing of any person in the Pulpit, was by him
made no scruple. If I shall therfore take licence by the
10 *right of nature, and that liberty wherin I was born, to de-*
fend my self publicly against a printed Calumny, and do
willingly appeal to those Judges to whom I am accus'd, it
can be no immoderate, or unallowable course of seeking so
just and needfull reparations. Which I had don long since,
15 *had not these employments, which are now visible, deferr'd*
me. It was preacht before ye, Lords and Commons, in Aug-
ust last upon a special day of humiliation, that there was
a wicked Book abroad, *and ye were taxt of sin that it was*
yet uncensur'd, the book deserving to be burnt, *and* im-
20 pudence *also was charg'd upon the Author,* who durst set
his name to it, and dedicate it to your selves. *First,*
Lords and Commons, I pray to that God, before whom ye
then were prostrate, so to forgive ye those omissions and
trespasses, which ye desire most should find forgivness,
25 *as I shall soon shew to the world how easily ye absolve your*
selves of that which this man calls your sin, and is indeed
your wisdome, and your Noblenesse, whereof to this day
ye have don well not to repent. He terms it a wicked book,

and why but for allowing other causes of Divorce, then Christ and his Apostles mention; *and with the same censure condemns of wickednesse not onely* Martin Bucer *that elect Instrument of Reformation, highly honour'd and*
5 *had in reverence by* Edward *the sixth, and his whole Parlament, whom also I had publisht in English by a good providence, about a week before this calumnious digression was preach'd; so that if he knew not* Bucer *then, as he ought to have known, he might at least have known him*
10 *some months after, ere the Sermon came in print, wherein notwithstanding he persists in his former sentence, and condemnes again of wickednesse, either ignorantly or wilfully, not onely* Martin Bucer, *and all the choisest and holiest of our Reformers, but the whole Parlament and Church*
15 *of England in those best and purest times of* Edward *the sixth. All which I shall prove with good evidence, at the end of these Explanations. And then let it be judg'd and seriously consider'd with what hope the affairs of our Religion are committed to one among others, who hath now*
20 *onely left him which of the twain he will choose, whether this shall be his palpable ignorance, or the same wickednesse of his own book, which he so lavishly imputes to the writings of other men: and whether this of his, that thus peremptorily defames and attaints of wickednesse unspotted*
25 *Churches, unblemisht Parlaments, and the most eminent restorers of Christian Doctrine, deserve not to be burnt first. And if his heat had burst out onely against the opinion, his wonted passion had no doubt bin silently born with*

wonted patience. But since against the charity of that sol-
emne place and meeting, it serv'd him furder to inveigh
opprobriously against the person, branding him with no
lesse then impudence, onely for setting his name to what
5 *he had writt'n, I must be excus'd not to be so wanting to*
the defence of an honest name, or to the reputation of those
good men who afford me their society, but to be sensible of
such a foule endeavour'd disgrace: not knowing ought either
in mine own deserts, or the Laws of this Land, why I
10 *should be subject, in such a notorious and illegal manner,*
to the intemperancies of this mans preaching choler. And
indeed to be so prompt and ready in the midst of his hum-
blenesse, to tosse reproaches of this bulk and size, argues
as if they were the weapons of his exercise, I am sure not
15 *of his Ministery, or of that dayes work. Certainly to sub-*
scribe my name at what I was to own, was what the State
had order'd and requires. And he who lists not to be mali-
cious, would call it ingenuity, cleer conscience, willing-
nesse to avouch what might be question'd, or to be better
20 *instructed. And if God were so displeas'd with those,* Isa.
58. *who* on the solemne fast were wont to smite with
the fist of wickednesse, *it could be no signe of his own*
humiliation accepted, which dispos'd him to smite so keenly
with a reviling tongue. But if onely to have writ my name
25 *must be counted* impudence, *how doth this but justifie an-*
other, who might affirm with as good warrant, that the late
Discourse of Scripture and Reason, *which is certain to be*
chiefly his own draught, was publisht without a name, out

*of base fear, and the sly avoidance of what might follow to
his detriment, if the party at Court should hap to reach
him. And I, to have set my name, where he accuses me to
have set it, am so far from recanting, that I offer my hand*
5 *also if need be, to make good the same opinion which I
there maintain, by inevitable consequences drawn parallel
from his own principal arguments in that of* Scripture
and Reason; *which I shall pardon him, if he can deny,
without shaking his own composition to peeces. The* im-
10 pudence *therfore, since he waigh'd so little what a grosse
revile that was to give his equall, I send him back again for
a* phylactery *to stitch upon his arrogance, that censures not
onely before conviction so bitterly without so much as one
reason giv'n, but censures the Congregation of his Governors*
15 *to their faces, for not being so hasty as himself to censure.*

*And whereas my other crime is, that I address'd the
Dedication of what I had studied, to the Parlament, how
could I better declare the loyalty which I owe to that supreme
and majestick Tribunal, and the opinion which I have of*
20 *the high-entrusted judgement, and personall worth assembl'd in that place. With the same affections therfore, and
the same addicted fidelity, Parlament of England, I here
again have brought to your perusal on the same argument
these following Expositions of Scripture. The former book,*
25 *as pleas'd some to think, who were thought judicious, had
of reason in it to a sufficiencie; what they requir'd, was
that the Scriptures there alleg'd, might be discuss'd more
fully. To their desires, thus much furder hath been labour'd*

in the Scriptures. Another sort also who wanted more au-
torities, and citations, have not been here unthought of. If
all this attain not to satisfie them, as I am confident that
none of those our great controversies at this day, hath had
5 *a more demonstrative explaining, I must confesse to ad-*
mire what it is, for doubtlesse it is not reason now adayes
that satisfies, or suborns the common credence of men, to
yeeld so easily, and grow so vehement in matters much
more disputable, and farre lesse conducing to the daily
10 *good and peace of life. Some whose necessary shifts have*
long enur'd them to cloak the defects of their unstudied
yeers, and hatred now to learn, under the appearance of a
grave solidity, which estimation they have gain'd among
weak perceivers, find the ease of slighting what they cannot
15 *refute, and are determin'd, as I hear, to hold it not worth*
the answering. In which number I must be forc'd to reck'n
that Doctor, who in a late equivocating Treatise plausibly
set afloat against the Dippers, *diving the while himself*
with a more deep prelatical malignance against the present
20 *state, & Church-government, mentions with ignominy* the
Tractate of Divorce; *yet answers nothing, but instead*
thereof (for which I do not commend his marshalling) sets
Moses *also among the crew of his Anabaptists; as one who*
to a holy Nation, the Common-wealth of Israel, gave Laws
25 breaking the bonds of mariage to inordinate lust. *These*
are no mean surges of blasphemy, not onely dipping Moses
the divine Lawgiver, but dashing with a high hand against
the justice and purity of God himself; as these ensuing

Scriptures plainly and freely handl'd shall verifie to the launcing of that old apostemated *error. Him therefore I leave now to his repentance.*

Others, which is their courtesie, confesse that wit and
5 *parts may do much to make that seem true which is not (as was objected to* Socrates *by them who could not resist his efficacy, that he ever made the worse cause seem the better) and thus thinking themselves discharg'd of the difficulty, love not to wade furder into the fear of a convincement.*
10 *These will be their excuses to decline the full examining of this serious point. So much the more I presse it and repeat it,* Lords *and* Commons, *that ye beware while time is, ere this grand secret, and onely art of ignorance affecting tyrany, grow powerfull and rule among us. For if*
15 *sound argument and reason shall be thus put off, either by an undervaluing silence, or the maisterly censure of a rayling word or two in the Pulpit, or by rejecting the force of truth, as the meer cunning of eloquence, and Sophistry, what can be the end of this, but that all good learning and*
20 *knowledge will suddenly decay: Ignorance, and illiterate presumption, which is yet but our disease, will turn at length into our very constitution, and prove the* hectic *evill of this age: worse to be fear'd, if it get once to reign over us, then any fift Monarchy. If this shall be the course, that*
25 *what was wont to be a chief commendation, and the ground of other mens confidence in an Author, his diligence, his learning, his elocution whether by right, or by ill meaning granted him, shall be turn'd now to a disadvantage and*

suspicion against him, that what he writes though uncon-
futed, must therefore be mistrusted, therfore not receiv'd
for the industry, the exactnesse, the labour in it, confess'd
to be more then ordnary; as if wisdome had now forsak'n
5 *the thirstie and laborious inquirer to dwell against her*
nature with the arrogant and shallow babler, to what pur-
pose all those pains and that continual searching requir'd
of us by Solomon *to the attainment of understanding; why*
are men bred up with such care and expence to a life of
10 *perpetual studies, why do your selves with such endeavour*
seek to wipe off the imputation of intending to discourage
the progresse and advance of learning? He therfore whose
heart can bear him to the high pitch of your noble enter-
prises, may easily assure himself that the prudence and
15 *farre-judging circumspectnesse of so grave a Magistracy*
sitting in Parlament, who have before them the prepar'd
and purpos'd Act of their most religious predecessors to
imitate in this question, cannot reject the cleernesse of these
reasons, and these allegations both here and formerly offer'd
20 *them; nor can over-look the necessity of ordaining more*
wholsomly and more humanly in the casualties of Divorce,
then our Laws have yet establisht: if the most urgent and
excessive grievances hapning in domestick life, be worth
the laying to heart, which, unlesse charity be farre from us,
25 *cannot be neglected. And that these things both in the right*
constitution, and in the right reformation of a Common-
wealth call for speediest redresse, and ought to be the first
consider'd, anough was urg'd in what was prefac'd to that

monument of Bucer *which I brought to your remembrance, and the other time before. Hence forth, except new cause be giv'n, I shall say lesse and lesse. For if the Law make not timely provision, let the Law, as reason is, bear the censure*
5 *of those consequences, which her own default now more evidently produces. And if men want manlinesse to expostulate the right of their due ransom, and to second their own occasions, they may sit hereafter and bemoan themselves to have neglected through faintnesse the onely remedy of their*
10 *sufferings, which a seasonable and well grounded speaking might have purchas'd them. And perhaps in time to come, others will know how to esteem what is not every day put into their hands, when they have markt events, and better weigh'd how hurtfull and unwise it is, to hide a secret and*
15 *pernicious rupture under the ill counsell of a bashfull silence. But who would distrust ought, or not be ample in his hopes of your wise and Christian determinations? who have the prudence to consider, and should have the goodnesse like gods, as ye are call'd, to find out readily, and by just Law*
20 *to administer those redresses which have of old, not without God ordaining, bin granted to the adversities of mankind, ere they who needed, were put to ask. Certainly, if any other have enlarg'd his thoughts to expect from this government so justly undertak'n, and by frequent assist-*
25 *ances from heaven so apparently upheld, glorious changes and renovations both in Church and State, he among the formost might be nam'd, who prayes that the fate of England may tarry for no other Deliverers.*

JOHN MILTON.

Tetrachordon,

Expositions upon the foure chiefe places in Scripture
which treat of Mariage, or nullities in Mariage.

Gen. 1. 27.

*So God created man in his owne image, in the image of God
created he him; male and female created he them.*

28. And God blessed them, and God said unto them be fruit-
5 *full, &c.*

Gen. 2. 18.

*And the Lord God said, It is not good that man should be
alone, I will make him a helpe meet for him.*

23. And Adam said, This is now bone of my bones, and flesh
10 *of my flesh; she shall be called Woman, because she was
taken out of Man.*

*24. Therefore shall a man leave his father and his mother,
and shall cleave unto his wife, and they shall be one flesh.*

Gen. 1. 27.

15 **S**O *God created man in his owne image.*] To be inform'd
aright in the whole History of Mariage, that we may
know for certain, not by a forc't yoke, but by an impartial definition, what Mariage is, and what is not Mariage;
it will undoubtedly be safest, fairest, and most with our obedi-
20 ence, to enquire, as our Saviours direction is, how it was in the
beginning. And that we begin so high as man created after

Gods owne Image, there want not earnest causes. For nothing
now adayes is more degenerately forgott'n, then the true dignity of man, almost in every respect, but especially in this
prime institution of Matrimony, wherein his native pre-emi-
5 nece ought most to shine. Although if we consider that just
and naturall privileges men neither can rightly seek, nor dare
fully claime, unlesse they be ally'd to inward goodnesse, and
stedfast knowledge, and that the want of this quells them to
a servile sense of their own conscious unworthinesse, it may
10 save the wondring why in this age many are so opposite both
to human and to Christian liberty, either while they understand not, or envy others that do; contenting, or rather prid-
ing themselves in a specious humility and strictnesse bred out
of low ignorance that never yet conceiv'd the freedome of the
15 Gospel; and is therefore by the Apostle to the Colossians
rankt with no better company, then Will-worship and the
meer shew of wisdome. And how injurious herein they are,
if not to themselves, yet to their neighbours, and not to them
only, but to the all-wise and bounteous grace offer'd us in our
20 redemption, will orderly appear.

[*In the Image of God created he him.*] It is anough determin'd, that this Image of God wherin man was created, is
meant Wisdom, Purity, Justice, and rule over all creatures.
All which being lost in *Adam,* was recover'd with gain by the
25 merits of Christ. For albeit our first parent had lordship over
sea, and land, and aire, yet there was a law without him, as a
guard set over him. But Christ having cancell'd the hand
writing of ordinances which was against us, *Coloss.* 2. 14.

and interpreted the fulfilling of all through charity, hath in
that respect set us over law, in the free custody of his love, and
left us victorious under the guidance of his living Spirit, not
under the dead letter; to follow that which most edifies, most
5 aides and furders a religious life, makes us holiest and likest to
his immortall Image, not that which makes us most conform-
able and captive to civill and subordinat precepts; whereof the
strictest observance may oftimes prove the destruction not
only of many innocent persons and families, but of whole
10 Nations. Although indeed no ordinance human or from
heav'n can binde against the good of man; so that to keep
them strictly against that end, is all one with to breake them.
Men of most renowned vertu have sometimes by transgressing, most truly kept the law; and wisest Magistrates have per-
15 mitted and dispenc't it; while they lookt not peevishly at the
letter, but with a greater spirit at the good of mankinde, if
alwayes not writt'n in the characters of law, yet engrav'n in
the heart of man by a divine impression. This Heathens could
see, as the well-read in story can recount of *Solon* and *Epam-*
20 *inondas,* whom *Cicero* in his first booke of *invention* nobly
defends. *All law,* saith he, *we ought referr to the common*
good, and interpret by that, not by the scrowl of letters. No
man observes law for laws sake, but for the good of them for
whom it was made. The rest might serv well to lecture these
25 times, deluded through belly-doctrines into a devout slavery.
The Scripture also affords us *David* in the shew-bread, *Heze-*
chiah in the passeover sound and safe transgressors of the
literall command, which also dispenc'd not seldom with it

self; and taught us on what just occasions to doe so: untill our
Saviour for whom that great and God-like work was reserv'd,
redeem'd us to a state above prescriptions by dissolving the
whole law into charity. And have we not the soul to under-
5 stand this, and must we against this glory of Gods transcend-
ent love towards us be still the servants of a literall indight-
ment?

[*Created he him.*] It might be doubted why he saith, *In
the Image of God created he him,* not them, as well as *male
10 and female* them; especially since that Image might be common to them both, but *male and female* could not, however
the Jewes fable, and please themselvs with the accidentall concurrence of *Plato*'s wit, as if man at first had bin created *Her-
maphrodite:* but then it must have bin male and female cre-
15 ated he him. So had the Image of God bin equally common
to them both, it had no doubt bin said, In the image of God
created he them. But St. *Paul* ends the controversie by explaining that the woman is not primarily and immediatly
the image of God, but in reference to the man. *The head of
20 the woman,* saith he, 1 *Cor.* 11. *is the man: he the image and
glory of God, she the glory of the man:* he not for her, but she
for him. Therefore his precept is, *Wives be subject to your
husbands as is fit in the Lord, Coloss.* 3. 18. *In every thing,
Eph.* 5. 24. Neverthelesse man is not to hold her as a servant,
25 but receives her into a part of that empire which God pro-
claims him to, though not equally, yet largely, as his own
image and glory: for it is no small glory to him, that a creature so like him, should be made subject to him. Not but that

particular exceptions may have place, if she exceed her husband in prudence and dexterity, and he contentedly yeeld, for then a superior and more naturall law comes in, that the wiser should govern the lesse wise, whether male or female.
5 But that which far more easily and obediently follows from this verse, is that, seeing woman was purposely made for man, and he her head, it cannot stand before the breath of this divine utterance, that man the portraiture of God, joyning to himself for his intended good and solace an inferiour sexe,
10 should so becom her thrall, whose wilfulnes or inability to be a wife frustrates the occasionall end of her creation, but that he may acquitt himself to freedom by his naturall birth-right, and that indeleble character of priority which God crown'd him with. If it be urg'd that sin hath lost him this, the answer
15 is not far to seek, that from her the sin first proceeded, which keeps her justly in the same proportion still beneath. She is not to gain by being first in the transgression, that man should furder loose to her, because already he hath lost by her means. Oft it happens that in this matter he is without fault; so that
20 his punishment herein is causeles: and God hath the praise in our speeches of him, to sort his punishment in the same kind with the offence. Suppose he err'd; it is not the intent of God or man, to hunt an error so to the death with a revenge beyond all measure and proportion. But if we argue thus,
25 this affliction is befaln him for his sin, therefore he must bear it, without seeking the only remedy, first it will be false that all affliction comes for sin, as in the case of *Job,* and of the man born blind, *Joh.* 9. 3, was evident: next by that reason,

all miseries comming for sin, we must let them all lye upon
us like the vermin of an Indian *Catharist,* which his fond religion forbids him to molest. Were it a particular punishment inflicted through the anger of God upon a person, or
5 upon a land, no law hinders us in that regard, no law but
bidds us remove it if we can: much more if it be a dangerous
temptation withall, much more yet, if it be certainly a temptation, and not certainly a punishment, though a pain. As for
what they say we must bear with patience, to bear with pa-
10 tience, and to seek effectuall remedies, implies no contradiction. It may no lesse be for our disobedience, our unfaithfulnes,
and other sins against God, that wives becom adulterous to the
bed, and questionles we ought to take the affliction as patiently,
as christian prudence would wish; yet hereby is not lost the
15 right of divorcing for adultery. No you say, because our Saviour excepted that only. But why, if he were so bent to punish our sins, and try our patience in binding on us a disastrous
mariage, why did he except adultery? Certainly to have bin
bound from divorce in that case also had bin as plentifull a
20 punishment to our sins, and not too little work for the pa-
tientest. Nay perhaps they will say it was too great a sufferance: And with as slight a reason, for no wise man but would
sooner pardon the act of adultery once and again committed
by a person worth pitty and forgivnes, then to lead a weari-
25 som life of unloving & unquiet conversation with one who
neither affects nor is affected, much lesse with one who exercises all bitternes, and would commit adultery too, but for
envy lest the persecuted condition should thereby get the ben-

efit of his freedom. 'Tis plain therefore that God enjoyns not this supposed strictnes of not divorcing either to punish us, or to try our patience.

Moreover, if man be the image of God, which consists in
5 holines, and woman ought in the same respect to be the image and companion of man, in such wise to be lov'd, as the Church is belov'd of Christ, and if, as God is the head of Christ, and Christ the head of man, so man is the head of woman; I cannot see by this golden dependance of headship
10 and subjection, but that Piety and Religion is the main tye of Christian Matrimony: So as if there be found between the pair a notorious disparity either of wickednes or heresie, the husband by all manner of right is disingag'd from a creature, not made and inflicted on him to the vexation of his right-
15 eousnes; the wife also, as her subjection is terminated in the Lord, being her self the redeem'd of Christ, is not still bound to be the vassall of him, who is the bondslave of Satan: she being now neither the image nor the glory of such a person, nor made for him, nor left in bondage to him; but hath re-
20 cours to the wing of charity, and protection of the Church; unless there be a hope on either side; yet such a hope must be meant, as may be a rationall hope, and not an endles servi- tude. Of which hereafter.

But usually it is objected, that if it be thus, then there can
25 be no true mariage between misbeleevers and irreligious per- sons? I might answer, let them see to that who are such; the Church hath no commission to judge those without, 1 *Cor.* 5. But this they will say perhaps, is but penuriously to resolv a

doubt. I answer therefore, that where they are both irreligious, the mariage may be yet true anough to them in a civill
relation. For there are left som remains of Gods image in
man, as he is meerly man; which reason God gives against
5 the shedding of mans bloud, *Gen*. 9. as being made in Gods
image, without expression whether he were a good man or a
bad, to exempt the slayer from punishment. So that in those
mariages where the parties are alike void of Religion, the
wife owes a civill homage and subjection, the husband owes
10 a civill loyalty. But where the yoke is mis-yok't, heretick with
faithfull, godly with ungodly, to the grievance and manifest
endangering of a brother or sister, reasons of a higher strain
then matrimoniall bear sway; unlesse the Gospel instead of
freeing us, debase it self to make us bondmen, and suffer evill
15 to controule good.

[*Male and female created he them.*] This contains another
end of matching man and woman, being the right, and law-
fulnes of the marige bed; though much inferior to the former end of her being his image and helpe in religious society.
20 And who of weakest insight may not see that this creating of
them male and female, cannot in any order of reason, or
Christianity, be of such moment against the better and higher
purposes of their creation, as to enthrall husband or wife to
duties or to sufferings, unworthy and unbeseeming the image
25 of God in them? Now when as not only men, but good men
doe stand upon their right, their estimation, their dignity in
all other actions and deportments with warrant anough and
good conscience, as having the image of God in them, it will

not be difficult to determin what is unworthy and unseemly
for a man to do or suffer in wedlock; and the like propor-
tionally may be found for woman: if we love not to stand disputing below the principles of humanity. He that said, *Male*
5 *and female created he them,* immediatly before that said also
in the same verse, *In the Image of God created he him,* and
redoubl'd it, that our thoughts might not be so full of dregs
as to urge this poor consideration of *male and female,* without remembring the noblenes of that former repetition; lest
10 when God sends a wise eye to examin our triviall glosses, they
be found extremly to creep upon the ground: especially since
they confesse that what here concerns mariage is but a brief
touch, only preparative to the institution which follows more
expressely in the next Chapter: and that Christ so took it, as
15 desiring to be briefest with them who came to tempt him,
account shall be given in due place.

V. 28. *And God blessed them, and God said unto them, be*
fruitfull, and multiply, and replenish the earth, &c.

This declares another end of Matrimony, the propagation
20 of mankind; and is again repeated to *Noah* and his sons.
Many things might be noted on this place not ordinary, nor
unworth the noting; but I undertook not a generall Comment. Hence therefore we see the desire of children is honest
and pious; if we be not lesse zealous in our Christianity, then
25 *Plato* was in his heathenism; who in the sixt *of his laws,*
counts off-spring therefore desirable, that we may leav in our
stead sons of our sons, continuall servants of God: a religious

and prudent desire, if people knew as well what were requir'd to breeding as to begetting; which desire perhaps was
a cause why the Jews hardly could endure a barren wedlock:
and *Philo* in his book of speciall laws esteems him only worth
5 pardon that sends not barrennes away. *Carvilius* the first recorded in Rome to have sought divorce, had it granted him
for the barrennes of his wife, upon his oath that he maried to
the end he might have children; as *Dionysius* and *Gellius* are
authors. But to dismisse a wife only for barrennes, is hard:
10 and yet in som the desire of children is so great, and so just,
yea somtime so necessary, that to condemn such a one to a
childles age, the fault apparently not being in him, might
seem perhaps more strict then needed. Somtimes inheritances,
crowns, and dignities are so interested and annext in their
15 common peace and good to such or such lineall descent, that
it may prove a great moment both in the affairs of men and
of religion, to consider throughly what might be don heerin,
notwithstanding the waywardnes of our School Doctors.

Gen. 2. 18.

20 *And the Lord said, It is not good that man should be alone;*
   I will make him a help meet for him.
   V. 23. *And Adam said,* &c. V. 24. *Therefore shall a man*
   leave, &c.

THIS second Chapter is granted to be a Commentary
25   on the first; and these verses granted to be an exposi-
      tion of that former verse, *Male and female created he*
them, and yet when this male and female is by the explicite

words of God himselfe heer declar'd to be not meant other
then a fit help, and meet society; som who would ingrosse
to themselves the whole trade of interpreting, will not suffer
the cleer text of God to doe the office of explaining it self.

5   [*And the Lord God said it is not good.*] A man would
think that the consideration of who spake, should raise up
the attention of our minds to enquire better, and obey the
purpos of so great a Speaker: for as we order the busines of
Mariage, that which he heer speaks is all made vain; and in
10 the decision of matrimony, or not matrimony, nothing at all
regarded. Our presumption, hath utterly chang'd the state and
condition of this ordinance: God ordain'd it in love and help-
fulnes to be indissoluble, and we in outward act and formality
to be a forc't bondage; so that being subject to a thousand
15 errors in the best men, if it prove a blessing to any, it is of meer
accident, as mans law hath handl'd it, and not of institution.

  [*It is not good for man to be alone.*] Hitherto all things
that have bin nam'd, were approv'd of God to be very good:
lonelines is the first thing which Gods eye nam'd not good:
20 whether it be a thing, or the want of somthing, I labour not;
let it be their tendance, who have the art to be industriously
idle. And heer *alone* is meant alone without woman; otherwise *Adam* had the company of God himself, and Angels
to convers with; all creatures to delight him seriously, or to
25 make him sport. God could have created him out of the
same mould a thousand friends and brother *Adams* to have
bin his consorts, yet for all this till *Eve* was giv'n him, God
reckn'd him to be alone.

[*It is not good.*] God heer presents himself like to a man deliberating; both to shew us that the matter is of high consequence, and that he intended to found it according to naturall reason, not impulsive command, but that the duty should arise from the reason of it, not the reason be swallow'd up in a reasonlesse duty. *Not good,* was as much to *Adam* before his fall, as not pleasing, not expedient; but since the comming of sin into the world, to him who hath not receiv'd the continence, it is not only not expedient to be alone, but plainly sinfull. And therefore he who wilfully abstains from mariage, not being supernaturally gifted, and he who by making the yoke of mariage unjust and intolerable, causes men to abhorr it, are both in a diabolicall sin, equall to that of Antichrist who forbids to marry. For what difference at all whether he abstain men from marying, or restrain them in a mariage hapning totally discommodious, distastfull, dishonest and pernicious to him without the appearance of his fault? For God does not heer precisely say, I make a female to this male, as he did briefly before, but expounding himselfe heer on purpos, he saith, because it is not good for man to be alone, I make him therefore a meet help. God supplies the privation of not good, with the perfect gift of a reall and positive good; it is mans pervers cooking who hath turn'd this bounty of God into a Scorpion, either by weak and shallow constructions, or by proud arrogance and cruelty to them who neither in their purposes nor in their actions have offended against the due honour of wedlock.

Now whereas the Apostle speaking in the Spirit, 1 *Cor.* 7.

pronounces quite contrary to this word of God, *It is good for a man not to touch a woman,* and God cannot contradict himself, it instructs us that his commands and words, especially such as bear the manifest title of som good to man, are not to
5 be so strictly wrung, as to command without regard to the most naturall and miserable necessities of mankind. Therefore the Apostle adds a limitation in the 26 v. of that chap. for the present necessity it is good; which he gives us doubtlesse as a pattern how to reconcile other places by the generall
10 rule of charity.

[*For man to be alone.*] Som would have the sense heerof to be in respect of procreation only: and *Austin* contests that manly friendship in all other regards had bin a more becomming solace for *Adam,* then to spend so many secret years in
15 an empty world with one woman. But our Writers deservedly reject this crabbed opinion; and defend that there is a peculiar comfort in the maried state besides the genial bed, which no other society affords. No mortall nature can endure either in the actions of Religion, or study of wisdome, with-
20 out somtime slackning the cords of intense thought and labour: which lest we should think faulty, God himself conceals us not his own recreations before the world was built; *I was,* saith the eternall wisdome, *dayly his delight, playing alwayes before him.* And to him indeed wisdom is as a high
25 towr of pleasure, but to us a steep hill, and we toyling ever about the bottom: he executes with ease the exploits of his omnipotence, as easie as with us it is to will: but no worthy enterprise can be don by us without continuall plodding and

wearisomnes to our faint and sensitive abilities. We cannot
therefore alwayes be contemplative, or pragmaticall abroad,
but have need of som delightfull intermissions, wherin the
enlarg'd soul may leav off a while her severe schooling; and
5 like a glad youth in wandring vacancy, may keep her holli-
daies to joy and harmles pastime: which as she cannot well
doe without company, so in no company so well as where the
different sexe in most resembling unlikenes, and most unlike
resemblance cannot but please best and be pleas'd in the apti-
10 tude of that variety. Wherof lest we should be too timorous,
in the aw that our flat sages would form us and dresse us,
wisest *Salomon* among his gravest Proverbs countenances a
kinde of ravishment and erring fondnes in the entertainment
of wedded leisures; and in the Song of Songs, which is gen-
15 erally beleev'd, even in the jolliest expressions to figure the
spousals of the Church with Christ, sings of a thousand rap-
tures between those two lovely ones farre on the hither side of
carnall enjoyment. By these instances, and more which might
be brought, we may imagine how indulgently God provided
20 against mans lonelines; that he approv'd it not, as by himself
declar'd not good; that he approv'd the remedy therof, as of
his own ordaining, consequently good; and as he ordain'd it,
so doubtles proportionably to our fal'n estate he gives it; els
were his ordinance at least in vain, and we for all his gift still
25 empty handed. Nay such an unbounteous giver we should
make him, as in the fables *Jupiter* was to *Ixion,* giving him *a*
cloud instead of *Juno,* giving him a monstrous issue by her,
the breed of *Centaures* a neglected and unlov'd race, the

fruits of a delusive mariage, and lastly giving him her with a
damnation to that wheele in hell, from a life thrown into the
midst of temptations and disorders. But God is no deceitfull
giver, to bestow that on us for a remedy of lonelines, which if
5 it bring not a sociable minde as well as a conjunctive body,
leavs us no lesse alone then before; and if it bring a minde
perpetually avers and disagreeable, betraies us to a wors condition then the most deserted lonelines. God cannot in the
justice of his own promise and institution so unexpectedly
10 mock us by forcing that upon us as the remedy of solitude,
which wraps us in a misery worse then any wildernes, as the
Spirit of God himself judges, Prov. 19. especially knowing
that the best and wisest men amidst the sincere and most cor-
diall designes of their heart doe dayly erre in choosing. We
15 may conclude therfore seeing orthodoxall Expositers confesse
to our hands, that by lonelines is not only meant the want of
copulation, and that man is not lesse alone by turning in a
body to him, unlesse there be within it a minde answerable,
that it is a work more worthy the care and consultation of
20 God to provide for the worthiest part of man which is his
minde, and not unnaturally to set it beneath the formalities
and respects of the body, to make it a servant of its owne vassall, I say we may conclude that such a mariage, wherin the
minde is so disgrac't and vilify'd below the bodies interest,
25 and can have no just or tolerable contentment, is not of Gods
institution, and therfore no mariage. Nay in concluding this,
I say we conclude no more then what the common Expositers
themselves give us, both in that which I have recited and

much more hereafter. But the truth is, they give us in such a manner, as they who leav their own mature positions like the eggs of an Ostrich in the dust; I do but lay them in the sun; their own pregnancies hatch the truth; and I am taxt of
5 novelties and strange producements, while they, like that inconsiderat bird, know not that these are their own naturall breed.

[*I will make him a help meet for him.*] Heer the heavnly instituter, as if he labour'd, not to be mistak'n by the super-
10 cilious hypocrisie of those that love to maister their brethren, and to make us sure that he gave us not now a servil yoke, but an amiable knot; contents not himself to say, I will make him a wife, but resolving to give us first the meaning before the name of a wife, saith graciously, *I will make him a help meet*
15 *for him.* And heer again, as before, I doe not require more full and fair deductions then the whole consent of our Divines usually raise from this text, that in matrimony there must be first a mutuall help to piety, next to civill fellowship of love and amity, then to generation, so to houshold affairs, lastly
20 the remedy of incontinence. And commonly they reck'n them in such order, as leavs generation and incontinence to be last consider'd. This I amaze me at, that though all the superior and nobler ends both of mariage and of the maried persons be absolutely frustrat, the matrimony stirs not, looses
25 no hold, remains as rooted as the center: but if the body bring but in a complaint of frigidity, by that cold application only, this adamantine *Alpe* of wedlock has leav to dissolve; which els all the machinations of religious or civill reason at the suit

of a distressed mind, either for divine worship or humane conversation violated, cannot unfasten. What courts of concupiscence are these, wherin fleshly appetite is heard before right reason, lust before love or devotion? They may be pious
5 Christians together, they may be loving and friendly, they may be helpfull to each other in the family, but they cannot couple; that shall divorce them though either party would not. They can neither serv God together, nor one be at peace with the other, nor be good in the family one to other, but
10 live as they were dead, or live as they were deadly enemies in a cage together; tis all one, they can couple, they shall not divorce till death, no though this sentence be their death. What is this, besides tryranny, but to turn nature upside down, to make both religion, and the minde of man wait upon the
15 slavish errands of the body, and not the body to follow either the sancity, or the sovranty of the mind unspeakably wrong'd, and with all equity complaining? what is this but to abuse the sacred and misterious bed of mariage to be the compulsive stie of an ingratefull and malignant lust, stirr'd up only from
20 a carnall acrimony, without either love or peace, or regard to any other thing holy or human. This I admire how possibly it should inhabit thus long in the sense of so many disputing *Theologians,* unlesse it be the lowest lees of a canonicall infection livergrown to their sides; which perhaps will never un-
25 cling, without the strong abstersive of som heroick magistrat, whose mind equall to his high office dares lead him both to know and to do without their frivolous case-putting. For certain he shall have God and this institution plainly on his side.

And if it be true both in divinity and law, that consent alone, though copulation never follow, makes a mariage, how can they dissolv it for the want of that which made it not, and not dissolv it for that not continuing which made it, and should
5 preserve it in love and reason, and difference it from a brute conjugality.

[*Meet for him.*] The originall heer is more expressive then other languages word for word can render it; but all agree effectuall conformity of disposition and affection to be heerby
10 signify'd; which God as it were not satisfy'd with the naming of a help, goes on describing *another self, a second self, a very self it self.* Yet now there is nothing in the life of man through our misconstruction, made more uncertain, more hazardous and full of chance then this divine blessing with such favor-
15 able significance heer conferr'd upon us, which if we do but erre in our choice the most unblamable error that can be, erre but one minute, one moment after those mighty syllables pronounc't which take upon them to joyn heavn and hell to-gether unpardnably till death pardon, this divine blessing
20 that lookt but now with such a human smile upon us, and spoke such gentle reason, strait vanishes like a fair skie and brings on such a scene of cloud and tempest, as turns all to shipwrack without havn or shoar but to a ransomles cap-tivity. And then they tell us it is our sin; but let them be told
25 again, that sin through the mercy of God hath not made such wast upon us, as to make utterly void to our use any temporall benefit, much lesse any so much availing to a peacefull and sanctify'd life, meerly for a most incident error which no

warines can certainly shun. And wherfore servs our happy
redemption, and the liberty we have in Christ, but to deliver
us from calamitous yokes not to be liv'd under without the
endangerment of our souls, and to restore us in som compe-
5 tent measure to a right in every good thing both of this life,
and the other. Thus we see how treatably and distinctly God
hath heer taught us what the prime ends of mariage are,
mutuall solace and help. That we are now, upon the most
irreprehensible mistake in choosing, defeated and defrauded
10 of all this originall benignity, was begun first through the
snare of Antichristian canons long since obtruded upon the
Church of Rome, and not yet scour'd off by reformation, out
of a lingring vain-glory that abides among us to make fair
shews in formall ordinances, and to enjoyn continence &
15 bearing of crosses in such a garb as no Scripture binds us,
under the thickest arrows of temptation, where we need not
stand. Now we shall see with what acknowledgement and
assent *Adam* receiv'd this new associat, which God brought
him.

20 V. 23. *And Adam said this is now bone of my bones, and*
flesh of my flesh, she shall be called Woman, because
she was tak'n out of Man.

That there was a neerer alliance between *Adam* and *Eve*,
then could be ever after between man and wife, is visible to
25 any. For no other woman was ever moulded out of her husbands rib, but of meer strangers for the most part they com to
have that consanguinity which they have by wedlock. And if

we look neerly upon the matter, though mariage be most
agreeable to holines, to purity and justice, yet is it not a naturall, but a civill and ordain'd relation. For if it were in nature,
no law or crime could disanull it, to make a wife, or husband,
5 otherwise then still a wife or husband, but only death; as
nothing but that can make a father no father, or a son no son.
But divorce for adultery or desertion, as all our Churches
agree but England, not only separats, but nullifies, and extinguishes the relation it self of matrimony, so that they are
10 no more man and wife; otherwise the innocent party could
not marry else-where, without the guilt of adultery; next
were it meerly naturall why was it heer ordain'd more then
the rest of morall law to man in his originall rectitude, in
whose brest all that was naturall or morall was engrav'n with-
15 out externall constitutions and edicts. *Adam* therfore in these
words does not establish an indissoluble bond of mariage in
the carnall ligaments of flesh and bones, for if he did, it would
belong only to himself in the literall sense; every one of us
being neerer in flesh of flesh, and bone of bones to our parents
20 then to a wife; they therfore were not to be left for her in that
respect. But *Adam* who had the wisdom giv'n him to know
all creatures, and to name them according to their properties,
no doubt but had the gift to discern perfectly, that which
concern'd him much more; and to apprehend at first sight
25 the true fitnes of that consort which God provided him. And
therfore spake in reference to those words which God pronounc't before; as if he had said, this is she by whose meet
help and society I shall no more be alone; this is she who was

made my image, ev'n as I the Image of God; not so much in
body, as in unity of mind and heart. And he might as easily
know what were the words of God, as he knew so readily
what had bin don with his rib, while he slept so soundly. He
5 might well know, if God took a rib out of his inside, to form
of it a double good to him, he would far sooner dis-joyn it
from his outside, to prevent a treble mischief to him: and far
sooner cut it quite off from all relation for his undoubted ease,
then nail it into his body again, to stick for ever there a thorn
10 in his heart. When as nature teaches us to divide any limb
from the body to the saving of his fellows, though it be the
maiming and deformity of the whole; how much more is it
her doctrin to sever by incision, not a true limb so much,
though that be lawfull, but an adherent, a sore, the gangrene
15 of a limb, to the recovery of a whole man. But if in these
words we shall make *Adam* to erect a new establishment of
mariage in the meer flesh, which God so lately had instituted,
and founded in the sweet and mild familiarity of love and
solace and mutuall fitnes, what do we but use the mouth of
20 our generall parent, the first time it opens, to an arrogant
opposition, and correcting of Gods wiser ordinance. These
words therfore cannot import any thing new in mariage, but
either that which belongs to *Adam* only, or to us in reference
only to the instituting words of God which made a meet help
25 against lonelines. *Adam* spake like *Adam* the words of flesh
and bones, the shell and rinde of matrimony; but God spake
like God, of love and solace and meet help, the soul both of
*Adam*s words and of matrimony.

*V. 24. Therefore shall a man leav his father and his mother,
and shall cleav unto his wife; and they shall be one
flesh.*

This vers, as our common heed expounds it, is the great
5 knot tier, which hath undon by tying, and by tangling, mil-
lions of guiltles consciences: this is that greisly Porter, who
having drawn men and wisest men by suttle allurement
within the train of an unhappy matrimony, claps the dun-
geon gate upon them, as irrecoverable as the grave. But if we
10 view him well, and hear him with not too hasty and prejudi-
cant ears, we shall finde no such terror in him. For first, it is
not heer said absolutely without all reason he shall cleave to
his wife, be it to his weal or to his destruction as it happens,
but he shall doe this upon the premises and considerations of
15 that meet help and society before mention'd. *Therefore he
shall cleave to his wife,* no otherwise a wife, then a fit help.
He is not bid to leave the dear cohabitation of his father,
mother, brothers and sisters, to link himself inseparably with
the meer carcas of a Mariage, perhaps an enemy. This joyn-
20 ing particle *Therefore* is in all equity, nay in all necessity of
construction to comprehend first and most principally what
God spake concerning the inward essence of Mariage in his
institution; that we may learn how far to attend what *Adam*
spake of the outward materials therof in his approbation.
25 For if we shall bind these words of *Adam* only to a corporall
meaning, and that the force of this injunction upon all us his
sons to live individually with any woman which hath befaln
us in the most mistak'n wedlock, shall consist not in those

morall and relative causes of *Eves* creation, but in the meer
anatomy of a rib, and that *Adams* insight concerning wedlock reacht no furder, we shall make him as very an idiot as
the Socinians make him; which would not be reverently don
5 of us. Let us be content to allow our great forefather so much
wisdom, as to take the instituting words of God along with
him into this sentence, which if they be well minded, wil
assure us that flesh and ribs are but of a weak and dead efficacy to keep Mariage united where there is no other fitnes. The
10 rib of Mariage, to all since *Adam,* is a relation much rather
then a bone; the nerves and sinews therof are love and meet
help, they knit not every couple that maries, and where they
knit they seldom break, but where they break, which for the
most part is where they never truly joyn'd, to such at the same
15 instant both flesh and rib cease to be in common; so that heer
they argue nothing to the continuance of a false or violated
Mariage, but must be led back to receive their meaning from
those institutive words of God which give them all the life
and vigor they have.

20   [*Therefore shall a man leav his father, &c.*] What to a
mans thinking more plain by this appointment, that the fatherly power should give place to conjugall prerogative? yet it
is generally held by reformed writers against the Papist, that
though in persons at discretion the Mariage in it self be never
25 so fit, though it be fully accomplisht with benediction, board
and bed, yet the father not consenting, his main will without
dispute shall dissolv all. And this they affirm only from col-
lective reason, not any direct law: for that in Exod. 22. 17.

which is most particular, speaks that a father may refuse to marry his daughter to one who hath deflour'd her, not that he may take her away from one who hath soberly married her. Yet because the generall honor due to parents is great, they hold he may, and perhaps hold not amisse. But again when the question is of harsh and rugged parents who deferr to bestow their childern seasonably, they agree joyntly that the Church or Magistrat may bestow them, though without the Fathers consent: and for this they have no express autority in Scripture. So that they may see by thir own handling of this very place, that it is not the stubborn letter must govern us, but the divine and softning breath of charity which turns and windes the dictat of every positive command, and shapes it to the good of mankind. Shall the outward accessory of a Fathers will wanting, rend the fittest and most affectionat mariage in twain, after all nuptial consummations, and shall not the want of love and the privation of all civil and religious concord, which is the inward essence of wedlock, doe as much to part those who were never truly wedded? shall a Father have this power to vindicate his own wilfull honour and autority to the utter breach of a most dearly-united mariage, and shall not a man in his own power have the permission to free his Soul, his life, and all his comfort of life from the disastre of a no-mariage. Shall fatherhood, which is but man, for his own pleasure dissolve matrimony, and shall not matrimony, which is Gods Ordinance, for its own honour and better conservation, dissolv it self, when it is wrong, and not fitted to any of the cheif ends which it owes us?

[*And they shall bee one flesh.*] These words also inferre that there ought to be an individualty in Mariage; but without all question presuppose the joyning causes. Not a rule yet that we have met with, so universall in this whole institution, 5 but hath admitted limitations and conditions according to human necessity. The very foundation of Matrimony, though God laid it so deliberately, *that it is not good for man to bee alone* holds not always, if the Apostle can secure us. Soon after wee are bid leav Father and Mother, and cleav to a 10 Wife, but must understand the Fathers consent withall, els not. *Cleav to a Wife,* but let her bee a wife, let her be a meet help, a solace, not a nothing, not an adversary, not a desertrice; can any law or command be so unreasonable as to make men cleav to calamity, to ruin, to perdition? In like manner 15 heer, *They shall be one flesh;* but let the causes hold, and be made really good, which only have the possibility to make them one flesh. Wee know that flesh can neither joyn, nor keep together two bodies of it self; what is it then must make them one flesh, but likenes, but fitnes of mind and disposi-20 tion, which may breed the Spirit of concord, and union between them? If that be not in the nature of either, and that there has bin a remediles mistake, as vain wee goe about to compell them into one flesh, as if wee undertook to weav a garment of drie sand. It were more easy to compell the veg-25 etable and nutritive power of nature to assimilations and mixtures which are not alterable each by other; or force the concoctive stomach to turn that into flesh which is so totally unlike that substance, as not to be wrought on. For as the unity

of minde is neerer and greater then the union of bodies, so doubtles, is the dissimilitude greater, and more dividuall, as that which makes between bodies all difference and distinction. Especially when as besides the singular and substantial
5 differences of every Soul, there is an intimat quality of good or evil, through the whol progeny of *Adam,* which like a radical heat, or mortal chilnes joyns them, or disjoyns them irresistibly. In whom therefore either the will, or the faculty is found to have never joyn'd, or now not to continue so, 'tis
10 not to say, they shall be one flesh, for they cannot be one flesh. God commands not impossibilities; and all the Ecclesiastical glue, that Liturgy, or Laymen can compound, is not able to soder up two such incongruous natures into the one flesh of a true beseeming Mariage. Why did *Moses* then set down thir
15 uniting into one flesh? And I again ask, why the Gospel so oft repeats the eating of our Saviours flesh, the drinking of his blood? *That wee are one body with him, the members of his body, flesh of his flesh and bone of his bone.* Ephes. 5. Yet lest wee should be Capernaitans, as wee are told there that
20 the flesh profiteth nothing, so wee are told heer, if we be not as deaf as adders, that this union of the flesh proceeds from the union of a fit help and solace. Wee know that there was never a more spiritual mystery then this Gospel taught us under the terms of body and flesh; yet nothing less intended
25 then that wee should stick there. What a stupidnes then is it, that in Mariage, which is the neerest resemblance of our union with Christ, wee should deject our selvs to such a sluggish and underfoot Philosophy, as to esteem the validity of

Mariage meerly by the flesh; though never so brokn and dis-
joynted from love and peace, which only can give a human
qualification to that act of the flesh, and distinguish it from
bestial. The Text therefore uses this phrase, that *they shall*
5 *bee one flesh,* to justify and make legitimat the rites of Mariage bed; which was not unneedfull, if for all this warrant,
they were suspected of pollution by some sects of Philosophy,
and Religions of old, and latelier among the Papists, and
other heretics elder then they. Som think there is a high mys-
10 tery in those words, from that which *Paul* saith of them,
Ephes. 5. *This is a great mystery, but I speak of Christ and
the Church:* and thence they would conclude mariage to be
inseparable. For me I dispute not now whether matrimony
bee a mystery or no; if it bee of Christ and his Church, cer-
15 tainly it is not meant of every ungodly and miswedded mariage, but then only mysterious, when it is a holy, happy, and
peacefull match. But when a Saint is joyn'd with a reprobate, or both alike, wicked with wicked, fool with fool, a hee
drunkard with a she, when the bed hath bin nothing els for
20 twenty yeares or more, but an old haunt of lust and malice
mixt together, no love, no goodnes, no loyalty, but counter-
plotting, and secret wishing one anothers dissolution, this is
to me the greatest mystery in the world, if such a mariage as
this, can be the mystery of ought, unless it bee the mystery of
25 iniquity: According to that which *Paræus* cites out of *Chrys-
ostom,* that a bad wife is a help for the devill, and the like
may be said of a bad husband. Since therfore none but a fit
and pious matrimony can signify the union of Christ and his

Church, ther cannot hence be any hindrance of divorce to that
wedlock wherin ther can be no good mystery. Rather it
might to a Christian Conscience bee matter of finding it self
so much less satisfy'd then before, in the continuance of an
5 unhappy yoke, wherein there can be no representation either
of Christ, or of his Church.

Thus having enquir'd the institution how it was in the beginning, both from the 1 Chap. of *Gen.* where it was only
mention'd in part, and from the second, where it was plainly
10 and evidently instituted, and having attended each clause and
word necessary, with a diligence not drousy, wee shall now
fix with som advantage; and by a short view backward gather
up the ground wee have gon; and summ up the strength wee
have, into one argumentative head, with that *organic* force
15 that *logic* proffers us. All arts acknowledge that then only
we know certainly, when we can define; for definition is that
which refines the pure essence of things from the circumstance. If therfore we can attain in this our Controversy to
define exactly what mariage is, wee shall soon lern, when
20 there is a nullity thereof, and when a divorce.

The part therfore of this Chapter which hath bin heer
treated, doth orderly and readily resolv it self into a definition of mariage, and a consectary from thence. To the definition these words cheifly contribute. *It is not good, &c. I will*
25 *make, &c.* Where the consectary begins this connexion
Therfore informs us, *Therfore shall a man, &c.* Definition
is decreed by Logicians to consist only of causes constituting
the essence of a thing. What is not therfore among the causes

constituting mariage, must not stay in the definition. Those
causes are concluded to be *matter,* and, as the Artist calls it,
Form. But inasmuch as the same thing may be a cause more
waies then one, and that in relations and institutions which
5 have no corporal subsistence, but only a respective beeing, the
Form by which the thing is what it is, is oft so slender and
undistinguishable, that it would soon confuse, were it not
sustain'd by the efficient and final causes, which concurre to
make up the form invalid otherwise of it self, it will bee need-
10 full to take in all the fowr causes into the definition. First
therfore the material cause of matrimony is man and woman;
the Author and efficient, God and their consent, the internal
Form and soul of this relation, is conjugal love arising from a
mutual fitnes to the final causes of wedlock, help and society
15 in Religious, Civil and Domestic conversation, which includes as an inferior end the fulfilling of natural desire, and
specifical increase; these are the final causes both moving the
efficient, and perfeting the *form.* And although copulation
be consider'd among the ends of mariage, yet the act therof
20 in a right esteem can no longer be matrimonial, then it is an
effect of conjugal love. When love findes it self utterly un-
matcht, and justly vanishes, nay rather cannot but vanish, the
fleshly act indeed may continue, but not holy, not pure, not
beseeming the sacred bond of mariage; beeing at best but an
25 animal excretion, but more truly wors and more ignoble then
that mute kindlyness among the heards and flocks: in that
proceeding as it ought from intellective principles, it par-
ticipates of nothing rational, but that which the feild and the

fould equalls. For in human actions the soule is the agent,
the body in a manner passive. If then the body doe out of sensitive force, what the soul complies not with, how can man,
and not rather somthing beneath man be thought the doer.

5   But to proceed in the persute of an accurat definition, it
will avail us somthing, and whet our thoughts, to examin
what fabric heerof others have already reard. *Paræus* on *Gen.*
defines Mariage to be *an indissoluble conjunction of one man
and one woman to an individual and intimat conversation,*
10 *and mutual benevolence, &c.* Wherin is to be markt his
placing of intimat conversation before bodily benevolence;
for bodily is meant, though indeed *benevolence* rather sounds
will then body. Why then shall divorce be granted for want
of bodily performance, and not for want of fitnes to intimat
15 conversation, when as corporal benevolence cannot in any human fashion bee without this? Thus his definition places the
ends of Mariage in one order, and esteems them in another.
His *Tautology* also of indissoluble and individual is not to be
imitated; especially since neither indissoluble, nor individual
20 hath ought to doe in the exact definition, beeing but a consectary flowing from thence, as appears by plain Scripture,
Therfore shall a man leav, &c. For Mariage is not true
mariage by beeing individual, but therfore individual, if it
be true Mariage. No argument but causes enter the defini-
25 tion; a Consectary is but the effect of those causes. Besides,
that Mariage is indissoluble, is not *Catholickly* true; wee
know it dissoluble for Adultery, and for desertion by the
verdit of all Reformed Churches. Dr. *Ames* defines it *an*

individual conjunction of one man and one woman, to com-
munion of body and mutual society of life; But this perverts
the order of God, who in the institution places meet help and
society of life before communion of body. And vulgar esti-
5 mation undervalues beyond comparison all society of life and
communion of minde beneath the communion of body;
granting no divorce, but to the want, or miscommunicat-
ing of that. *Hemingius,* an approved Author, *Melanchtons*
Scholler, and who next to *Bucer* and *Erasmus* writes of di-
10 vorce most like a Divine, thus comprises, *Mariage is a con-*
junction of one man and one woman lawfully consenting,
into one flesh, for mutual helps sake, ordain'd of God. And
in his explanation stands punctually upon the conditions of
consent, that it be not in any main matter deluded, as beeing
15 the life of wedloc, and no true marriage without a true consent. *Into one flesh* he expounds into one minde, as well as
one body, and makes it the formal cause: Heerin only missing, while he puts the effect into his definition instead of the
cause which the Text affords him. For *one flesh* is not the
20 formal essence of wedloc, but one end, or one effect of *a meet*
help; The end oft times beeing the effect and fruit of the
form, as Logic teaches: Els many aged and holy matrimonies,
and more eminently that of *Joseph* and *Mary,* would bee no
true mariage. And that *maxim* generally receiv'd, would be
25 fals, that *consent alone, though copulation never follow,*
makes the mariage. Therefore to consent lawfully into one
flesh, is not the formal cause of Matrimony, but only one of
the effects. The Civil Lawyers, and first *Justinian* or *Tri-*

bonian defines Matrimony a *conjunction of man and woman
containing individual accustom of life.* Wherin first, individual is not so bad as indissoluble put in by others: And
although much cavil might be made in the distinguishing be-
5 tween indivisible, and individual, yet the one tak'n for possible, the other for actuall, neither the one nor the other can
belong to the essence of mariage; especially when a Civilian
defines, by which Law mariage is actually divorc't for many
causes, and with good leav, by mutual consent. Therfore
10 where *conjunction* is said, they who comment the *Institutes,*
agree that conjunction of minde is by the Law meant, not
necessarily conjunction of body. That Law then had good
reason attending to its own definition, that divorce should be
granted for the breaking of that conjunction which it holds
15 necessary, sooner then for the want of that conjunction which
it holds not necessary. And wheras *Tuningus* a famous Law-
yer excuses individual as the purpos of Mariage, not always
the success, it suffices not. Purpos is not able to constitute the
essence of a thing. Nature her self the universal Mother in-
20 tends nothing but her own perfection and preservation; yet is
not the more indissoluble for that. The *Pandects* out of *Mo-
destinus,* though not define, yet well describe Mariage, *the
conjunction of male and female, the society of all life, the
communion of divine and human right:* which *Bucer* also
25 imitates on the fifth to the *Ephesians.* But it seems rather to
comprehend the several ends of Mariage, then to contain the
more constituting cause that makes it what it is.

That I therefore among others (for who sings not *Hylas*)

may give as well as take matter to be judg'd on, it will be
lookt I should produce another definition then these which
have not stood the tryal. Thus then I suppose that Mariage by
the natural and plain order of Gods institution in the Text
5 may be more demonstratively and essentially defin'd. *Mariage is a divine institution joyning man and woman in a love
fitly dispos'd to the helps and comforts of domestic life. A
divine institution.* This contains the prime efficient cause of
Mariage; as for consent of Parents and Guardians, it seems
10 rather a concurrence then a cause; for as many, that marry
are in thir own power as not; and where they are not thir
own, yet are they not subjected beyond reason. Now though
efficient causes are not requisite in a definition, yet divine institution hath such influence upon the *Form,* and is so a con-
15 serving cause of it, that without it the *Form* is not sufficient
to distinguish matrimony from other conjunctions of male
and female, which are not to be counted mariage. *Joyning
man and woman in a love, &c.* This brings in the parties
consent; until which be, the mariage hath no true beeing.
20 When I say *consent,* I mean not error, for error is not properly consent: And why should not consent be heer understood with equity and good to either part, as in all other
freindly covnants, and not be strain'd and cruelly urg'd to
the mischeif and destruction of both? Neither doe I mean
25 that singular act of consent which made the contract, for that
may remain, and yet the mariage not true nor lawful; and
that may cease, and yet the mariage both true and lawful, to
their sin that break it. So that either as no efficient at all, or

but a transitory, it comes not into the definition. That consent I mean which is a love fitly dispos'd to mutual help and comfort of life; this is that happy *Form* of mariage naturally arising from the very heart of divine institution in the Text, 5 in all the former definitions either obscurely, and under mistak'n terms exprest, or not at all. This gives mariage all her due, all her benefits, all her beeing, all her distinct and proper beeing. This makes a mariage not a bondage, a blessing not a curse, a gift of God not a snare. Unless ther be a love, and 10 that love born of fitnes, how can it last? unless it last how can the best and sweetest purposes of mariage be attain'd, and they not attain'd, which are the cheif ends, and with a lawful love constitute the formal cause it self of mariage, how can the essence thereof subsist, how can it bee indeed what it goes 15 for? Conclude therfore by all the power of reason, that where this essence of mariage is not, there can bee no true mariage; and the parties either one of them, or both are free, and without fault rather by a nullity, then by a divorce may betake them to a second choys; if thir present condition be not tol- 20 erable to them. If any shall ask, why *domestic* in the definition? I answer, that because both in the Scriptures, and in the gravest Poets and Philosophers I finde the properties and excellencies of a wife set out only from domestic vertues; if they extend furder, it diffuses them into the notion of som more 25 common duty then matrimonial.

Thus farre of the definition; the *Consectary* which flows from thence, and altogether depends theron, is manifestly brought in by this connexive particle *Therfore;* and branches

it self into a double consequence; First individual Society,
therfore shall a man leav father and mother: Secondly conjugal benevolence, *and they shall bee one flesh.* Which as was
shewn, is not without cause heer mention'd, to prevent and
5 to abolish the suspect of pollution in that natural and unde-
filed act. These consequences therfore cannot either in Religion, Law, or Reason bee bound, and posted upon mankind
to his sorrow and misery, but receiv what force they have
from the meetnes of help and solace, which is the *formal*
10 cause and end of that definition that sustains them. And although it be not for the Majesty of Scripture to humble her
self in artificial *theorems,* and definitions, and *Corollaries,*
like a professor in the Schools, but looks to be *analys'd,* and
interpreted by the logical industry of her Disciples and fol-
15 lowers, and to bee reduc't by them, as oft as need is, into those
Sciential rules, which are the implements of instruction, yet
Moses, as if foreseeing the miserable work that mans ignorance and pusillanimity would make in this matrimonious
busines, and endevouring his utmost to prevent it, conde-
20 scends in this place to such a methodical and School-like way
of defining, and consequencing, as in no place of the whole
Law more.

Thus wee have seen, and if wee be not contentious, may
know what was Mariage in the beginning, to which in the
25 Gospel wee are referr'd; and what from hence to judge of
nullity, or divorce. Heer I esteem the work don; in this field
the controversie decided; but because other places of Scripture seem to look aversly upon this our decision, although in-

deed they keep all harmony with it, and because it is a better work to reconcile the seeming diversities of Scripture, then the reall dissentions of neerest friends, I shall assay in three following Discourses to perform that Office.

5   Deut. 24. 1, 2.

1. *When a man hath taken a Wife, and married her, and it come to pass that she find no favour in his eyes, because he hath found som uncleannes in her, then let him write her a bill of divorcement, and give it in her hand, and send her*
10   *out of his house.*

2. *And when she is departed out of his house, she may goe and be another mans wife.*

THAT which is the only discommodity of speaking in a cleer matter, the abundance of argument that
15   presses to bee utter'd, and the suspence of judgement what to choose, and how in the multitude of reason, to be not tedious, is the greatest difficulty which I expect heer to meet with. Yet much hath bin said formerly concerning this Law in *the Doctrine of divorce;* Wherof I shall repeat no more
20   then what is necessary. Two things are heer doubted: First, and that but of late, whether this bee a Law or no, next what this reason of *uncleannes* might mean for which the Law is granted; That it is a plain Law no man ever question'd, till *Vatablus* within these hunder'd years profess'd Hebrew at
25   *Paris,* a man of no Religion, as *Beza* deciphers him. Yet som there be who follow him, not only against the current of all antiquity, both Jewish and Christian, but the evidence of Scripture also, Malach. 2. 16. *Let him who hateth put away*

saith the Lord God of Israel. Although this place also hath
bin tamper'd with, as if it were to be thus render'd, *The Lord
God saith, that hee hateth putting away.* But this new interpretation rests only in the autority of *Junius;* for neither
5 *Calvin,* nor *Vatablus* himself, nor any other known Divine
so interpreted before. And they of best note who have translated the Scripture since, and *Diodati* for one, follow not his
reading. And perhaps they might reject it, if for nothing els,
for these two reasons: First, it introduces in a new manner
10 the person of God speaking less Majestic then he is ever
wont; When God speaks by his Profet, he ever speaks in the
first person; thereby signifying his Majesty and omni-pres-
ence. Hee would have said, I hate putting away, saith the
Lord; and not sent word by *Malachi* in a sudden faln stile,
15 The *Lord God saith that hee hateth putting away:* that were
a phrase to shrink the glorious omnipresence of God speaking, into a kind of circumscriptive absence. And were as if a
Herald in the *Atcheivment* of a King, should commit the *in-
decorum* to set his helmet sidewaies and close, not full fac't
20 and open in the posture of direction and command. Wee cannot think therfore that this last Profet would thus in a new
fashion absent the person of God from his own words as if he
came not along with them. For it would also be wide from
the proper scope of this place: hee that reads attentively will
25 soon perceav, that God blames not heer the Jews for putting
away thir wives, but for keeping strange Concubines, to the
profaning of Juda's holines, and the vexation of thir Hebrew
wives, v. 11. and 14. *Judah hath maried the daughter of a*

strange God: And exhorts them rather to put thir wives away whom they hate, as the Law permitted, then to keep them under such affronts. And it is receiv'd that this Profet livd in those times of *Ezra* and *Nehemiah* (nay by som is 5 thought to bee *Ezra* himself) when the people were forc't by these two Worthies to put thir strange wives away. So that what the story of those times, and the plain context of the 11 verse, from whence this rebuke begins, can give us to conjecture of the obscure and curt *Ebraisms* that follow, this Profet 10 does not forbid putting away, but forbids keeping, and commands putting away according to Gods Law, which is the plainest interpreter both of what God will, and what he can best suffer. Thus much evinces that God there commanded divorce by *Malachi,* and this confirmes that he commands it 15 also heer by *Moses.*

I may the less doubt to mention by the way an Author, though counted Apocryphal, yet of no small account for piety and wisdom, the Author of *Ecclesiasticus.* Which Book begun by the Grand-father of that *Jesus* who is call'd the Son 20 of *Sirach,* might have bin writt'n in part, not much after the time when *Malachi* livd; if wee compute by the Reigne of *Ptolemæus Euergetes.* It professes to explain the Law and the Profets; and yet exhorts us to divorce for incurable causes, and to cut off from the flesh those whom it there describes, 25 *Ecclesiastic.* 25. 26. Which doubtles that wise and ancient Writer would never have advis'd, had either *Malachi* so lately forbidd'n it, or the Law by a full precept not left it lawful; But I urge not this for want of better prooff; our

Saviour himself allows divorce to be a command, *Mark* 10.
3. 5. Neither doe they weak'n this assertion, who say it was
only a sufferance, as shall be prov'd at large in that place of
Matthew. But suppose it were not a writt'n Law, they never
5 can deny it was a custom, and so effect nothing. For the same
reasons that induce them why it should not bee a law, will
strait'n them as hard why it should bee allow'd a custom. All
custom is either evil or not evil; if it be evil, this is the very
end of Law-giving, to abolish evil customs by wholsom
10 Laws; unless wee imagin *Moses* weaker then every negligent
and startling Politician. If it be, as they make this of divorce
to be, a custom against nature, against justice, against chastity, how, upon this most impure custom tolerated, could the
God of purenes erect a nice and precise Law, that the wife
15 marryed after divorce could not return to her former husband, as beeing defil'd? What was all this following nicenes
worth, built upon the leud foundation of a wicked thing allow'd? In few words then, this custom of divorce either was
allowable, or not allowable; if not allowable, how could it be
20 allow'd? if it were allowable, all who understand Law will
consent, that a tolerated custom hath the force of a Law, and
is indeed no other but an unwritt'n Law, as *Justinian* calls it,
and is as prevalent as any writt'n statute. So that thir shift of
turning this Law into a custom wheels about, and gives the
25 onset upon thir own flanks; not disproving, but concluding
it to be the more firm law, because it was without controversy
a granted custom; as cleer in the reason of common life, as
those giv'n rules wheron *Euclides* builds his propositions.

Thus beeing every way a Law of God, who can without blasphemy doubt it to be a just and pure Law. *Moses* continually disavows the giving them any statute, or judgement, but what hee learnt of God; of whom also in his Song hee
5 saith, Deut. 32. *Hee is the rock, his work is perfet, all his waies are judgement, a God of truth and without iniquity, just and right is hee.* And *David* testifies, the judgements of the Lord *are true and righteous altogether.* Not partly right and partly wrong, much less wrong altogether, as Divines of
10 now adaies dare censure them. *Moses* again of that people to whom hee gave this Law saith, Deut. 14. *Yee are the childern of the Lord your God, the Lord hath chosen thee to bee a peculiar people to himself above all the nations upon the earth, that thou shouldst keep all his Commandements; and*
15 *be high in praise, in name, and in honour, holy to the Lord,* Chap. 26. And in the fourth, *Behold I have taught you statutes and judgements, eevn as the Lord my God commanded mee, keep therfore and doe them. For this is your wisdom and your understanding in the sight of Nations that shall*
20 *hear all these Statutes and say, surely this great Nation is a wise and understanding people. For what Nation is ther so great, who hath God so nigh to them? and what Nation that hath Statutes and Judgements so righteous as all this Law which I set before you this day?* Thus whether wee look at
25 the purity and justice of God himself, the jealousy of his honour among other Nations, the holines and moral perfection which hee intended by his Law to teach this people, wee cannot possibly think how he could indure to let them slugg

& grow inveteratly wicked, under base allowances, & whole
adulterous lives by dispensation. They might not eat, they
might not touch an unclean thing; to what hypocrisy then
were they train'd up, if by prescription of the same Law, they
5 might be unjust, they might be adulterous for term of life?
forbid to soile thir garments with a coy imaginary pollution,
but not forbid, but countnanc't and animated by Law to soile
thir soules with deepest defilements. What more unlike to
God, what more like that God should hate, then that his
10 Law should bee so curious to wash vessels, and vestures, and
so careles to leav unwasht, unregarded, so foul a scab of
Egypt in thir Soules? what would wee more? the Statutes of
the Lord are all pure and just: and if all, then this of Divorce.

[*Because hee hath found som uncleannes in her.*] That
15 wee may not esteem this law to bee a meer authorizing of
licence, as the Pharises took it, *Moses* adds the reason, for *som
uncleannes found.* Som heertofore have bin so ignorant, as to
have thought, that this *uncleannes* means adultery. But *Erasmus,* who for having writ an excellent Treatise of Divorce,
20 was wrote against by som burly standard Divine, perhaps of
Cullen, or of *Lovain,* who calls himself *Phimostomus,* shews
learnedly out of the Fathers with other Testimonies and Reasons, that *uncleannes* is not heer so understood; defends his
former work, though new to that age, and perhaps counted
25 licentious, and fears not to ingage all his fame on the Argument. Afterward, when Expositers began to understand the
Hebrew Text, which they had not done of many ages before,
they translated word for word not *uncleannes,* but *the naked-*

nes of any thing; and considering that nakednes is usually referr'd in Scripture to the minde as well as to the body, they constantly expound it any defect, annoyance, or ill quality in nature, which to bee joyn'd with, makes life tedious, and such
5 company wors then solitude. So that heer will be no cause to vary from the generall consent of exposition, which gives us freely that God permitted divorce, for whatever was unalterably distastful, whether in body or mind. But with this admonishment, that if the *Roman* law especially in contracts
10 and dowries left many things to equity with these cautions, *ex fide bonâ, quod æquius melius erit, ut inter bonos bene agier,* wee will not grudge to think that God intended not licence heer to every humor, but to such remediles greevances as might move a good, and honest, and faithfull man then to
15 divorce, when it can no more bee peace or comfort to either of them continuing thus joyn'd. And although it could not be avoided, but that men of hard hearts would abuse this liberty, yet doubtles it was intended as all other privileges in Law are, to good men principally, to bad only by accident.
20 So that the sin was not in the permission, nor simply in the action of divorce (for then the permitting also had bin sin) but only in the abuse. But that this Law should, as it were, bee wrung from God and *Moses,* only to serve the hard heartednes, and the lust of injurious men, how remote it is
25 from all sense, and law, and honesty, and therfore surely from the meaning of Christ, shall abundantly be manifest in due order.

Now although *Moses* needed not to adde other reason of

this law then that one there exprest, yet to these ages wherin
Canons, and *Scotisms,* and *Lumbard* Laws, have dull'd, and
almost obliterated the lively Sculpture of ancient reason, and
humanity, it will be requisit to heap reason upon reason, and
5 all little enough to vindicat the whitenes and the innocence of
this divine Law, from the calumny it findes at this day, of
beeing a dore to licence and confusion. When as indeed there
is not a judicial point in all *Moses,* consisting of more true
equity, high wisdom, and God-like pitty then this Law; not
10 derogating, but preserving the honour and peace of Mariage,
and exactly agreeing with the sense and mind of that institution in *Genesis.*

 For first, if Mariage be but an ordain'd relation, as it seems
not more, it cannot take place above the prime dictats of na-
15 ture; and if it bee of natural right, yet it must yeeld to that
which is more natural, and before it by eldership and prece-
dence in nature. Now it is not natural that *Hugh* marries
Beatrice, or *Thomas Rebecca,* beeing only a civill contract,
and full of many chances, but that these men seek them meet
20 helps, that only is natural; and that they espouse them such,
that only is mariage. But if they find them neither fit helps,
nor tolerable society, what thing more natural, more original
and first in nature then to depart from that which is irksom,
greevous, actively hateful, and injurious eevn to hostility,
25 especially in a conjugal respect, wherin antipathies are invincible, and wher the forc't abiding of the one, can bee no
true good, no real comfort to the other. For if hee find no
contentment from the other, how can he return it from him-

self, or no acceptance, how can hee mutually accept? what
more equal, more pious then to untie a civil knot for a natural enmity held by violence from parting, to dissolv an accidental conjunction of this or that man & woman, for the
5 most natural and most necessary disagreement of meet from
unmeet, guilty from guiltles, contrary from contrary? It beeing certain that the mystical and blessed unity of mariage can
bee no way more unhallow'd and profan'd, then by the forcible uniting of such disunions and separations. Which if wee
10 see oft times they cannot joyn or peece up to a common
friendship, or to a willing conversation in the same house,
how should they possibly agree to the most familiar and
united amity of wedlock? *Abraham* and *Lot,* though dear
friends and brethren in a strange Country, chose rather to
15 part asunder, then to infect thir friendship with the strife of
thir servants: *Paul* and *Barnabas* joyn'd together by the Holy
Ghost to a Spiritual work, thought it better to separate when
once they grew at variance. If these great Saints joynd by nature, friendship, religion, high providence, and revelation,
20 could not so govern a casual difference, a sudden passion, but
must in wisdom divide from the outward duties of a friendship, or a Collegueship in the same family, or in the same
journey, lest it should grow to a wors division, can any thing
bee more absurd and barbarous then that they whom only
25 error, casualty, art or plot hath joynd, should be compell'd,
not against a sudden passion but against the permanent and
radical discords of nature, to the most intimat and incorporating duties of love and imbracement, therin only rational

and human, as they are free and voluntary; beeing els an abject and servile yoke, scars not brutish. And that there is in man such a peculiar sway of liking, or disliking in the affairs of matrimony is evidently seen before mariage among those
5 who can bee freindly, can respect each other, yet to marry each other would not for any perswasion. If then this unfitnes and disparity bee not till after mariage discover'd, through many causes, and colours, and concealements, that may overshadow; undoubtedly it will produce the same effects and
10 perhaps with more vehemence, that such a mistakn pair, would give the world to be unmarried again. And thir condition *Solomon* to the plain justification of divorce expresses, *Prov.* 30. 21. 23. Where hee tells us of his own accord, that a *hated,* or a *hatefull* woman, *when shee is married, is a thing*
15 *for which the earth is disquieted and cannot bear it;* thus giving divine testimony to this divine Law, which bids us nothing more then is the first and most innocent lesson of nature, to turn away peaceably from what afflicts and hazards our destruction; especially when our staying can doe no good,
20 and is expos'd to all evil.

Secondly, It is unjust that any Ordinance ordain'd to the good and comfort of man, where that end is missing, without his fault, should be forc't upon him to an unsufferable misery and discomfort, if not commonly ruin. All Ordi-
25 nances are establisht in thir end; the end of Law is the vertu, is the righteousnes of Law. And therfore him wee count an ill Expounder who urges Law against the intention therof. The general end of every Ordinance, of every severest, every

divinest, eevn of Sabbath, is the good of man, yea his temporal good not excluded. But marriage is one of the benignest ordinances of God to man, wherof both the general and particular end is the peace and contentment of mans mind, as 5 the institution declares. Contentment of body they grant, which if it bee defrauded, the plea of frigidity shall divorce: But heer lies the fadomles absurdity, that granting this for bodily defect, they will not grant it for any defect of the mind, any violation of religious or civil society. When as, if the ar-
10 gument of Christ bee firm against the ruler of the Synagogue, Luk. 13. *Thou hypocrite, doth not each of you on the Sabbath day loos'n his Oxe or his Asse from the stall, and lead him to watering, and should not I unbind a daughter of Abraham from this bond of Satan?* it stands as good heer, yee
15 have regard in mariage to the greevance of body; should you not regard more the greevances of the mind, seeing the Soul as much excells the body, as the outward man excells the Ass and more; for that *animal* is yet a living creature, perfet in it self; but the body without the Soul is a meer senseles trunck.
20 No Ordinance therfore givn particularly to the good both spiritual and temporal of man, can bee urg'd upon him to his mischeif, and if they yeeld this to the unworthier part, the body, wherabout are they in thir principles, that they yeeld it not to the more worthy, the mind of a good man?
25 Thirdly, As no Ordinance, so no Covnant, no not between God and man, much less between man and man, beeing as all are, intended to the good of both parties, can hold to the deluding or making miserable of them both. For equity is

understood in every Covnant, eevn between enemies, though
the terms bee not exprest. If equity therfore made it, extremity may dissolv it. But Mariage, they use to say, is the Covnant of God. Undoubted: and so is any covnant frequently
5 call'd in Scripture, wherin God is call'd to witness: the covnant of freindship between *David* and *Jonathan,* is call'd *the*
Covnant of the Lord, 1 Sam. 20. The covnant of *Zedechiah*
with the King of *Babel,* a Covnant to bee doubted whether
lawfull or no, yet in respect of God invok't thereto, is call'd
10 *the Oath, and the Covnant of God,* Ezech. 17. Mariage also
is call'd the *Covnant of God,* Prov. 2. 17. Why, but as before,
because God is the witnes therof, Malach. 2. 14. So that this
denomination adds nothing to the Covnant of Mariage, above
any other civil and solemn contract: nor is it more indisso-
15 luble for this reason then any other against the end of its own
ordination, nor is any vow or Oath to God exacted with such
a rigor, where superstition reignes not. For look how much
divine the Covnant is, so much the more equal; So much the
more to bee expected that every article therof should bee
20 fairly made good, no fals dealing, or unperforming should be
thrust upon men without redress, if the covnant bee so divine.
But faith they say must be kept in Covnant, though to our
dammage. I answer, that only holds true, where the other
side performs, which failing, hee is no longer bound. Again,
25 this is true, when the keeping of faith can bee of any use, or
benefit to the other. But in Mariage a league of love and willingnes, if faith bee not willingly kept, it scars is worth the
keeping; nor can bee any delight to a generous minde, with

whom it is forcibly kept: and the question still supposes the
one brought to an impossibility of keeping it as hee ought, by
the others default, and to keep it formally, not only with a
thousand shifts and dissimulations, but with open anguish,
5 perpetual sadnes and disturbance, no willingnes, no cheer-
fulnes, no contentment, cannot bee any good to a minde not
basely poor and shallow, with whom the contract of love is
so kept. A Covnant therfore brought to that passe, is on the
unfaulty side without injury dissolv'd.

10   Fourthly, The Law is not to neglect men under greatest
sufferances, but to see Covnants of greatest moment faith-
fullest perform'd. And what injury comparable to that sustain'd in a frustrat and fals dealing Mariage, to loose, for anothers fault against him, the best portion of his temporal
15 comforts, and of his spiritual too, as it may fall out. It was
the Law, that for mans good and quiet, reduc't things to propriety, which were at first in common; how much more Law-
like were it to assist nature in disappropriating that evil which
by continuing proper becomes destructive. But hee might
20 have bewar'd. So hee might in any other covnant, wherin the
Law does not constrain error to so dear a forfeit. And yet in
these matters wherin the wisest are apt to erre, all the warines
that can bee, oft times nothing avails. But the Law can compell the offending party to bee more duteous. Yes, if all these
25 kind of offences were fit in public to bee complain'd on, or
beeing compell'd were any satisfaction to a mate not sottish,
or malicious. And these injuries work so vehemently, that if
the Law remedy them not, by separating the cause when no

way els will pacify, the person not releev'd betakes him either
to such disorderly courses, or to such a dull dejection, as renders him either infamous, or useles to the service of God and
his Country. Which the Law ought to prevent as a thing per-
5 nicious to the Common wealth; and what better prevention
then this which *Moses* us'd?

Fifthly, The Law is to tender the liberty and the human
dignity of them that live under the Law, whether it bee the
mans right above the woman, or the womans just appeal
10 against wrong, and servitude. But the duties of mariage contain in them a duty of benevolence, which to doe by compulsion against the Soul, where ther can bee neither peace, nor
joy, nor love, but an enthrallment to one who either cannot,
or will not bee mutual in the godliest and the civilest ends of
15 that society, is the ignoblest, and the lowest slavery that a human shape can bee put to. This Law therfor justly and piously provides against such an unmanly task of bondage as
this. The civil Law, though it favour'd the setting free of a
slave, yet if hee prov'd ungratefull to his Patron, reduc't him
20 to a servil condition. If that Law did well to reduce from
liberty to bondage for an ingratitude not the greatest, much
more became it the Law of God to enact the restorement of a
free born man from an unpurpos'd, and unworthy bondage
to a rightfull liberty for the most unnatural fraud and in-
25 gratitude that can be committed against him. And if that
Civilian Emperour in his title of *Donations,* permit the giver
to recall his guift from him who proves unthankful towards
him, yea, though hee had subscrib'd and sign'd in the deed

of his guift, not to recall it though for this very cause of ingratitude, with much more equity doth *Moses* permit heer
the giver to recall no petty guift, but the guift of himself from
one who most injuriously & deceitfully uses him against the
5 main ends and conditions of his giving himself, exprest in
Gods institution.

Sixthly, Although ther bee nothing in the plain words of
this Law, that seems to regard the afflictions of a wife, how
great so ever, yet Expositers determin, and doubtles determin
10 rightly, that God was not uncompassionat of them also in the
framing of this Law. For should the rescript of *Antoninus* in
the Civil Law give release to servants flying for refuge to the
Emperours statue, by giving leav to change thir cruel Maisters, and should God who in his Law also is good to injur'd
15 servants, by granting them thir freedom in divers cases, not
consider the wrongs and miseries of a wife which is no servant. Though heerin the counter sense of our Divines, to me,
I must confesse seems admirable; who teach that God gave
this as a mercifull Law, not for man whom he heer names,
20 and to whom by name hee gives this power, but for the wife
whom hee names not, and to whom by name hee gives no
power at all. For certainly if man be liable to injuries in mariage, as well as woman, and man be the worthier person, it
were a preposterous law to respect only the less worthy; her
25 whom God made for mariage, and not him at all for whom
mariage was made.

Seventhly, The Law of mariage gives place to the power
of Parents: for wee hold that consent of Parents not had may

break the wedlock, though els accomplisht. It gives place to
maisterly power, for the Maister might take away from an
Hebrew servant the wife which hee gave him, *Exod*. 21. If
it be answer'd that the mariage of servants is no matrimony:
5 tis reply'd, that this in the ancient *Roman* Law is true, not in
the *Mosaic*. If it bee added, she was a stranger not an Hebrew,
therfore easily divorc't, it will be answerd that strangers not
beeing *Canaanites,* and they also beeing Converts might bee
lawfully maryed, as *Rahab* was. And her conversion is heer
10 suppos'd; for an Hebrew maister could not lawfully give a
heathen wife to an Hebrew servant. However, the divorcing
of an Israelitish woman was as easy by the Law, as the divorcing of a stranger, and almost in the same words permitted,
Deut. 24. and *Deut*. 21. Lastly, it gives place to the right of
15 warr, for a captiv woman lawfully maryed, and afterward
not belov'd, might bee dismist, only without ransom, *Deut*.
21. If mariage may bee dissolv'd by so many exterior powers,
not superior, as wee think, why may not the power of mariage it self for its own peace and honour dissolv it self, wher
20 the persons wedded be free persons, why may not a greater
and more natural power complaining dissolv mariage? for
the ends why matrimony was ordain'd, are certainly and by
all Logic above the Ordinance it self, why may not that dissolv mariage without which that institution hath no force at
25 all? for the prime ends of mariage, are the whole strength
and validity therof, without which matrimony is like an Idol,
nothing in the world. But those former allowances were all
for hardnes of heart. Be that granted, untill we come where

to understand it better: if the Law suffer thus farr the obstinacy of a bad man, is it not more righteous heer, to doe willingly what is but equal, to remove in season the extremities
of a good man?

5   Eightly, If a man had deflowr'd a Virgin, or brought an ill
name on his wife that shee came not a Virgin to him, hee was
amerc't in certain shekles of Silver, and bound never to divorce her all his daies, *Deut.* 22. which shews that the Law
gave no liberty to divorce, wher the injury was palpable; and
10 that the absolute forbidding to divorce, was in part the punishment of a deflowrer, and a defamer. Yet not so but that the
wife questionles might depart when shee pleas'd. Otherwise
this cours had not so much righted her, as deliverd her up to
more spight and cruel usage. This Law therfore doth justly
15 distinguish the privilege of an honest and blameles man in the
matter of divorce from the punishment of a notorious offender.

Ninthly, Suppose it might bee imputed to a man, that hee
was too rash in his choyse and why took hee not better heed,
let him now smart, and bear his folly as he may; although the
20 Law of God, that terrible law doe not thus upbraid the infirmities and unwilling mistakes of man in his integrity: But
suppose these and the like proud aggravations of som stern
hypocrite, more merciles in his mercies, then any literall
Law in the vigor of severity, must be patiently heard; yet all
25 Law, and Gods Law especially grants every where to error
easy remitments, eevn where the utmost penalty exacted were
no undoing. With great reason therfore and mercy doth it
heer not torment an error, if it be so, with the endurance of

a whole life lost to all houshold comfort and society, a punishment of too vast and huge dimension for an error, and the
more unreasonable for that the like objection may be oppos'd against the plea of divorcing for adultery; hee might
5 have lookt better before to her breeding under religious
Parents: why did hee not then more diligently inquire into
her manners, into what company she kept? every glaunce of
her eye, every step of her gate would have propheci'd adultery, if the quick sent of these discerners had bin took along;
10 they had the divination to have foretold you all this; as they
have now the divinity to punish an error inhumanly. As good
reason to be content, and forc't to be content with your adultress, if these objecters might be the judges of human frailtie.
But God more mild and good to man, then man to his
15 brother, in all this liberty givn to divorcement, mentions not
a word of our past errors and mistakes, if any were, which
these men objecting from their own inventions prosecute
with all violence and iniquity. For if the one bee to look so
narrowly what hee takes, at the peril of ever keeping, why
20 should not the other bee made as wary what is promis'd, by
the peril of loosing? for without those promises the treaty of
mariage had not proceeded. Why should his own error bind
him, rather then the others fraud acquit him? Let the buyer
beware, saith the old Law-beaten termer. Belike then, ther
25 is no more honesty, nor ingenuity in the bargain of a wedloc,
then in the buying of a colt: Wee must it seems drive it on as
craftily with those whose affinity wee seek, as if they were a
pack of sale men and complotters. But the deceiver deceivs

himself in the unprosperous mariage, and therin is sufficiently
punisht. I answer, that the most of those who deceiv, are such
as either understand not, or value not the true purposes of
mariage; they have the prey they seek, not the punishment:
5 yet say it prove to them som cross, it is not equal that error and
fraud should bee linkt in the same degree of forfeture, but
rather that error should be acquitted, and fraud bereav'd his
morsel: if the mistake were not on both sides, for then on
both sides the acquitment will be reasonable, if the bondage
10 be intolerable; which this Law graciously determins, not un-
mindful of the wife, as was granted willingly to the common
Expositers, though beyond the letter of this law, yet not beyond the spirit of charity.

Tenthly, Mariage is a solemn thing, som say a holy, the
15 resemblance of Christ and his Church; and so indeed it is
where the persons are truly religious; and wee know all Sacred things not perform'd sincerely as they ought, are no way
acceptable to God in thir outward formality. And that wherin
it differs from personal duties, if they be not truly don, the
20 fault is in our selves; but mariage to be a true and pious mariage is not in the single power of any person; the essence
whereof, as of all other Covnants is in relation to another, the
making and maintaining causes thereof are all mutual, and
must be a communion of spiritual and temporal comforts. If
25 then either of them cannot, or obstinatly will not be answerable in these duties, so as that the other can have no peaceful
living, or enduring the want of what he justly seeks, and sees
no hope, then strait from that dwelling love, which is the soul

of wedloc, takes his flight, leaving only som cold perform-
ances of civil and common respects, but the true bond of mariage, if there were ever any there, is already burst like a rott'n
thred. Then follows dissimulation, suspicion, fals colours, fals
5 pretences, and wors then these, disturbance, annoyance, vexation, sorrow, temtation eevn in the faultles person, weary of
himself, and of all action public or domestic; then comes disorder, neglect, hatred, and perpetual strife, all these the enemies of holines and christianity, and every one of these per-
10 sisted in, a remediles violation to matrimony. Therfore God
who hates all faining and formality, wher there should bee
all faith and sincerenes, and abhorrs to see inevitable discord,
wher there should be greatest concord, when through anothers default, faith and concord cannot bee, counts it neither
15 just to punish the innocent with the transgressor, nor holy, nor
honourable for the sanctity of mariage, that should bee the
union of peace and love, to be made the commitment, and
close fight of enmity and hate. And therfore doth in this Law,
what best agrees with his goodnes, loosning a sacred thing to
20 peace and charity, rather then binding it to hatred and contention; loosning only the outward and formal tie of that
which is already inwardly, and really brokn, or els was really
never joyn'd.

Eleventhly, One of the cheif matrimonial ends is said to
25 seek a holy seed; but where an unfit mariage administers continual cause of hatred and distemper, there, as was heard before, cannot choose but much unholines abide. Nothing more
unhallows a man, more unprepares him to the service of God

in any duty, then a habit of wrath and perturbation, arising
from the importunity of troublous causes never absent. And
wher the houshold stands in this plight, what love can ther
bee to the unfortunat issue, what care of thir breeding, which
5 is of main conducement to their beeing holy. God therfore
knowing how unhappy it would bee for children to bee born
in such a family, gives this Law either as a prevention, that
beeing an unhappy pair, they should not adde to bee unhappy
parents, or els as a remedy that if ther be childern, while they
10 are fewest, they may follow either parent, as shall bee agreed,
or judg'd, from the house of hatred and discord, to a place of
more holy and peaceable education.

Twelfthly, All Law is available to som good end, but the
final prohibition of divorce avails to no good end, causing
15 only the endles aggravation of evil, and therfore this permission of divorce was givn to the Jews by the wisdom and fatherly providence of God; who knew that Law cannot command love, without which, matrimony hath no true beeing,
no good, no solace, nothing of Gods instituting, nothing but
20 so sordid and so low, as to bee disdain'd of any generous person. Law cannot inable natural inability either of body, or
mind, which gives the greevance; it cannot make equal those
inequalities, it cannot make fit those unfitnesses; and where
there is malice more then defect of nature, it cannot hinder
25 ten thousand injuries, and bitter actions of despight too suttle
and too unapparent for Law to deal with. And while it seeks
to remedy more outward wrongs, it exposes the injur'd person to other more inward and more cutting. All these evils

unavoidably will redound upon the children, if any be, and
the whole family. It degenerates and disorders the best spirits, leavs them to unsettl'd imaginations, and degraded hopes,
careles of themselvs, their houshold and their freinds, un-
5 active to all public service, dead to the Common-wealth;
wherin they are by one mishapp, and no willing trespas of
theirs, outlaw'd from all the benefits and comforts of married
life and posterity. It conferrs as little to the honour and in-
violable keeping of Matrimony, but sooner stirrs up tempta-
10 tions, and occasions to secret adulteries, and unchast roaving.
But it maintaines public honesty. Public folly rather, who
shall judge of public honesty? the Law of God, and of ancientest Christians, and all Civil Nations, or the illegitimat
Law of Monks and Canonists, the most malevolent, most un-
15 experienc't, and incompetent judges of Matrimony?

These reasons, and many more that might bee alleg'd,
afford us plainly to perceav, both what good cause this Law
had to doe for good men in mischances, and what necessity it
had to suffer accidentally the hard heartednes of bad men,
20 which it could not certainly discover, or discovering could not
subdue, no nor indeavour to restrain without multiplying sorrow to them, for whom all was indeavour'd. The guiltles
therfore were not depriv'd thir needful redresses, and the
hard hearts of others unchastisable in those judicial Courts,
25 were so remitted there, as bound over to the higher Session
of Conscience.

Notwithstanding all this, ther is a loud exception against
this Law of God, nor can the holy Author save his Law from

this exception, that it opens a dore to all licence and confusion. But this is the rudest, I was almost saying the most graceles objection, and with the least reverence to God and *Moses,* that could bee devis'd: This is to cite God before mans
5 Tribunal, to arrogate a wisdom and holines above him. Did not God then foresee what event of licence or confusion could follow? did not hee know how to ponder these abuses with more prevailing respects, in the most eevn ballance of his justice and purenes, till these correctors came up to shew him
10 better? The Law is, if it stirre up sin any way, to stirre it up by forbidding, as one contrary excites another, *Rom.* 7. but if it once come to provoke sin, by granting licence to sin, according to Laws that have no other honest end, but only to permit the fulfilling of obstinat lust, how is God not made the
15 contradicter of himself? No man denies that best things may bee abus'd: but it is a rule resulting from many pregnant experiences, that what doth most harm in the abusing, us'd rightly doth most good. And such a good to take away from honest men, for beeing abus'd by such as abuse all things, is
20 the greatest abuse of all. That the whole Law is no furder usefull, then as a man uses it lawfully, St. *Paul* teaches, 1 *Tim.* 1. And that Christian liberty may bee us'd for an occasion to the flesh, the same Apostle confesses, *Galat.* 5. yet thinks not of removing it for that, but bidds us rather *Stand*
25 *fast in the liberty wherwith Christ hath freed us, and not bee held again in the yoke of bondage.* The very permission which Christ gave to divorce for adultery, may bee fouly abus'd, by any whose hardnes of heart can either fain adultery, or dares

committt, that hee may divorce. And for this cause the Pope, and hitherto the Church of *England,* forbid all divorce from the bond of mariage, though for openest adultery. If then it bee righteous to hinder for the fear of abuse, that which Gods Law notwithstanding that caution, hath warranted to bee don, doth not our righteousnes come short of Antichrist, or doe we not rather heerin conform our selvs to his unright-eousnes in this undue and unwise fear. For God regards more to releev by this Law the just complaints of good men, then to curb the licence of wicked men, to the crushing withall, and the overwhelming of his afflicted servants. He loves more that his Law should look with pitty upon the difficulties of his own, then with rigor upon the boundlesse riots of them who serv another Maister, and hinder'd heer by strictnes, will break another way to wors enormities. If this Law therfore have many good reasons for which God gave it, and no intention of giving scope to leudnes, but as abuse by accident comes in with every good Law, and every good thing, it cannot be wis-dom in us, while we can content us with Gods wisdom, nor can be purity, if his purity will suffice us, to except against this Law, as if it foster'd licence. But if they affirm this Law had no other end, but to permitt obdurat lust, because it would bee obdurat, making the Law of God intentionally to pro-clame and enact sin lawful, as if the will of God were becom sinfull, or sin stronger then his direct and Law-giving will, the men would bee admonisht to look well to it, that while they are so eager to shut the dore against licence, they doe not open a wors dore to blasphemy. And yet they shall bee heer

furder shewn thir iniquity; what more foul and common sin among us then drunkennes, and who can bee ignorant, that if the importation of Wine, and the use of all strong drink were forbid, it would both clean ridde the possibility of com-
5 mitting that odious vice, and men might afterwards live happily and healthfully, without the use of those intoxicating licors. Yet who is ther the severest of them all, that ever propounded to loos his Sack, his Ale, toward the certain abolishing of so great a sin, who is ther of them, the holiest, that less
10 loves his rich Canary at meals, though it bee fetcht from places that hazard the Religion of them who fetch it, and though it make his neighbour drunk out of the same Tunne? While they forbid not therfore the use of that liquid Marchandise, which forbidd'n would utterly remove a most loath-
15 som sin, and not impair either the health, or the refreshment of mankind, suppli'd many other wayes, why doe they forbid a Law of God, the forbidding wherof brings into an excessive bondage, oft times the best of men, and betters not the wors? Hee to remove a Nationall vice, will not pardon his cupps,
20 nor think it concerns him to forbear the quaffing of that outlandish Grape, in his unnecessary fullnes, though other men abuse it never so much, nor is hee so abstemious as to intercede with the Magistrate that all matter of drunkennes be banisht the Common-wealth, and yet for the fear of a less
25 inconvenience unpardnably requires of his brethren, in thir extreme necessity to debarre themselves the use of Gods permissive Law, though it might bee thir saving, and no mans indangering the more. Thus this peremptory strictnes we

may discern of what sort it is, how unequal, and how unjust.

But it will breed confusion. What confusion it would breed, God himself took the care to prevent in the fourth verse of this Chapter, that the divorc't beeing maried to an-
5 other, might not return to her former Husband. And *Justinians* law counsels the same in his Title of *Nuptials*. And what confusion els can ther bee in separation, to separat, upon extrem urgency, the Religious from the irreligious, the fit from the unfit, the willing from the wilfull, the abus'd from
10 the abuser, such a separation is quite contrary to confusion. But to binde and mixe together holy with Atheist, hevnly with hellish, fitnes with unfitnes, light with darknes, antipathy with antipathy, the injur'd with the injurer, and force them into the most inward neernes of a detested union, this
15 doubtles is the most horrid, the most unnatural mixture, the greatest confusion that can be confus'd!

Thus by this plain and Christian *Talmud* vindicating the Law of God from irreverent and unwary expositions, I trust, wher it shall meet with intelligible perusers, som stay at least
20 of mens thoughts will bee obtain'd, to consider these many prudent and righteous ends of this divorcing permission. That it may have, for the great Authors sake, heerafter som competent allowance to bee counted a little purer then the prerogative of a legal and public ribaldry, granted to that
25 holy seed. So that from hence wee shall hope to finde the way still more open to the reconciling of those places which treat this matter in the Gospel. And thether now without interruption the cours of method brings us.

TETRACHORDON,

Matt. 5. 31, 32.

31. *It hath beene said whosoever shall put away his wife, let
him give her a writing of divorcement.*
32. *But I say unto you that whosoever shall put away his*
5   *wife, &c.*

Matt. 19, 3, 4, &c.

3. *And the Pharises also came unto him tempting him, &c.*

IT *hath beene said.*] What hitherto hath beene spoke
upon the law of God touching Matrimony or divorce,
10 hee who will deny to have bin argu'd according to reason, and all equity of Scripture, I cannot edifie how, or by
what rule of proportion that mans vertue calculates, what his
elements are, nor what his *analytics*. Confidently to those who
have read good bookes, and to those whose reason is not an
15 illiterate booke to themselves I appeale, whether they would
not confesse all this to be the commentary of truth and justice,
were it not for these recited words of our Saviour. And if they
take not backe that which they thus grant, nothing sooner
might perswade them that Christ heer teaches no new pre-
20 cept, and nothing sooner might direct them to finde his meaning, then to compare and measure it by the rules of nature
and eternall righteousnes, which no writt'n law extinguishes,
and the Gospel least of all. For what can be more opposite

and disparaging to the cov'nant of love, of freedom, & of our
manhood in grace, then to bee made the yoaking pedagogue
of new severities, the scribe of syllables and rigid letters, not
only greevous to the best of men, but different and strange
5 from the light of reason in them, save only as they are fain to
stretch & distort their apprehensions, for feare of displeasing
the verbal straightnesse of a text, which our owne servil feare
gives us not the leisure to understand aright. If the law of
Christ shall be writt'n in our hearts, as was promis'd to the
10 Gospel, *Jer.* 31, how can this in the vulgar and superficiall
sense be a law of Christ, so farre from beeing writt'n in our
hearts, that it injures and dissallowes not onely the free dic-
tates of nature and morall law, but of charity also and religion in our hearts. Our Saviours doctrine is, that the end, and
15 the fulfilling of every command is charity; no faith without
it, no truth without it, no worship, no workes pleasing to
God but as they partake of charity. He himselfe sets us an
example, breaking the solemnest and the strictest ordinance
of religious rest, and justify'd the breaking, not to cure a
20 dying man, but such whose cure might without danger have
beene deferr'd. And wherefore needes must the sick mans bed
be carried home on that day by his appointment, and why
were the Disciples who could not forbeare on that day to
pluck the corne, so industriously defended, but to shew us
25 that if he preferr'd the slightest occasions of mans good before
the observing of highest and severest ordinances, hee gave us
much more easie leave to breake the intolerable yoake of a
never well joyn'd wedlocke for the removing of our heaviest

afflictions. Therefore it is that the most of evangelick precepts are given us in proverbiall formes, to drive us from the
letter, though we love ever to be sticking there. For no other
cause did Christ assure us that whatsoever things wee binde,
5 or slacken on earth, are so in heaven, but to signifie that the
christian arbitrement of charity is supreme decider of all controversie, and supreme resolver of all Scripture; not as the
Pope determines for his owne tyrany, but as the Church ought
to determine for its owne true liberty. Hence *Eusebius* not
10 far from beginning his History, compares the state of Christians to that of *Noah* and the Patriarkes before the Law. And
this indeede was the reason, why *Apostolick* tradition in the
antient Church was counted nigh equall to the writt'n word,
though it carried them at length awry, for want of consider-
15 ing that tradition was not left to bee impos'd as law, but to be
a patterne of that Christian prudence, and liberty which holy
men by right assum'd of old, which truth was so evident, that
it found entrance even into the Councell of *Trent,* when the
point of tradition came to be discusst. And *Marinaro* a learned
20 *Carmelite* for approaching too neere the true cause that gave
esteeme to tradition, that is to say, the difference betweene
the Old and New Testament, the one punctually prescribing
writt'n Law, the other guiding by the inward spirit, was reprehended by Cardinall *Poole* as one that had spoken more
25 worthy a *German Colloquie,* then a generall councell. I omit
many instances, many proofes and arguments of this kind,
which alone would compile a just volume, and shall content
me heer to have shew'n breifly, that the great and almost

only commandment of the Gospel, is to command nothing
against the good of man, and much more no civil command,
against his civil good. If we understand not this, we are but
crackt cimbals, we do but tinckle, we know nothing, we doe
5 nothing, all the sweat of our toilsomest obedience will but
mock us. And what wee suffer superstitiously returnes us no
thankes. Thus med'cining our eyes wee neede not doubt to see
more into the meaning of these our Saviours words, then
many who have gone before us.

10   [*It hath beene said, whosoever shall put away his wife.*]
Our Saviour was by the doctors of his time suspected of intending to dissolve the law. In this chapter he wipes off this
aspersion upon his accusers, and shewes how they were the
law breakers. In every common wealth when it decayes, cor-
15 ruption makes two maine steps; first when men cease to doe
according to the inward and uncompell'd actions of vertue,
caring only to live by the outward constraint of law, and
turne the Simplicity of reall good, into the craft of seeming
so by law. To this hypocritical honesty was *Rome* declin'd in
20 that age, wherein *Horace* liv'd and discover'd it to *Quintius*.

> *Whom doe we count a good man, whom but he*
> *Who keepes the lawes and statutes of the Senate,*
> *Who judges in great suits and controversies,*
> *Whose witnesse and opinion winnes the cause;*
> 25 *But his owne house, and the whole neighbourhood*
> *Sees his foule inside through his whited skin.*

The next declining is, when law becomes now too straight for the secular manners, and those too loose for the cincture of law. This brings in false and crooked interpretations to eeke out law, and invents the suttle encroachment of obscure
5 traditions hard to be disprov'd. To both these descents the Pharises themselves were fall'n. Our Saviour therefore shews them both where they broke the law in not marking the divine intent thereof, but onely the letter, and where they deprav'd the letter also with sophisticall expositions. This law
10 of divorse they had deprav'd both waies. First, by teaching that to give a bill of divorse was all the duty which that law requir'd, what ever the cause were. Next by running to divorse for any triviall, accidentall cause; whenas the law evidently stayes in the grave causes of naturall and immu-
15 table dislike. *It hath been said,* saith he. Christ doth not put any contempt or disesteeme upon the law of *Moses,* by citing it so briefly; for in the same manner God himselfe cites a law of greatest caution, *Jer. 3. They say if a man put away his wife, shall he returne to her againe, &c.* Nor
20 doth hee more abolish it then the law of swearing, cited next with the same brevity, and more appearance of contradicting. For divorce hath an exception left it, but we are charg'd there, as absolutely as words can charge us, *not to sweare at all:* yet who denies the lawfulnesse of an oath,
25 though here it be in no case permitted? And what shall become of his solemne protestation not to abolish one law, or one tittle of any law, especially of those which hee mentions in this chapter. And that hee meant more particularly the not

abolishing of *Mosaic* divorse, is beyond all cavill manifest in
Luke 16. 17, 18. where this clause against abrogating is inserted immediately before the sentence against divorse, as if
it were call'd thither on purpose to defend the equity of this
5 particular law against the foreseene rashnesse of common
textuaries, who abolish lawes, as the rable demolish images,
in the zeale of their hammers oft violating the Sepulchers of
good men, like *Pentheus* in the tragedies, they see that for
Thebes which is not, and take that for superstition, as these
10 men in the heate of their annulling perceive not how they
abolish right, and equall, and justice under the appearance of
judicial. And yet are confessing all the while, that these sayings of Christ stand not in contradiction to the law of *Moses,*
but to the false doctrine of the Pharises rais'd from thence;
15 that the law of God is perfect, not liable to additions or dimi-
nutions, & *Paræus* accuses the Jesuite *Maldonatus* of greatest
falsity for limiting the perfection of that law only to the rudenes of the Jewes. He adds *that the law promiseth life to the*
performers thereof; therefore needs not perfecter precepts,
20 *then such as bring to life; that if the corrections of Christ*
stand opposite, not to the corruptions of the Pharises, but to
the law it selfe of God, the heresie of Manes would follow,
one God of the old Testament, and another of the New. That
Christ saith not here except your righteousnesse exceede the
25 *righteousnesse of Moses law, but of the Scribes and Pharises.*
That all this may be true, whether is common sense flown
asquint, if we can maintaine that Christ forbid the Mosaic
divorse utterly, and yet abolisht not the law that permits it?

For if the conscience onely were checkt, and the law not repeal'd, what meanes the *fanatic* boldnesse of this age that
dares tutor Christ to be more strict then he thought fit? Ye
shall have the evasion, it was a judiciall law. What could
5 infancy and slumber have invented more childish? Judiciall
or not judiciall, it was one of those lawes expresly, which he
forewarn'd us with protestation, that his mind was not to
abrogate: and if we marke the stearage of his words, what
course they hold, wee may perceive that what he protested not
10 to dissolve (that he might faithfully & not deceitfully remove
a suspition from himselfe) was principally concerning the
judiciall law; for of that sort are all these here which he vin-
dicates; except the last. Of the Ceremonial law he told them
true, that nothing of it should passe *untill all were fullfill'd*.
15 Of the morall law he knew the Pharises did not suspect he
meant to nullifie that: for so doing would soone have undone
his authority, and advanc'd theirs. Of the judiciall law therefore cheifly this Apologie was meant: For how is that fullfill'd longer then the common equity thereof remaines in
20 force? And how is this our Saviours defence of himselfe, not
made fallacious, if the Pharises chiefe feare be, least he should
abolish the judiciall law, and he to satisfie them, protests his
good intention to the Moral law. It is the generall grant of
Divines, that what in the Judicial law is not meerely *judaicall,*
25 but reaches to human equity in common, was never in the
thought of being abrogated. If our Saviour tooke away ought
of law, it was the burthensome of it, not the ease of burden,
it was the bondage, not the liberty of any divine law that he

remov'd: this he often profest to be the end of his comming.
But what if the law of divorce be a morall law, as most certainly it is fundamentally, and hath been so prov'd in the
reasons thereof. For though the giving of a bill may be ju-
5 diciall, yet the act of divorce is altogether conversant in good
or evill, and so absolutely moral. So farr as it is good it never
can be abolisht being morall; so farr as it is simply evil it
never could be judiciall, as hath beene shewen at large in *the
Doctrine of divorce,* and will be reassum'd anon. Whence
10 one of these two necessities follow, that either it was never
establisht, or never abolisht. Thus much may be enough to
have said on this place. The following verse will be better
unfolded in the 19. Chapter, where it meets us againe, after
a large debatement on the question, between our Saviour and
15 his adversaries.

Mat. 19. 3, 4, &c.

V. 3. *And the Pharises came unto him tempting him and
saying unto him.*

[*Tempting him.*] The manner of these men comming to
20 our Saviour, not to learne, but to tempt him, may give us to
expect that their answer will bee such as is fittest for them,
not so much a teaching, as an intangling. No man though
never so willing or so well enabl'd to instruct, but if he discerne his willingnesse and candor made use of to intrapp
25 him, will suddainly draw in himselfe, and laying aside the
facil vein of perspicuity, will know his time to utter clouds
and riddles; if he be not lesse wise then that noted Fish, when

as he should bee not unwiser then the Serpent. Our Saviour
at no time exprest any great desire to teach the obstinate and
unteachable Pharises; but when they came to tempt him, then
least of all. As now about the liberty of divorce, so another
5 time about the punishment of adultery they came to sound
him, and what satisfaction got they from his answer, either
to themselves or to us, that might direct a law under the Gospel, new from that of *Moses,* unlesse we draw his absolution
of adultery into an edict. So about the tribute, who is there
10 can picke out a full solution, what and when we must give to
Cæsar, by the answer which he gave the Pharises? If we must
give to *Cæsar* that which is *Cæsars,* and all be *Cæsars,* which
hath his image, wee must either new stamp our Coine, or we
may goe new stamp our Foreheads with the superscription
15 of slaves instead of freemen. Besides it is a generall precept,
not only of Christ, but of all other Sages, not to instruct the
unworthy and the conceited who love tradition more then
truth, but to perplex and stumble them purposely with con-
triv'd obscurities. No wonder then if they who would deter-
20 mine of divorce by this place, have ever found it difficult, and
unsatisfying through all the ages of the Church, as *Austine*
himselfe and other great writers confesse. Lastly it is manifest to be the principal scope of our Saviour both here, and in
the 5. of *Mat.* to convince the Pharises of what they being
25 evill did licentiously, not to explaine what others being good
and blamelesse men might be permitted to doe in case of
extremity. Neither was it seasonable to talke of honest and
conscientious liberty among them who had abused legall and

civil liberty to uncivil licence. We doe not say to a servant
what we say to a sonne; nor was it expedient to preach freedome to those who had transgrest in wantonnesse. When we
rebuke a Prodigal, we admonish him of thrift, not of mag-
5 nificence, or bounty. And to school a proud man we labour
to make him humble, not magnanimous. So Christ to retort
these arrogant inquisitors their own, tooke the course to lay
their hautinesse under a severity which they deserv'd; not to
acquaint them, or to make them judges either of the just
10 mans right and privilege, or of the afflicted mans necessity.
And if wee may have leave to conjecture, there is a likelyhood
offer'd us by *Tertullian* in his 4. against *Marcion,* whereby it
may seeme very probable that the Pharises had a private drift
of malice against our Saviours life in proposing this question;
15 and our Saviour had a peculiar aim in the rigor of his answer,
both to let them know the freedome of his spirit, and the
sharpenesse of his discerning. *This I must now shew,* saith
*Tertullian, Whence our Lord deduc'd this sentence, and
which way he directed it, whereby it will more fully appeare
20 that he intended not to dissolve Moses.* And there upon tells
us that the vehemence of this our Saviours speech was cheifly
darted against *Herod* and *Herodias.* The story is out of *Josephus: Herod* had beene a long time married to the daughter of *Aretas* King of *Petra,* til hapning on his jorney to-
25 wards *Rome* to be entertain'd at his brother *Philip*s house, he
cast his eye unlawfully and unguestlike upon *Herodias* there,
the wife of *Philip,* but daughter to *Aristobulus* their common
brother, and durst make words of marrying her his Neece

from his brothers bed. She assented upon agreement he
should expell his former wife. All was accomplisht, and by
the *Baptist* rebuk't with the losse of his head. Though doubtlesse that staid not the various discourses of men upon the
5 fact, which while the *Herodian* flatterers, and not a few perhaps among the Pharises endevour'd to defend by wresting
the law, it might be a meanes to bring the question of divorce
into a hot agitation among the people, how farre *Moses* gave
allowance. The Pharises therefore knowing our Saviour to
10 be a friend of *John the* Baptist, and no doubt but having heard
much of his Sermon in the Mount, wherein he spake rigidly
against the licence of divorce, they put him this question both
in hope to find him a contradicter of *Moses,* and a condemner of *Herod;* so to insnare him within compasse of the
15 same accusation which had ended his friend; and our Saviour
so orders his answer, as that they might perceive *Herod* and
his Adultresse only not nam'd; so lively it concern'd them
both what he spake. No wonder then if the sentence of our
Saviour sounded stricter then his custome was; which his
20 conscious attempters doubtlesse apprehended sooner then his
other auditors. Thus much we gaine from hence to informe
us, that what Christ intends to speake here of divorce, will be
rather the forbidding of what we may not doe herein passionately and abusively, as *Herod* and *Herodias* did, then the
25 discussing of what herein we may doe reasonably and necessarily.

[*Is it lawfull for a man to put away his wife.*] It might be
render'd more exactly from the Greeke, *to loosen or to set*

free; which though it seeme to have a milder signification
then the two Hebrew words commonly us'd for divorce, yet
Interpreters have noted, that the Greeke also is read in the
Septuagint, for an act which is not without constraint. As
5 when *Achish* drove from his presence *David* counterfeting
madnesse, *Psal.* 34. the Greeke word is the same with this
here, to put away. And *Erasmus* quotes *Hilary* rendering it
by an expression, not so soft. Whence may be doubted,
whether the Pharises did not state this question in the strict
10 right of the man, not tarrying for the wives consent. And if
our Saviour answer directly according to what was askt in the
tearm of putting away, it may be questionable, whether the
rigor of his sentence did not forbid only such putting away as
is without mutuall consent, in a violent and harsh manner,
15 or without any reason, but will, as the *Tetrarch* did. Which
might be the cause that those Christian Emperours fear'd not
in their constitutions to dissolve mariage by mutuall consent; In that our Saviour seemes here, as the case is most
likely, not to condemne all divorce but all injury and violence
20 in divorce. But no injury can be done to them who seeke it,
as the *Ethics* of *Aristotle* sufficiently prove. True it is, that an
unjust thing may be done to one though willing, and so may
justly be forbid'n: But divorce being in it selfe no unjust or
evill thing, but only as it is joyn'd with injury, or lust, injury
25 it cannot be at law, if consent be, and *Aristotle* erre not. And
lust it may as frequently not be, while charity hath the judging of so many private greevances in a misfortun'd Wedlock,
which may pard'nably seeke a redemption. But whether it

be or not, the law cannot discerne, or examine lust, so long
as it walkes from one lawfull terme to another, from divorce
to marriage both in themselves indifferent. For if the law
cannot take hold to punish many actions apparently covetous,
5 ambitious, ingratefull, proud, how can it forbid and punish
that for lust, which is but only surmis'd so, and can no more
be certainly prov'd in the divorcing now, then before in the
marrying. Whence if divorce be no unjust thing, but through
lust, a cause not discernable by law, as law is wont to discerne
10 in other cases, and can be no injury where consent is, there
can be nothing in the equity of law, why divorce by consent
may not be lawfull: leaving secrecies to conscience, the thing
which our Saviour here aimes to rectifie, not to revoke the
statutes of *Moses*. In the meane while the word *To put away,*
15 being in the Greeke, to loosen or disolve, utterly takes away
that vaine papisticall distinction of divorce from bed, and divorce from bond, evincing plainly that both Christ and the
Pharises meane here that divorce which finally disolves the
bond and frees both parties to a second marriage.

20   [*For every cause.*] This the Pharises held, that for every
cause they might divorce, for every accidentall cause, any
quarrell or difference that might happ'n. So both *Josephus*
and *Philo,* men who liv'd in the same age, explain; and the
Syriac translater, whose antiquity is thought parallel to the
25 *Evangelists* themselves, reads it conformably *upon any occasion or pretence.* Divines also generally agree that thus the
Pharises meant. *Cameron* a late writer much applauded,
commenting this place not undiligently, affirmes that the

Greeke preposition Κατὰ translated unusually (for) hath a
force in it implying the suddennesse of those Pharisaic divorces; and that their question was to this effect, *whether for*
any cause, whatever it chanc'd to be, straight as it rose, the
5 *divorse might be lawfull.* This he freely gives what ever
mov'd him, and I as freely take, nor can deny his observation
to be acute & learned. If therfore we insist upon the word of
putting away, that it imports a constraint without consent, as
might be insisted, and may enjoy what *Cameron* bestowes on
10 us, that for every cause is to be understood, *according as any*
cause may happen, with a relation to the speedinesse of those
divorces and that *Herodian* act especially, as is already brought
us, the sentence of our Saviour wil appeare nothing so strict
a prohibition as hath beene long conceiv'd, forbidding only
15 to divorce for casuall & temporary causes, that may be soon
ended, or soone remedied; & likewise forbidding to divorce
rashly, & on the sudden heate, except it be for adultery. If
these qualifications may be admitted, as partly we offer them,
partly are offer'd them by some of their own opinion, and that
20 where nothing is repugnant why they should not bee admitted,
nothing can wrest them from us, the severe sentence of our
Saviour will straight unbend the seeming frowne into that
gentlenesse and compassion which was so abundant in all his
actions, his office and his doctrine, from all which otherwise
25 it stands off at no meane distance.

Vers. 4. *And he answered and said unto them, have ye not*
read that he which made them at the beginning,
made them Male and Female?

Vers. 5. *And said, for this cause shall a man leave Father and Mother, and shall cleave to his wife, and they twaine shall be one flesh?*

Vers. 6. *Wherefore they are no more twaine but one flesh, what therefore God hath joyned together, let no man put asunder.*

[4. and 5. *Made them Male and Female, And said for this cause, & c.*] We see it here undeniably, that the law which our Saviour cites to prove that divorce was forbidd'n, is not an absolute and tyrannicall command without reason, as now adaies wee make it little better, but is grounded upon some rationall cause not difficult to be apprehended, being in a matter which equally concernes the meanest and the plainest sort of persons in a houshold life. Our next way then will be to inquire if there bee not more reasons then one, and if there be, whether this be the best and cheifest. That we shall finde by turning to the first institution, to which Christ referrs our owne reading; He himselfe having to deale with treacherous assailants, useth brevity, and lighting on the first place in *Genesis* that mentions any thing tending to Marriage in the first chapter, joynes it immediately to the 24. verse of the 2 chapter, omitting all the prime words between, which create the institution, and containe the noblest and purest ends of Matrimony, without which attain'd, that conjunction hath nothing in it above what is common to us with beasts. So likewise beneath in this very chapter, to the young man who came not tempting him, but to learne of him, asking him which com-

mandments hee should keepe, he neither repeates the first
table, nor all the second, nor that in order which he repeates.
If heere then being tempted, hee desire to bee the shorter, and
the darker in his conference, and omitt to cite that from the
5 second of *Genesis*, which all Divines confesse is a commentary to what he cites out of the first, the *making them Male
and Female;* what are we to doe, but to search the institution
our selves; and we shall finde there his owne authority giving
other manner of reasons why such firme union is to bee in
10 matrimony, without which reasons their being male and female can be no cause of joyning them unseparably: for if it
be, then no Adultery can sever. Therefore the prohibition of
divorce depends not upon this reason heere exprest to the
Pharises, but upon the plainer & more eminent causes omitted
15 heere and referr'd to the institution; which causes not being
found in a particular and casuall Matrimony, this sensitive
and materious cause alone can no more hinder a divorce
against those higher and more human reasons urging it, then
it can alone without them to warrant a copulation, but leaves
20 it arbitrary to those who in their chance of marriage finde not
why divorce is forbidd them, but why it is permitted them;
and finde both here and in *Genesis*, that the forbidding is not
absolute, but according to the reasons there taught us, not
here. And that our Saviour taught them no better, but uses
25 the most vulgar, most animal and corporal argument, to convince them, is first to shew us, that as through their licentious
divorces they made no more of mariage then as if to marry,
were no more then to be male and female, so hee goes no

higher in his confutation; deeming them unworthy to be talkt
with in a higher straine, but to bee ty'd in marriage by the
meere material cause thereof, since their owne licence testify'd that nothing matrimonial was in their thought but to be
5 male and female. Next it might be don to discover the brute
ignorance of these carnall Doctors, who taking on them to
dispute of marriage and divorce, were put to silence with such
a slender opposition as this, and outed from their hold with
scarce one quarter of an argument. That we may beleeve this,
10 his entertainment of the young man soon after may perswade
us. Whom, though he came to preach eternall life by faith
only, he dismisses with a salvation taught him by workes
only. On which place *Paræus* notes, *That this man was to be
convinc't by a false perswasion; and that Christ is wont oth-*
15 *erwise to answer hypocrites, otherwise those that are docible.*
Much rather then may we thinke that in handling these
tempters, he forgot not so to frame his prudent ambiguities
and concealements, as was to the troubling of those perem-
tory disputants most wholsome. When therefore we would
20 know what right there may be, in ill accidents, to divorce,
wee must repaire thither where God professes to teach his
servants by the prime institution, and not where we see him
intending to dazle sophisters: Wee must not reade *hee made*
them Male and Female, & not understand he made them
25 more intendedly *a meet helpe* to remove the evill of being
alone. We must take both these together, and then we may
inferre compleatly as from the whole cause why a man shall
cleave to his wife, and they twaine shall be one flesh: but if

the full and cheife cause why we may not divorce, be wanting
heer, this place may skirmish with the rabbies while it will,
but to the true christian it prohibits nothing beyond the full
reason of it's own prohibiting, which is best knowne by the
5 institution.

Vers. 6. [*Wherefore they are no more twaine, but one
flesh.*] This is true in the generall right of marriage, but not
in the chance medley of every particular match. For if they
who were once undoubtedly one flesh, yet become twain by
10 adultery, then sure they who were never one flesh rightly,
never helps meete for each other according to the plain pre-
script of God, may with lesse adoe then a volume be concluded still twaine. And so long as we account a Magistrate
no Magistrate, if there be but a flaw in his election, why
15 should we not much rather count a Matrimony no Matrimony, if it cannot be in any reasonable manner according to
the words of Gods institution.

[*What therefore God hath joyned, let no man put asunder.*] But heare the christian prudence lies to consider what
20 God hath joyn'd; shall wee say that God hath joyn'd error,
fraud, unfitnesse, wrath, contention, perpetuall lonelinesse,
perpetuall discord; what ever lust, or wine, or witchery,
threate, or inticement, avarice or ambition hath joyn'd together, faithfull with unfaithfull, christian with antichris-
25 tian, hate with hate, or hate with love, shall we say this is
Gods joyning?

[*Let not man put asunder.*] That is to say, what God hath
joyn'd; for if it be, as how oft we see it may be, not of Gods

joyning, and his law tells us he joynes not unmachable things but hates to joyne them, as an abominable confusion, then the divine law of *Moses* puts them asunder, his owne divine will in the institution puts them asunder, as oft as the reasons be
5 not extant, for which only God ordain'd their joyning. Man only puts asunder when his inordinate desires, his passion, his violence, his injury makes the breach: not when the utter want of that which lawfully was the end of his joyning, when wrongs and extremities, and unsupportable greevances com-
10 pell him to disjoyne: when such as *Herod* & the pharises divorce beside law, or against law, then only man separates, and to such only this prohibition belongs. In a word, if it be unlawful for man to put asunder that which God hath joyn'd, let man take heede it be not detestable to joyne that by com-
15 pulsion which God hath put assunder.

Vers. 7. *They say unto him, why did Moses then command to give a writing of divorcement, and to put her away?*
Vers. 8. *He saith unto them, Moses because of the hardnesse of your hearts suffered you to put away your wives,*
20 *but from the beginning it was not so.*

[*Moses because of the hardnesse of your hearts suffered you.*] Hence the divinity now current argues that this judiciall *Moses* is abolisht. But suppose it were so, though it hath bin prov'd otherwise, the firmenesse of such right to divorce
25 as here pleads, is fetcht from the prime institution, does not stand or fall with the judiciall Jew, but is as morall as what is moralest. Yet as I have shewn positively that this law can-

not bee abrogated, both by the words of our Saviour pronouncing the contrary, and by that unabolishable equity
which it convaies to us, so I shall now bring to view those ap-
pearances of strength which are levied from this text to main-
5 taine the most grosse and massy paradox that ever did violence to reason and religion, bred onely under the shadow of
these words, to all other piety or philosophy strange and insolent, that God by act of law drew out a line of adultery
almost two thousand yeares long: although to detect the
10 prodigy of this surmise, the former booke set forth on this
argument hath already beene copious. I shall not repeate
much though I might borrow of mine own, but shall endeavour to adde something either yet untoucht, or not largely
anough explain'd. First it shal be manifest that the common
15 exposition cannot possibly consist with christian doctrine:
next a truer meaning of this our Saviours reply shall be left
in the roome. The receiv'd exposition is, that God though
not approving did enact a law to permit adultery by divorcement simply unlawfull. And this conceit they feede with
20 fond supposals that have not the least footing in Scripture.
As that the Jews learnt this custome of divorce in *Egypt,* and
therefore God would not unteach it them till Christ came,
but let it stick as a notorious botch of deformity in the midst
of his most perfect and severe law. And yet he saith, *Levit.*
25 the 18th *after the doings of Egypt ye shall not do.* Another
while they invent a slander (as what thing more bold then
teaching Ignorance when he shifts to hide his nakednes) that
the Jews were naturally to their wives the cruellest men in the

world; would poison, braine, and doe I know not what, if
they might not divorce. Certain, if it were a fault heavily
punisht, to bring an evill report upon the land which God
gave, what is it to raise a groundles calumny against the
5 people which God made choise of? But that this bold inter-
pretament, how commonly so ever sided with, cannot stand
a minute with any competent reverence to God or his law, or
his people, nor with any other maxim of religion, or good
manners, might bee prov'd through all the heads and *Topics*
10 of argumentation: but I shall willingly bee as concise as possible. First the law, not onely the moral, but the judicial
given by *Moses* is just and pure; for such is God who gave it.
Harken O Israel, saith *Moses, Deut.* 4. *unto the statutes and
the judgements which I teach you, to doe them, that ye may*
15 *live, &c. ye shall not adde unto the word which I command
you, neither shall ye diminish ought from it, that ye may
keepe the commandements of the Lord your God which I
command you.* And onward in the chapter, *Behold I have
taught you statutes and judgements, even as the Lord my*
20 *God commanded me. Keepe therefore and doe them, for this
is your wisedome and your understanding. For what nation
hath God so nigh unto them, and what nation hath statutes
and judgements so righteous as all this law which I set before
ye this day.* Is it imaginable there should bee among these a
25 law which God allow'd not, a law giving permissions laxative
to unmarry a wife and marry a lust, a law to suffer a kind of
tribunall adultery? Many other scriptures might be brought
to assert the purity of this judicial law, and many I have al-

leg'd before; this law therefore is pure and just. But if it permit, if it teach, if it defend that which is both unjust and impure, as by the common doctrine it doth, what thinke we?
The three generall doctrines of *Justinians* law, are *To live in*
5 *honesty, To hurt no man, To give every one his due.* Shall
the *Roman civil* law observe these three things, as the onely
end of law, and shall a statute be found in the civil law of
God, enacted simply and totally against all these three precepts of nature and morality?

10   Secondly, the gifts of God are all perfet, and certainely the
law is of all his other gifts one of the perfetest. But if it give
that outwardly which it takes away really, & give that seem-
ingly, which, if a man take it, wraps him into sinne and
damns him, what gift of an enemy can be more dangerous
15 and destroying then this.

    Thirdly, *Moses* every where commends his lawes, preferrs
them before all of other nations, and warrants them to be the
way of life and safety to all that walke therein, *Levit.* 18. But
if they containe statutes which God approves not, and traine
20 men unweeting to committ injustice and adultery, under the
shelter of law, if those things bee sin, and death sins wages,
what is this law but the snare of death?

    Fourthly, the statutes and judgements of the Lord, which
without exception are often told us to be such, as doing wee
25 may live by them, are doubtles to be counted the rule of
knowledge and of conscience. *For I had not known lust,* saith
the Apostle, *but by the law.* But if the law come downe from
the state of her incorruptible majesty to grant lust his boon,

palpably it darkns and confounds both knowledge and conscience; it goes against the common office of all goodnes and
freindlinesse, which is at lest to counsel and admonish; it
subverts the rules of all sober education; and is it selfe a most
5 negligent and debaushing tutor.

Fiftly, if the law permit a thing unlawfull it permitts that
which else where it hath forbid; so that hereby it contradicts
it selfe, and transgresses it selfe. But if the law become a
transgressor, it stands guilty to it selfe, and how then shall it
10 save another; it makes a confederacy with sin, how then can
it justly condemne a sinner? and thus reducing it selfe to the
state of neither saving nor condemning, it will not faile to
expire solemnely ridiculous.

Sixtly, the Prophets in Scripture declare severely against
15 the decreeing of that which is unjust, *Psal.* 94. 20. *Isaiah* the
10th. But it was done, they say, for heardnesse of heart; To
which objection the Apostles rule, *not to doe evill that good
may come thereby,* gives an invincible repuls; and here especially, where it cannot be shewn how any good came by
20 doing this evil, how rather more evil did not hereon abound;
for the giving way to hardnesse of heart hard'ns the more,
and adds more to the number. God to an evil and adulterous generation would not *grant a signe;* much lesse would
he for their hardnesse of heart pollute his law with an adul-
25 terous permission. Yea but to permitt evil is not to doe evil.
Yes, it is in a most eminent manner to doe evil: where else
are all our grave and faithfull sayings, that he whose office
is to forbid and forbids not, bids, exhorts, encourages. Why

hath God denounc'd his anger against parents, maisters,
freinds, magistrates neglectfull of forbidding what they
ought, if law the common father, maister, friend, and perpetuall magistrate shall not onely not forbidd, but enact, ex-
5 hibit, and uphold with countnance and protection a deede
every way dishonest, what ever the pretence be. If it were
of those inward vices, which the law cannot by outward constraint remedy, but leaves to conscience and perswasion, it
had bin guiltlesse in being silent: but to write a decree of that
10 which can be no way lawfull, and might with ease be hinder'd, makes law by the doome of law it selfe accessory in the
highest degree.

Seventhly, it makes God the direct author of sin, For although he bee not made the authour of what he silently per-
15 mitts in his providence, yet in his law, the image of his will,
when in plaine expression he constitutes and ordaines a fact
utterly unlawfull, what wants hee to authorize it, and what
wants that to be the author?

Eightly, to establish by law a thing wholy unlawfull and
20 dishonest, is an affirmation was never heard of before in any
law, reason, philosophy, or religion, till it was rais'd by inconsiderat glossists from the mistake of this text. And though
the Civilians have bin contented to chew this opinion, after
the canon had subdu'd them, yet they never could bring ex-
25 ample or authority either from divine writt, or human learning, or human practice in any nation, or well-form'd repub-
lick, but only from the customary abuse of this text. Usually
they allege the Epistle of *Cicero* to *Atticus;* wherein *Cato* is

blam'd for giving sentence to the scumme of *Romulus,* as if
he were in *Plato*'s common wealth. *Cato* would have call'd
some great one into judgement for bribery, *Cicero* as the
time stood, advis'd against it. *Cato,* not to endammage the
public treasury, would not grant to the Roman Knights, that
the *Asian* taxes might bee farm'd them at a lesse rate. *Cicero*
wisht it granted. Nothing in all this will bee like the establishing of a law to sinne: here are no lawes made, here onely
the execution of law is crav'd might be suspended: between
which and our question is a broad difference. And what if
human law givers have confest they could not frame their
lawes to that perfection which they desir'd, we heare of no
such confession from *Moses* concerning the lawes of God,
but rather all praise and high testimony of perfection given
them. And although mans nature cannot beare exactest lawes,
yet still within the confines of good it may and must; so long
as lesse good is far anough from altogether evil. As for what
they instance of usury, let them first prove usury to be wholly
unlawfull, as the law allowes it; which learned men as nu-
merous on the other side will deny them. Or if it be altogether unlawfull, why is it tolerated more then divorce? he
who said divorse not, said also *lend hoping for nothing
againe,* Luk. 6. 35. But then they put in, that trade could
not stand. And so to serve the commodity of insatiable trading, usury shall be permitted, but divorce, the onely meanes
oft times to right the innocent, & outrageously wrong'd, shall
be utterly forbid. This is egregious doctrine, and for which
one day charity will much thanke them. *Beza* not finding

how to salve this perplexity, and *Cameron* since him, would
secure us; although the latter confesses that to *permit a*
wicked thing by law, is a wickednesse from which God ab-
horrs; yet to limit sin, and prescribe it a certaine measure, is
5 *good.* First this evasion will not helpe heere; for this law
bounded no man; he might put away whatever found not
favour in his eyes. And how could it forbid to divorce, whom
it could not forbidd to dislike, or command to love. If these
be the limits of law to restraine sinne, who so lame a sinner
10 but may hoppe over them more easily then over those *Rom-*
ulean circumscriptions, not as *Remus* did with hard succes,
but with all indemnity. Such a limiting as this were not
worth the mischeif that accompanies it. This law therefore
not bounding the supposed sinne, by permitting enlarges it,
15 gives it enfranchisement. And never greater confusion, then
when law and sin move their land markes, mixe their terri-
tories, and correspond, have intercourse and traffic together.
When law contracts a kindred and hospitality with transgression, becomes the godfather of sinne and names it Law-
20 full; when sin revels and gossips within the arcenal of law,
plaies, and dandles the artillery of justice that should be bent
against her, this is a faire limitation indeede. Besides it is an
absurdity to say that law can measure sin, or moderate sin;
sin is not in a predicament to be measur'd and modify'd, but
25 is alwaies an excesse. The least sinne that is, exceeds the
measure of the largest law that can bee good; and is as boundlesse as that vacuity beyond the world. If once it square to
the measure of Law, it ceases to be an excesse, and conse-

quently ceases to be a sinne; or else law conforming it selfe
to the obliquity of sin, betraies it selfe to be not strait, but
crooked and so immediatly no law. And the improper conceit of moderating sin by law will appeare, if wee can imagin
5 any lawgiver so senselesse as to decree that so farre a man
may steale, and thus farre bee drunk, that moderately he may
cozen, and moderatly committ adultery. To the same extent
it would be as pithily absurd to publish that a man may moderately divorce, if to doe that be intirely naught. But to end
10 this moot, the law of *Moses* is manifest to fixe no limit therein
at all, or such at lest as impeaches the fraudulent abuser no
more then if it were not set; only requires the dismissive
writing without other caution, leaves that to the inner man,
and the barre of conscience. But it stopt other sins. This is
15 as vaine as the rest, and dangerously uncertain: the contrary
to be fear'd rather, that one sin admitted courteously by law,
open'd the gate to another. However evil must not be don for
good. And it were a fall to be lamented, an indignity unspeakable, if law should becom tributary to sin her slave, and
20 forc't to yeild up into his hands her awfull minister Punishment, should buy out her peace with sinne for sinne, paying
as it were her so many *Philistian* foreskins to the proud demand of Trangression. But suppose it any way possible to
limit sinne, to put a girdle about that *Chaos,* suppose it also
25 good; yet if to permitt sin by Law bee an abomination in the
eyes of God, as *Cameron* acknowledges, the evil of permitting will eate out the good of limiting. For though sin be not
limited, there can but evil come out of evil; but if it be per-

mitted & decreed lawfull by divine law, of force then sin must
proceed from the infinit Good, which is a dreadfull thought.
But if the restraining of sinne by this permission beeing good,
as this author testifies, be more good then the permission of
5 more sin by the restraint of divorce, and that God waighing
both these like two ingots in the perfet scales of his justice and
providence found them so, and others coming without authority from God, shall change this counterpoise, and judge
it better to let sin multiply by setting a judicial restraint upon
10 divorce, which Christ never set, then to limit sin by this permission, as God himselfe thought best to permitt it, it will
behoove them to consult betimes whether these their bal-
lances be not fals and abominable; and this their limiting that
which God loosen'd, and their loosning the sinnes that he
15 limited, which they confesse was good to doe: and were it
possible to doe by law, doubtlesse it would be most morally
good; and they so beleeving, as we heare they doe, and yet
abolishing a law so good and moral, the limiter of sin, what
are they else but contrary to themselves? for they can never
20 bring us to that time wherein it will not be good to limit
sinne, and they can never limit it better then so as God prescrib'd in his law.

Others conceav it a more defensible retirement to say this
permission to divorce sinfully for hardnesse of heart was a
25 dispensation. But surely they either know not, or attend not
what a dispensation meanes. A dispensation is for no long
time, is particular to som persons rather then generall to a
whole people; alwaies hath charity the end, is granted to

necessities and infirmities, not to obstinat lust. This permission is another creature, hath all those evils and absurdities
following the name of a dispensation, as when it was nam'd
a law; and is the very *antarctic pole* against charity, nothing
5 more advers, ensnaring and ruining those that trust in it, or
use it; so leud and criminous as never durst enter into the
head of any Politician, Jew, or Proselyte, till they became the
apt Schollers of this canonistic exposition. Ought in it, that
can allude in the lest manner to charity, or goodnes, belongs
10 with more full right to the christian under grace and liberty,
then to the Jew under law and bondage. To Jewish ignorance it could not be dispenc't, without a horrid imputation
laid upon the law, to dispence fouly, in stead of teaching
fairly; like that dispensation that first polluted Christendom
15 with Idolatry, permitting to lay men images in stead of
bookes and preaching. Sloth or malice in the law would they
have this calld? But what ignorance can be pretended for
the Jewes, who had all the same precepts about mariage, that
we now: for Christ referrs all to the institution. It was as rea-
20 sonable for them to know then as for us now, and concern'd
them alike: for wherein hath the gospel alter'd the nature of
matrimony? All these considerations, or many of them have
bin furder amplify'd in *the doctrine of divorce*. And what
Rivetus and *Paræus* hath objected, or giv'n over as past cure
25 hath bin there discusst. Whereby it may be plain anough to
men of eyes, that the vulgar exposition of a permittance by
law to an entire sin, what ever the colour may be, is an opinion both ungodly, unpolitic, unvertuous, and void of all hon-

esty & civil sense. It appertaines therefore to every zealous
Christian both for the honour of Gods law, & the vindication
of our Saviours words, that such an irreligious depravement
no longer may be sooth'd and flatter'd through custome, but
5 with all diligence and speed solidly refuted, and in the room
a better explanation giv'n; which is now our next endeavour.

[*Moses suffer'd you to put away, &c.*] Not commanded
you, saies the common observer, and therefore car'd not how
soon it were abolisht, being but suffer'd; heerin declaring his
10 annotation to be slight & nothing law prudent. For in this
place *commanded and suffer'd* are interchangeably us'd in
the same sense both by our Saviour and the Pharises. Our
Saviour who heer saith, *Moses suffer'd you,* in the 10th of
Marke saith, *Moses wrote you this command.* And the Phar-
15 isees who heer say, *Moses commanded,* and would mainly
have it a command, in that place of *Marke* say *Moses suffer'd,*
which had made against them in their owne mouthes, if the
word of *suffering* had weakn'd the command. So that *suffer'd*
and *commanded* is heer taken for the same thing on both
20 sides of the controversy: as *Cameron* also and others on this
place acknowledge. And Lawyers know that all the precepts
of law are devided into obligatorie and permissive, containing
either what we must doe, or what wee may do; and of this
latter sort are as many precepts, as of the former, and all as
25 lawfull. Tutelage, an ordainment then which nothing more
just, being for the defence of Orfanes, the *Institutes* of *Justinian,* say *is given and permitted by the civil law:* and *to parents it is permitted to choose and appoint by will the guar-*

dians of their children. What more equall, and yet the civil law calls this *permission.* So likewise to *manumise,* to adopt, to make a will, and to be made an heire is call'd *permission* by law. Marriage it selfe, and this which is already granted, 5 to divorce for adultery, obliges no man, is but a permission by law, is but suffer'd. By this we may see how weakly it hath bin thought that all divorce is utterly unlawfull, because the law is said to suffer it: whenas to *suffer* is but the legall phrase denoting what by law a man may doe or not doe.

10 [*Because of the hardnesse of your hearts.*] Hence they argue that therefore he allowd it not; and therefore it must be abolisht. But the contrary to this will sooner follow, that because he suffer'd it for a cause, therefore in relation to that cause he allow'd it. Next, if he in his wisedome, and in the 15 midst of his severity allow'd it for hardnesse of heart, it can be nothing better then arrogance and presumption to take stricter courses against hardnes of heart then God ever set an example, and that under the Gospel which warrants them to no judicial act of compulsion in this matter, much lesse to be 20 more severe against hardnes of extremity, then God thought good to bee against hardnes of heart. He suffer'd it, rather then worse inconveniences; these men wiser as they make themselves, will suffer the worst and hainousest inconveniences to follow, rather then they will suffer what God suf-25 fer'd. Although they can know when they please, that Christ spake only to the conscience, did not judge on the civil bench, but alwaies disavow'd it. What can be more contrary to the waies of God then these their doings. If they bee such ene-

mies to hardnes of heart, although this groundlesse rigor pro-
claims it to be in themselves, they may yet learne, or consider
that hardnesse of heart hath a twofould acception in the
Gospel. One, when it is in a good man taken for infirmity,
5 and imperfection, which was in all the Apostles, whose weak-
nesse only, not utter want of beleef is call'd hardnes of heart,
Marke 16. partly for this hardnesse of heart, the imperfection and decay of man from original righteousnesse, it was
that God suffer'd not divorce onely, but all that which by
10 Civilians is term'd the *secondary law of nature and of nations*. He suffer'd his owne people to wast and spoyle and
slay by warre, to lead captives, to be som maisters, som servants, som to be princes, others to be subjects, hee suffer'd
propriety to divide all things by severall possession trade and
15 commerce, not with out usury; in his comon wealth some
to bee undeservedly rich, others to bee undeservingly poore.
All which till hardnesse of heart came in, was most unjust;
whenas prime Nature made us all equall, made us equall
coheirs by common right and dominion over all creatures. In
20 the same manner, and for the same cause hee suffer'd divorce
as well as mariage, our imperfet and degenerat condition of
necessity requiring this law among the rest, as a remedy
against intolerable wrong and servitude above the patience of
man to beare. Nor was it giv'n only because our infirmity, or
25 if it must be so call'd, hardnesse of heart could not endure all
things, but because the hardnes of anothers heart might not
inflict all things upon an innocent person, whom far other
ends brought into a league of love and not of bondage and

indignity. If therefore we abolish divorce as only suffer'd for
hardnes of heart, we may as well abolish the whole law of
nations, as only sufferd for the same cause; it being shewn us
by Saint *Paul* 1 *Cor.* 6. that the very seeking of a mans right
5 by law, and at the hands of a worldly magistrat, is not without the hardnesse of our hearts. *For why doe ye not rather
take wrong,* saith he, *why suffer ye not rather your selves to
be defrauded?* If nothing now must be suffer'd for hardnes
of heart, I say the very prosecution of our right by way of
10 civil justice can no more bee suffer'd among Christians, for
the hardnes of heart wherwith most men persue it. And that
would next remove all our judiciall lawes, and this restraint
of divorce also in the number; which would more then halfe
end the controversy. But if it be plaine that the whole ju-
15 ridical law and civil power is only suffer'd under the Gospel,
for the hardnes of our hearts, then wherefore should not that
which *Moses* suffer'd, be suffer'd still by the same reason?

In a second signification hardnes of heart is tak'n for a
stubborne resolution to doe evil. And that God ever makes
20 any law purposely to such, I deny; for he voutsafes not to
enter cov'nant with them, but as they fortune to be mixt with
good men, and passe undiscover'd; much lesse that he should
decree an unlawfull thing only to serve their licentiousnes.
But that God *suffers* this reprobate hardnes of heart I affirm,
25 not only in this law of divorce, but throughout all his best
and purest commandements. He commands all to worship
in singlenes of heart according to all his Ordinances; and yet
suffers the wicked man to performe all the rites of religion

hypocritically and in the hardnes of his heart. He gives us
generall statutes & privileges in all civil matters, just & good
of themselves, yet suffers unworthiest men, to use them & by
them to prosecute their own right, or any colour of right,
5 though for the most part maliciously, covetously, rigorously,
revengefully. He allow'd by law the discreet father and husband to forbidd, if he thought fit, the religious vows of his
wife or daughter: *Num.* 30. and in the same law suffer'd the
hard heartednes of impious and covetous fathers or husbands
10 abusing this law to forbidd their wives or daughters in their
offrings and devotions of greatest zeal. If then God suffer
hardnes of heart equally in the best laws as in this of divorce,
there can be no reason that for this cause this law should be
abolisht. But other lawes, they object, may be well us'd, this
15 never. How often shall I answer both from the institution of
mariage, and from other general rules in Scripture, that this
law of divorce hath many wise and charitable ends besides the
being suffer'd for hardnes of heart; which is indeed no end,
but an accident happning through the whole law; which
20 gives to good men right, and to bad men who abuse right
under false pretences, gives only sufferance. Now although
Christ express no other reasons here, but only what was
suffer'd, it nothing followes that this law had no other reason
to be permitted but for hardnes of heart. The Scripture sel-
25 dome, or never in one place sets down all the reasons of what
it grants or commands, especially when it talks to enemies
and tempters. St. *Paul* permitting mariage, 1 *Cor.* 7, seems
to permit even that also for hardnes of heart only, lest we

should run into fornication; yet no intelligent man thence
concludes mariage allow'd in the Gospel only to avoid an
evill, because no other end is there exprest. Thus *Moses* of
necessity suffer'd many to put away their wives for hardnesse
5 of heart; but enacted the law of divorce doubtles for other
good causes, not for this only sufferance. He permitted not
divorce by law as an evil, for that was impossible to divine
law, but permitted by accident the evil of them who divorc't
against the lawes intention undiscoverably. This also may be
10 thought not improbably, that Christ stirr'd up in his spirit
against these tempting Pharises, answer'd them in a certain
forme of indignation usual among good authors; wherby the
question, or the truth is not directly answer'd, but som thing
which is fitter for them, who aske, to heare. So in the eccle-
15 siastical stories one demanding how God imploy'd himself
before the world was made, had answer; that he was making
hel for curious questioners. Another (and *Libanius* the
Sophist as I remember) asking in derision som Christian,
what the Carpenter, meaning our Saviour, was doing, now
20 that *Julian* so prevail'd, had it return'd him, that the Carpenter was making a coffin for the *Apostat.* So Christ being
demanded maliciously why *Moses* made the law of divorce,
answers them in a vehement *scheme,* not telling them the
cause why he made it, but what was fittest to be told them,
25 that *for the hardnes of their hearts* he suffer'd them to abuse
it. And all beit *Mark* say not he suffer'd you, but *to you he
wrote this precept; Mark* may be warrantably expounded by
Mathew the larger. And whether he suffer'd, or gave pre-

cept, being all one as was heard, it changes not the *trope* of
indignation, fittest account for such askers. Next for the
hardnes of *your hearts to you he wrote this precept,* inferrs
not therfore for this cause only he wrote it, as was parallell'd
5 by other Scriptures. Lastly, It may be worth the observing,
that Christ speaking to the Pharises does not say in general
that for hardnes of heart he gave this precept, but *you he
suffer'd, & to you he gave this precept for your* hardnes of
heart. It cannot be easily thought that Christ heer included
10 all the children of Israel under the person of these tempting
Pharises but that he conceals wherefore he gave the better sort
of them this law, and expresses by saying emphatically *To
you* how he gave it to the worser, such as the Pharises best
represented, that is to say for the hardnes of your hearts: as
15 indeed to wicked men and hardn'd hearts he gives the whole
law and the Gospel also, to hard'n them the more. Thus
many waies it may orthodoxally be understood how God or
Moses suffer'd such as the demanders were, to divorce for
hardnes of heart. Whereas the vulgar expositer beset with
20 contradictions and absurdities round, and resolving at any
peril to make an exposition of it, as there is nothing more
violent and boistrous then a reverend ignorance in fear to be
convicted, rushes brutely and impetuously against all the
principles both of nature, piety, and moral goodnes; and in
25 the fury of his literal expounding overturns them all.

[*But from the beginning it was not so.*] Not how from
the beginning doe they suppose, that men might not divorce at all, not necessarily, not deliberatly except for adul-

tery, but that som law, like canon law presently attacht them
both before and after the flood, till stricter *Moses* came, and
with law brought licence into the world? that were a fancy
indeed to smile at. Undoubtedly as to point of judiciall law,
5 divorce was more permissive from the beginning before
Moses then under *Moses*. But from the beginning, that is to
say, by the institution in Paradice it was not intended that
matrimony should dissolve for every trivial cause as you
Pharises accustome. But that it was not thus suffer'd from
10 the beginning ever since the race of men corrupted, & laws
were made, he who will affirme, must have found out other
antiquities then are yet known. Besides we must consider
now, what can be so as from the beginning, not only what
should be so. In the beginning, had men continu'd perfet, it
15 had bin just that all things should have remain'd, as they
began to *Adam* & *Eve*. But after that the sons of men grew
violent & injurious, it alter'd the lore of justice, and put the
goverment of things into a new frame. While man and
woman were both perfet each to other, there needed no di-
20 vorce; but when they both degenerated to imperfection, &
oft times grew to be an intolerable evil each to other, then law
more justly did permitt the alienating of that evil which mistake made proper, then it did the appropriating of that good
which Nature at first made common. For if the absence of
25 outward good be not so bad as the presence of a close evil, &
that propriety, whether by cov'nant or possession, be but the
attainment of some outward good, it is more natural & righteous that the law should sever us from an intimat evil, then

appropriate any outward good to us from the community of
nature. The Gospel indeed tending ever to that which is perfetest, aim'd at the restorement of all things, as they were in
the beginning. And therefore all things were in common to
5 those primitive Christians in the Acts, which *Ananias &*
Sapphira dearly felt. That custome also continu'd more or
less till the time of *Justin Martyr,* as may be read in his 2ᵈ
Apology, which might be writt after that act of communion
perhaps some 40. yeares above a hunder'd. But who will be
10 the man shall introduce this kind of common wealth, as
christianity now goes? If then mariage must be as in the beginning, the persons that marry must be such as then were,
the institution must make good, in som tolerable sort, what it
promises to either party. If not, it is but madnes to drag this
15 one ordinance back to the beginning, and draw down all
other to the present necessity, and condition farre from the
beginning even to the tolerating of extortions and oppres-
sions. Christ only told us that from the beginning it was not
so; that is to say, not so as the Pharises manur'd the busines;
20 did not command us that it should be forcibly so again in all
points, as at the beginning; or so at least in our intentions and
desires, but so in execution, as reason, and present nature can
bear. Although we are not to seek, that the institution it selfe
from the first beginning was never but conditional, as all
25 cov'nants are: because thus and thus, therefore so and so; if
not thus, then not so. Then moreover was perfetest to fulfill
each law in it selfe; now is perfetest in this estate of things,
to ask of charity how much law may be fulfill'd: els the ful-

filling, oft times is the greatest breaking. If any therefore demand, which is now most perfection, to ease an extremity by
divorce, or to enrage and fester it by the greevous observance
of a miserable wedloc, I am not destitute to say which is most
5 perfection (although som who beleev they thinke favourably
of divorce, esteem it only venial to infirmity). Him I hold
more in the way to perfection who forgoes an unfit ungodly
& discordant wedloc, to live according to peace & love, &
Gods institution in a fitter chois, then he who debarrs him-
10 self the happy experience of all godly, which is peaceful conversation in his family, to live a contentious, and unchristian
life not to be avoided, in temptations not to be liv'd in, only
for the fals keeping of a most unreal nullity, a mariage that
hath no affinity with Gods intention, a daring phantasm, a
15 meer toy of terror awing weak senses, to the lamentable superstition of ruining themselves, the remedy wherof God in
his law voutsafes us. Which not to dare use, he warranting,
is not our perfection, is our infirmity, our little faith, our
timorous and low conceit of charity: and in them who force
20 us, it is their masking pride and vanity, to seem holier & more
circumspect then God. So far is it that we need impute to him
infirmity, who thus divorces: since the rule of perfection is
not so much that which was don in the beginning, as that
which now is nearest to the rule of charity. This is the great-
25 est, the perfetest, the highest commandment.

V. 9. *And I say unto you, who so shall put away his wife,*
except it be for Fornication, and shall marry another,

committeth adultery; and who so marrieth her which is
put away, doth commit adultery.

[*And I say unto you.*] That this restrictive denouncement
of Christ contradicts and refutes that permissive precept of
5 *Moses,* common expositers themselves disclaime: and that it
does not traverse from the closet of conscience to the courts
of civil or canon law, with any Christian rightly commenc't
requires not long evincing. If Christ then did not heer check
permissive *Moses,* nor did reduce matrimony to the begin-
10 ning more then all other things, as the reason of mans condition could beare, we would know precisely what it was which
he did, and what the end was of his declaring thus austerely
against divorce. For this is a confesst oracle in law, that he
who lookes not at the intention of a precept, the more super-
15 stitious he is of the letter, the more he misinterprets. Was it
to shame *Moses?* that had beene monstrous: or all those purest ages of Israel, to whom the permission was granted? that
were as incredible. Or was it that he who came to abrogate
the burden of law, not the equity, should put this yoke upon
20 a blamelesse person, to league himselfe in chaines with a be-
girting mischeif, not to separat till death? hee who taught us
that no man puts a peece of new cloth upon an old garment,
nor new wine into old bottles, that he should sow this patch
of strictnes upon the old apparel of our frailty, to make a rent
25 more incurable, when as in all other amendments his doctrine still charges, that regard be had to the garment, and to
the vessel, what it can endure; this were an irregular and

single peece of rigor, not onely sounding disproportion to the whole Gospel, but outstretching the most rigorous nervs of law and rigor it selfe. No other end therefore can bee left imaginable of this excessive restraint, but to bridle those er-
5 roneous and licentious postillers the Pharises; not by telling them what may bee done in necessity, but what censure they deserve who divorce abusively, which their Tetrarch had done. And as the offence was in one extreme, so the rebuke, to bring more efficaciously to a rectitude and mediocrity,
10 stands not in the middle way of duty, but in the other extreme. Which art of powerfull reclaiming, wisest men have also taught in their ethical precepts and *gnomologies;* resembling it, as when wee bend a crooked wand the contrary way; not that it should stand so bent, but that the overbending
15 might reduce it to a straitnesse by its own reluctance. And as the Physician cures him who hath tak'n down poyson, not by the middling temper of nourishment, but by the other extreme of *antidote,* so Christ administers heer a sharpe & corrosive sentence against a foul and putrid licence; not to eate
20 into the flesh, but into the sore. And knowing that our divines through all their comments make no scruple, where they please, to soften the high and vehement speeches of our Saviour, which they call *hyperbolies,* why in this one text should they be such crabbed *masorites* of the Letter, as not to
25 mollifie a transcendence of literal rigidity, which they confesse to find often elsewhere in his manner of delivery, but must make their exposition heer such an obdurat *Cyclops,* to have but one eye for this text, and that onely open to cruelty

and enthralment, such as no divine, or human law before
ever heard of. No, let the foppish canonist with his fardel of
matrimonial cases goe and be vendible where men bee so unhappy as to cheap'n him; the words of Christ shall be asserted
5 from such elementall notaries, and resolv'd by the now-only
lawgiving mouth of charity; which may be done undoubtedly by understanding them as followes.

[*Whosoever shall put away his wife.*] That is to say, shall
so put away as the propounders of this question, the Pharisees
10 were wont to doe and covertly defended *Herod* for so doing;
whom to rebuke, our Saviour heer mainely intends, and not
to determine all the cases of divorce, as appeares by Saint
Paul. Whosoever shall put away, either violently without
mutuall consent for urgent reasons, or conspiringly by plot
15 of lust, or cunning malice, shall put away for any sudden
mood, or contingency of disagreement, which is not daily
practice, but may blow soone over, and be reconcil'd, except
it bee fornication; whosoever shall put away rashly, as his
choler prompts him, without due time of deliberating, and
20 thinke his conscience discharg'd only by the bill of divorce
giv'n, and the outward law satisfi'd; whosoever lastly shall
put away his wife, that is a wife indeede, & not in name only,
such a one who both can and is willing to bee a meet helpe
toward the cheif ends of mariage both civil, and sanctify'd,
25 except fornication be the cause, that man, or that pair committ adultery. Not he who puts away by mutuall consent,
with all the considerations and respects of humanity and gentlenesse without malicious or lustfull drift. Not he who after

sober and coole experience, and long debate within himself,
puts away whom though he cannot love or suffer as a wife,
with that sincere affection that marriage requires, yet loves at
lest with that civility and goodnesse, as not to keepe her under
5 a neglected and unwelcom residence, where nothing can be
hearty, and not beeing, it must needs bee both unjoyous and
injurious to any perceaving person so detain'd, and more injurious, then to be freely, and upon good termes dismist. Nor
doth hee put away adulterously who complaines of causes
10 rooted in immutable nature, utter unfitnesse, utter disconformity, not concileable, because not to be amended without
a miracle. Nor hee who puts away an unquenchable vexation
from his bosom, and flies an evil then which a greater cannot
befall human society. Nor hee who puts away with the full
15 suffrage and applause of his conscience, not relying on the
writt'n bill of law, but claiming by faith and fulnes of perswasion the rights and promises of Gods institution, of which
hee finds himselfe in a mistak'n wedlock defrauded. Doubtlesse this man hath baile anough to bee no adulterer giving
20 divorce for these causes.

[*His Wife.*] This word is not to be idle here, a meere
word without a sense, much lesse a fallacious word signifying
contrary to what it pretends; but faithfully signifies a wife,
that is, a comfortable helpe and society, as God instituted;
25 does not signify deceitfully under this name, an intolerable
adversary, not a helpelesse, unaffectionate and sullen masse
whose very company represents the visible and exactest figure
of lonelines it selfe. Such an associate he who puts away, di-

vorces not a wife, but disjoyns a nullity which God never
joyn'd, if she be neither willing, nor to her proper and requisite duties sufficient, as the words of God institute her. And
this also is *Bucers* explication of this place.

5 [*Except it bee for fornication, or saving for the cause of
fornication, as Matt.* 5th.] This declares what kind of causes
our Saviour meant; fornication being no natural and perpetual cause, but onely accidental and temporary; therefore
shewes that head of causes from whence it is excepted, to bee
10 meant of the same sort. For exceptions are not logically deduc't from a divers kind, as to say who so puts away for any
naturall cause except fornication, the exception would want
salt. And if they understand it, who so for any cause what
ever, they cast themselves; granting divorce for frigidity a
15 naturall cause of their own allowing, though not heer exprest,
and for desertion without infidelity when as he who marries,
as they allow him for a desertion, deserts as well as is deserted,
and finally puts away, for another cause besides adultery. It
will with all due reason therefore be thus better understood,
20 who so puts away for any accidental and temporary causes,
except one of them, which is fornication. Thus this exception
finds out the causes from whence it is excepted, to be of the
same kind, that is, casuall, not continuall.

[*Saving for the cause of fornication.*] The New Testa-
25 ment, though it be said originally writt in Greeke, yet hath
nothing neer so many *Atticisms* as *Hebraisms,* & *Syriacisms*
which was the Majesty of God, not filing the tongue of Scripture to a Gentilish *Idiom,* but in a princely manner offring

to them as to Gentiles and Foreiners grace and mercy, though
not in forein words, yet in a forein stile that might induce
them to the fountaines; and though their calling were high
and happy, yet still to acknowledge Gods ancient people their
5 betters, and that language the *Metropolitan* language. He
therefore who thinks to *Scholiaze* upon the Gospel, though
Greek, according to his Greek *Analogies,* and hath not bin
Auditor to the oriental dialects, shall want in the heat of his
Analysis no accomodation to stumble. In this place, as the 5th
10 of *Matth.* reads it, *Saving for the cause of fornication,* the
Greek, such as it is, sounds it, except for the *word, report,
speech, or proportion* of fornication. In which regard with
other inducements, many ancient and learned writers have
understood this exception as comprehending any fault equiv-
15 alent and proportional to fornication. But truth is, the Evangelist heer *Hebraizes,* taking *word* or *speech* for *cause* or
matter in the common eastern phrase, meaning perhaps no
more then if he had said for fornication, as in this 19th chapter. And yet the word is found in the 5th of *Exodus* also sig-
20 nifying *Proportion;* where the Irsaelites are commanded to
doe their tasks, *The matter of each day in his day.* A task we
know is a proportion of work, not doing the same thing absolutely every day, but so much. Whereby it may be doubtfull
yet, whether heer be not excepted not only fornication it self,
25 but other causes equipollent, and proportional to fornication.
Which very word also to understand rightly, wee must of
necessity have recours again to the Ebrew. For in the Greek
and Latin sense by fornication is meant the common prosti-

tution of body for sale. So that they who are so exact for the letter, shall be dealt with by the *Lexicon,* and the *Etymologicon* too if they please, and must be bound to forbidd divorce for adultery also, untill it come to open whoredom and
5 trade, like that for which *Claudius* divorc't *Messalina*. Since therfore they take not heer the word fornication in the common significance, for an open exercise in the stews, but grant divorce for one single act of privatest adultery, notwithstanding that the word speakes a public and notorious frequency
10 of fact, not without price, we may reason with as good leav, and as little straining to the text, that our Saviour on set purpose chose this word *Fornication,* improperly appli'd to the lapse of adultery, that we might not think our selvs bound from all divorce, except when that fault hath bin actually
15 committed. For the language of Scripture signifies by fornication (and others beside St. *Austin* so expounded it) not only the trespas of body nor perhaps that between maried persons, unlesse in a degree or quality as shameles as the *Bordello,* but signifies also any notable disobedience, or intract-
20 able cariage of the wife to the husband, as *Judg.* the 19. 2. Whereof at large *in the Doctrin of Divorce, l. 2. c.* 18. Secondly signifies the apparent alienation of mind not to idolatry, (which may seeme to answer the act of adultery) but farre on this side, to any point of will worship, though to the
25 true God; some times it notes the love of earthly things, or worldly pleasures though in a right beleever, some times the least suspicion of unwitting idolatry. As *Num.* 15. 39. willfull disobedience to any the least of Gods commandements is

call'd fornication. *Psal.* 73. 26, 27. A distrust only in God,
and withdrawing from that neernes of zeal and confidence
which ought to be, is call'd fornication. We may be sure it
could not import thus much less then Idolatry in the bor-
5 row'd metaphor between God and man, unless it signifi'd as
much less then adultery in the ordinary acception between
man and wife. Adde also that there was no need our Saviour
should grant divorce for adultery, it being death by law, and
law then in force. Which was the cause why *Joseph* sought
10 to put away his betrothed wife privately, least he should make
her an example of capitall punishment, as lernedest ex-
pounders affirm, *Herod* being a great zelot of the Mosaic law,
and the Pharises great maisters of the text, as the woman
tak'n in adultery doubtless had cause to fear. Or if they can
15 prove it was neglected, which they cannot doe, why did our
Saviour shape his answer to the corruption of that age, and
not rather tell them of their neglect? If they say he came not
to meddle with their judicatures, much less then was it in his
thought to make them new ones, or that divorce should be
20 judicially restrain'd in a stricter manner by these his words,
more then adultery judicially acquitted by those his words
to the adultres. His sentence doth no more by law forbidd
divorce heer, then by law it doth absolve adultery there. To
them therefore, who have drawn this yoke upon Christians
25 from his words thus wrested, nothing remaines but the guilt
of a presumption and perversnes which will be hard for them
to answer. Thus much that the word fornication is to be understood as the language of Christ understands it, for a con-

stant alienation and disaffection of mind, or for the continual
practise of disobedience and crossnes from the duties of love
and peace, that is in summ, when to be a tolerable wife is
either naturally not in their power, or obstinatly not in their
5 will, and this opinion also is St. *Austins*, least it should hap to
be suspected of novelty. Yet grant the thing heer meant were
only adultery, the reason of things will afford more to our
assertion, then did the reason of words. For why is divorce
unlawfull but only for adultery? because, say they, that crime
10 only breaks the matrimony. But this, I reply, the institution
it selfe gainsaies: for that which is most contrary to the words
and meaning of the institution, that most breaks the matrimony; but a perpetuall unmeetnes and unwillingnesse to all
the duties of helpe, of love and tranquillity is most contrary
15 to the words and meaning of the institution; that therefore
much more breaks matrimony then the act of adultery
though repeated. For this, as it is not felt, nor troubles him
who perceaves it not, so beeing perceav'd, may be soon re-
pented, soon amended, soon, if it can be pardon'd, may be
20 redeem'd with the more ardent love and duty in her who
hath the pardon. But this naturall unmeetnes both cannot
be unknown long, and ever after cannot be amended, if it be
natural, and will not, if it be farre gon obstinat. So that wanting ought in the instant to be as great a breach as adultery, it
25 gains it in the perpetuity to be greater. Next adultery does
not exclude her other fitnes, her other pleasingnes; she may
be otherwise both loving and prevalent, as many adultresses
be; but in this general unfitnes or alienation she can be noth-

ing to him that can please. In adultery nothing is given
from the husband, which he misses, or enjoyes the less, as it
may be suttly giv'n: but this unfitnes defrauds him of the
whole contentment which is sought in wedloc. And what
5 benefit to him, though nothing be giv'n by the stealth of
adultery to another, if that which there is to give, whether it
be solace, or society, be not such as may justly content him?
and so not only deprives him of what it should give him, but
gives him sorrow and affliction, which it did not ow him.
10 Besides is adultery the greatest breach of matrimony in respect of the offence to God, or of the injury to man? if in the
former, then other sins may offend God more, and sooner
cause him to disunite his servant from being one flesh with
such an offender. If in respect of the latter, other injuries are
15 demonstrated therein more heavy to mans nature then the
iterated act of adultery. God therfore in his wisedom would
not so dispose his remedies, as to provide them for the less
injuries, and not allow them for the greater. Thus is won
both from the word fornication, & the reason of adultery, that
20 the exception of divorce is not limitted to that act, but enlarg'd
to the causes above specify'd.

[*And who so marieth her which is put away doth committ
adultery.*]

By this clause alone, if by nothing els, we may assure us,
25 that Christ intended not to deliver heer the whole doctrin of
divorce, but only to condemn abuses. Otherwise to marry
after desertion, which the Apostle, and the reformed Churches
at this day permitt, is heer forbid, as adultery. Be she never

so wrongfully deserted, or put away, as the law then suffer'd, if thus forsak'n and expulst, she accept the refuge and
protection of any honester man who would love her better,
and give her self in mariage to him, by what the letter guides
5 us, it shall be present adultery to them both. This is either
harsh and cruel, or all the Churches teaching as they doe the
contrary, are loos and remiss; besides that the Apostle himselfe stands deeply fin'd in a contradiction against our Saviour. What shall we make of this? what rather the com-
10 mon interpreter can make of it, for they be his own markets,
let him now trie; let him trie which way he can wind in his
Vertumnian distinctions and evasions, if his canonical gabar-
dine of text and letter do not now sit too close about him, and
pinch his activity; which if I erre not, hath heer hamper'd it
15 selfe in a springe fitt for those who put their confidence in
Alphabets. *Spanheim* a writer of *Evangelic doubts* comes
now and confesses that our Saviours words *are to be limited*
beyond the limitation there exprest, and excepted beyond
their own exception, as not speaking of what happn'd rarely,
20 but what most commonly. Is it so rare *Spanheim,* to be deserted, or was it then so rare to put away injuriously, that a
person so hatefully expell'd, should to the heaping of more
injury be turn'd like an infectious thing out of all maried
fruition upon pain of adultery, as not considerable to the
25 brevity of this halfe sentence? Of what then speakes our Saviour? of *that collusion,* saith he, *which was then most fre-*
quent among the Jews of changing wives and husbands,
through inconstancy and unchast desires. Colluders your

selves, as violent to this law of God by your unmercifull binding, as the Pharises by their unbounded loosning! Have thou-
sands of Christian souls perisht as to this life, and God knows
what hath betided their consciences, for want of this healing
5 explanation, and is it now at last obscurely drawn forth, only
to cure a scratch, and leave the main wound spouting? *Who
so ever putteth away his wife except for fornication committeth adultery;* That shall be spoke of all ages, and all men,
though never so justly otherwise mov'd to divorce: in the
10 very next breath, *And who so marieth her which is put away
committeth adultery,* the men are new and miraculous, they
tell you now *you are to limit it to that age, when it was in
fashion to chop matrimonies; and must be meant of him who
puts away with his wives consent through the lightnes, and
15 leudnes of them both.* But what rule of Logic, or indeed of
reason is our commission to understand the *Antecedent* one
way and the *Consequent* another; for in that habitude this
whole vers may be consider'd: or at least to take the parts of
a *copulat axiom,* both absolutely affirmative, and to say the
20 first is absolutely true, the other not, but must bee limited
to a certain time and custome; which is no lesse then to say
they are both false. For in this *compound axiom,* be the parts
never so many, if one of them doe but falter, & be not equally
absolute and generall, the rest are all fals. If therefore,
25 that *he who marries her which is put away committs adultery,*
be not generally true, neither is it generally true that *he
committs adultery who puts away for other cause then fornication.* And if the marrying her which is put away, must be

understood limited, which they cannot but yeild it must, with the same limitation must be understood the putting away. Thus doth the common exposition confound it selfe, and justify this which is heer brought; that our Saviour as well in the first part of this sentence as in the second, prohibited onely such divorses as the Jewes then made through malice or through plotted licence, not those which are for necessary and just causes; where charity and wisedome disjoyns, that which not God, but Error and Disastre joyn'd.

And there is yet to this our exposition, a stronger siding freind, then any can be an adversary, unlesse Saint *Paul* be doubted, who repeating a command concerning divorce, 1 *Cor.* 7. which is agreed by writers to be the same with this of our Saviour, and appointing that the *wife remaine unmaried, or be reconcil'd to her husband,* leavs it infallible that our Saviour spake cheifly against putting away for casual and choleric disagreements, or any other cause which may with human patience and wisedom be reconcil'd, not hereby meaning to hale and dash together the irreconcilable aversations of nature, nor to tie up a faultlesse person like a parricide, as it were into one sack with an enemy, to be his causelesse tormenter and executioner the length of a long life. Lastly, let this sentence of Christ bee understood how it will, yet that it was never intended for a judicial law, to be inforc'd by the Magistrat, besides that the office of our Saviour had no such purpose in the Gospel, this latter part of the sentence may assure us, *And who so marrieth her which is put away com-*

mitts adultery. Shall the exception for adultery belong to this clause or not? if not, it would be strange, that he who marries a woman really divorc't for adultery, as Christ permitted, should becom an adulter by marrying one who is now no other
5 mans wife, himself being also free, who might by this meanes reclaim her from common whordome. And if the exception must belong hither, then it followes that he who marries an adultresse divorc'd, commits no adultry; which would soone discover to us what an absurd and senseles peece of injustice
10 this would be, to make a civil statute of, in penal courts: whereby the adultresse put away may marry another safely, and without a crime to him that marries her: but the innocent and wrongfully divorc'd shall not marry again without the guilt of adultery both to her selfe and to her second husband.
15 This saying of Christ therefore cannot be made a temporal law, were it but for this reason. Nor is it easie to say what coherence there is at all in it from the letter, to any perfet sense not obnoxious to som absurdity, and seems much lesse agreeable to what ever els of the Gospel is left us written; doubtles
20 by our Saviour spok'n in that fiercenes and abstruse intricacy, first to amuse his tempters, and admonish in general the abusers of that Mosaic law; next to let *Herod* know a second knower of his unlawfull act, though the Baptist were beheaded; last that his Disciples and all good men might learne
25 to expound him in this place, as in all other his precepts, not by the written letter, but by that unerring paraphrase of Christian love and Charity, which is the summe of all commands, and the perfection.

Vers. 10. *His Disciples say unto him, if the case of the man be so with his wife, it is not good to marry.*

This verse I adde, to leave no objection behind unanswer'd: for some may thinke, if this our Saviours sentence be so faire,
5 as not commanding ought that patience or nature cannot brook, why then did the Disciples murmur and say, *it is not good to marry*. I answer that the Disciples had bin longer bred up under the Pharisæan doctrin, then under that of Christ, and so no marvel though they yet retain'd the infec-
10 tion of loving old licentious customs; no marvel though they thought it hard they might not for any offence that throughly anger'd them, divorce a wife, as well as put away a servant; since it was but giving her a bill, as they were taught. Secondly, it was no unwonted thing with them not to understand
15 our Saviour in matters farre easier. So that bee it granted their conceit of this text was the same which is now commonly conceiv'd, according to the usuall rate of their capacity then, it will not hurt a better interpretation. But why did not Christ seeing their error informe them? for good cause; it was his
20 profest method not to teach them all things at all times, but each thing in due place and season. Christ said *Luke* 22. that *hee who had no sword should sell his garment and buy one:* the Disciples tooke it in a manifest wrong sense, yet our Saviour did not there informe them better. He told them *it was*
25 *easier for a Camell to go through a needles eye,* then a rich man in at heav'n gate. They were *amaz'd exceedingly:* he explain'd himselfe to meane of those *who trust in riches,*

Mark 10. *They were amaz'd then out of measure,* for so *Marke* relates it; as if his explaining had increas'd their amazement, in such a plaine case, and which concern'd so neerely their calling to be inform'd in. Good reason therefore, 5 if Christ at that time did not stand amplifying, to the thick prejudice and tradition wherein they were, this question of more difficulty, and lesse concernment to any perhaps of them in particular. Yet did he not omitt to sow within them the seeds of a sufficient determining, agen the time that his prom-10 is'd spirit should bring all things to their memory. Hee had declar'd in their hearing not long before, how distant hee was from abolishing the law it selfe of divorce; hee had referr'd them to the institution; and after all this, gives them a set answer, from which they might collect what was cleer anough, 15 that *all men cannot receive all sayings,* verse 11. If such re-gard bee had to each mans receiving of mariage or single life, what can arise, that the same christian regard should not bee had in most necessary divorce? All which instructed both them and us, that it beseem'd his Disciples to learne the decid-20 ing of this question, which hath nothing new in it, first by the institution, then by the generall grounds of religion, not by a particular saying here or there, temper'd and level'd only to an incident occasion, the riddance of a tempting assault. For what can this bee but weake and shallow apprehension, to for-25 sake the standard principles of institution, faith, & charity; then to be blanke & various at every occurrence in Scripture, and in a cold *Spasm* of scruple, to reare peculiar doctrines upon the place; that shall bid the gray autority of most un-

changeable and sovran rules to stand by & be contradicted.
Thus to this Evangelic precept of famous difficulty, which for
these many ages weakly understood, and violently put in practice, hath made a shambles rather then an ordinance of mat-
5 rimony, I am firme a truer exposition cannot be given. If this
or that argument heer us'd, please not every one, there is no
scarsity of arguments, any halfe of them will suffice. Or
should they all faile, as Truth it selfe can faile as soon, I
should content me with the institution alone to wage this con-
10 troversie, and not distrust to evince. If any need it not, the
happier; yet Christians ought to study earnestly what may be
anothers need. But if, as mortall mischances are, som hap to
need it, let them be sure they abuse not, and give God his
thanks, who hath reviv'd this remedy, not too late for them,
15 and scowr'd off an inveterat misexposition from the Gospel:
a work not to perish by the vaine breath or doome of this age.
Our next industry shall bee, under the same guidance, to try
with what fidelity that remaining passage in the *Epistles*
touching this matter, hath bin commented.

20   1 Cor. 7. 10, &c.

    10. *And unto the maried I command, &c.*
    11. *And let not the husband put away his wife.*

    This intimates but what our Saviour taught before, that
divorce is not rashly to be made, but reconcilement to be
25 persuaded and endevor'd, as oft as the cause can have to
doe with reconcilement, & is not under the dominion of

blameles nature; which may have reason to depart though
seldomest and last from charitable love, yet somtimes from
friendly, and familiar, and somthing oftner from conjugal
love, which requires not only moral, but natural causes to the
5 making and maintayning; and may be warrantably excus'd to
retire from the deception of what it justly seeks, and the ill re-
quitals which unjustly it finds. For Nature hath her *Zodiac*
also, keepes her great annual circuit over human things as truly
as the Sun and Planets in the firmament; hath her *anomalies,*
10 hath her obliquities in ascensions and declinations, accesses and
recesses, as blamelesly as they in heaven. And sitting in her
planetary Orb with two rains in each hand, one strait, the
other loos, tempers the cours of minds as well as bodies to
several conjunctions and oppositions, freindly, or unfreindly
15 aspects, consenting oftest with reason, but never contrary.
This in the effect no man of meanest reach but daily sees; and
though to every one it appeare not in the cause, yet to a cleare
capacity, well nurtur'd with good reading and observation, it
cannot but be plaine and visible. Other exposition therefore
20 then hath bin given to former places that give light to these
two summary verses, will not be needfull: save onely that these
precepts are meant to those maried who differ not in religion.

[*But to the rest speake I, not the Lord; if any brother hath
a wife that beleeveth not, and she be pleased to dwell with*
25 *him, let him not put her away.*]

Now followes what is to be done, if the persons wedded be
of a different faith. The common beleef is, that a christian is
heer commanded not to divorce, if the infidel please to stay,

though it be but to vexe, or to deride, or to seduce the christian. This doctrin will be the easie worke of a refutation. The
other opinion is, that a christian is heer conditionally permitted to hold wedloc with a misbeleever only upon hopes lim-
5 ited by christian prudence, which without much difficulty
shall be defended. That this heer spoken by *Paul,* not by the
Lord cannot be a command, these reasons avouch. First the law
of *Moses, Exod.* 34. 16. *Deut.* 7. 3. 6. interpreted by *Ezra,* and
Nehemiah two infallible authors, commands to divorce an
10 infidel not for the feare onely of a ceremonious defilement,
but of an irreligious seducement, fear'd both in respect of the
beleever himselfe, and of his children in danger to bee per-
verted by the misbeleeving parent. *Nehem.* 13. 24. 26. and
Peter Martyr thought this a convincing reason. If therefore
15 the legal pollution vanishing have abrogated the ceremony of
this law, so that a christian may be permitted to retaine an
infidel without uncleannes, yet the moral reason of divorcing
stands to eternity, which neither Apostle nor Angel from
heaven can countermand. All that they reply to this, is their
20 human warrant, that God will preserve us in our obedience
to this command against the danger of seducement. And so
undoubtedly he will, if we understand his commands aright;
if we turn not this evangelic permission into a legal, and yet
illegal command: if we turne not hope into bondage, the
25 charitable and free hope of gaining another, into the forc't
and servil temptation of loosing our selves; but more of this
beneath. Thus these words of *Paul* by common doctrin made
a command, are made a contradiction to the morall law.

Secondly, not the law only, but the Gospel from the law, and from it selfe requires even in the same chapter, where divorce between them of one religion is so narrowly forbidd, rather then our christian love should come into danger of
5 backsliding, to forsake all relations how neer so ever, and the wife expresly, with promise of a high reward, *Mat.* 19. And he who hates not father or mother, wife, or children hindring his christian cours, much more, if they despise or assault it, cannot be a Disciple, *Luke* 14. How can the Apostle then
10 command us, to love and continue in that matrimony, which our Saviour bids us hate, and forsake? They can as soon teach our faculty of respiration to contract and to dilate it selfe at once, to breath and to fetch breath in the same instant, as teach our minds how to doe such contrary acts as these, towards the
15 same object, and as they must be done in the same moment. For either the hatred of her religion, & her hatred to our religion will work powerfully against the love of her society, or the love of that will by degrees flatter out all our zealous hatred and forsaking and soone ensnare us to unchristianly
20 compliances.

Thirdly, In mariage there ought not only to be a civil love, but such a love as Christ loves his Church; but where the religion is contrary without hope of conversion, there can be no love, no faith, no peacefull society, (they of the other opinion
25 confess it) nay there ought not to be, furder then in expectation of gaining a soul; when that ceases, we know God hath put enmity between the seed of the woman, and the seed of the Serpent. Neither should *we love them that hate the Lord,*

as the Prophet told *Jehosaphat. 2 Chron.* 19. And this Apostle himselfe in another place, warns us *that we be not unequally yokt with Infidels,* 2 *Cor.* 6. for that there can be no fellowship, no communion, no concord between such. Outward commerce and civil intercours cannot perhaps be avoided; but true friendship and familiarity there can be none. How vainly therefore, not to say how impiously would the most inward and dear alliance of mariage or continuance in mariage be commanded, where true friendship is confest impossible. For say they, wee are forbidd heer to marry with an infidel, not bid to divorce. But to rob the words thus of their full sense will not be allow'd them: it is not said, enter not into yoke, but *be not unequally yokt;* which plainly forbids the thing in present act, as well as in purpose; and his manifest conclusion is, not only that *we should not touch,* but that having toucht, *we should come out from among them, and be separat;* with the promise of a blessing thereupon that *God will receave us, will be our father, and we his sons and daughters.* v. 17. 18. Why we should stay with an Infidel after the expence of all our hopes, can be but for a civil relation; but why we should depart from a seducer, setting aside the misconstruction of this place, is from a religious necessity of departing. The wors cause therefore of staying (if it be any cause at all, for civil government forces it not) must not overtop the religious cause of separating, executed with such an urgent zeal, & such a prostrate humiliation by *Ezra* and *Nehemiah.* What God hates to joyn, certainly he cannot love should continue joyn'd: it being all one

in matter of ill consequence, to marry, or to continue maried
with an Infidel, save only so long as we wait willingly, and
with a safe hope. St. *Paul* therefore citing heer a command
of *the Lord Almighty,* for so he terms it, that we should *sep-*
5 *arate,* cannot have bound us with that which he calls his own
whether command or counsel that we should not separate.

Which is the fourth reason, for he himselfe takes care least
we should mistake him, [*But to the rest speak I, not the
Lord.*] If the Lord spake not, then man spake it and man
10 hath no Lordship to command the conscience: yet modern
interpreters will have it a command maugre St. *Paul* himselfe, they will make him a Prophet like *Caiaphas* to speak the
word of the Lord not thinking, nay denying to think; though
he disavow to have receav'd it from the Lord, his word shall
15 not be tak'n, though an Apostle, he shall be born down in his
own Epistle, by a race of expositers who presume to know
from whom he spake, better then he himselfe. *Paul* deposes
that the Lord speaks not this, they, that the Lord speaks it:
can this be less then to brave him with a full fac't contradic-
20 tion? Certainly to such a violence as this, for I cannot call it
an expounding, what a man should answer I know not, unless
that if it be their pleasure next to put a gag into the Apostles
mouth, they are already furnisht with a commodious audac-
ity toward the attempt. *Beza* would seem to shun the contra-
25 dictory by telling us that the Lord spake it not in person, as he
did the former precept. But how many other doctrines doth
St. *Paul* deliver which the Lord spake not in person, and yet
never uses this preamble but in things indifferent? So long as

we receave him for a messenger of God, for him to stand sort-
ing sentences what the Lord spake in person, and what he,
not the Lord in person, would be but a chill trifling, and his
readers might catch an ague the while. But if we shall supply
5 the grammatical *Ellipsis* regularly, and as we must in the
sam *tense,* all will be then cleer, for we cannot supply it thus,
to the rest I speake, the Lord spake not, but I speake, the Lord
speaks not. If then the Lord neither spake in person, nor
speakes it now, the Apostle testifying both, it follows duely,
10 that this can be no command. Forsooth the fear is, least this
not being a command, would prove an evangelic counsel, & so
make way for supererogations. As if the Apostle could not
speak his mind in things indifferent, as he doth in fowr or five
several places of this chapter with the like preface of not com-
15 manding, but that the doubted inconvenience of supererero-
gating must needs rush in. And how adds it to the word of the
Lord, (for this also they object) when as the Apostle by his
christian prudence guids us in the liberty which God hath left
us to, without command? could not the spirit of God instruct
20 us by him what was free, as well as what was not? But what
need I more, when *Cameron* an ingenuous writer, and in high
esteem, solidly confutes the surmise of a command heer, and
among other words hath these. That *when Paul speaks as an
Apostle, he uses this forme,* The Lord saith, not I, v. 10. *but
25 as a privat man he saith,* I speak, not the Lord. And thus also
all the prime fathers *Austin, Jerom,* and the rest understood
this place.

Fiftly, The very stating of the question declares this to be

no command; *If any brother hath an unbeleeving wife, and she be pleased to dwell with him, let him not put her away.* For the Greek word συνευδοκεῖ does not imply only her being pleas'd to stay, but his being pleas'd to let her stay; it must
5 be a consent of them both. Nor can the force of this word be render'd less, without either much negligence or iniquity of him that otherwise translates it. And thus the Greek Church also and their Synods understood it, who best knew what their own language meant, as appeares by *Matthæus Monachus* an
10 author set forth by *Leunclavius* and of antiquity perhaps not inferior to *Balsamon* who writes upon the canons of the Apostles; this Author in his chap. *that mariage is not to be made with heretics,* thus recites the second canon of the 6. Synod, *As to the Corinthians Paul determins, If the beleeving wife choos*
15 *to live with the unbeleeving husband, or the beleeving husband with the unbeleeving wife. Mark* saith he, *how the Apostle heer condescends, if the beleever please to dwell with the unbeleever; so that if he please not, out of doubt the mariage is dissolv'd. And I am perswaded it was so in the begin-*
20 *ning, and thus preach't.* And thereupon gives an example of one, who though not deserted, yet by the decree of *Theodotus* the Patriarch divorc't an unbeleeving wife. What therefore depends in the plain state of this question on the consent and well liking of them both, must not be a command. Lay next
25 the latter end of the 11. v. to the twelf (for wherefore els is Logic taught us) in a *discrete axiom,* as it can be no other by the phrase, *The Lord saith, let not the husband put away his wife, But I say let him not put away a misbeleeving wife;* this

sounds as if by the judgement of *Paul,* a man might put away
any wife but the misbeleeving; or els the parts are not *discrete,*
or *dissentanie,* for both conclude not putting away, and consequently in such a form the proposition is ridiculous. Of ne-
5 cessity therfore the former part of this sentence must be conceav'd, as understood, and silently granted, that although the
Lord command to divorce an infidel, yet I, not the Lord command you? No, but give my judgement, that for som evangelic
reasons a christian may be permitted not to divorce her. Thus
10 while we reduce the brevity of St. *Paul* to a plainer sense, by
the needfull supply of that which was granted between him
and the Corinthians, the very logic of his speech extracts him
confessing that the Lords command lay in a seeming contrariety to this his counsel: and that he meant not to thrust out
15 a command of the Lord by a new one of his own, as one nail
drives another, but to release us from the rigor of it, by the
right of the Gospel, so farre forth as a charitable cause leads
us on in the hope of winning another soule without the peril
of loosing our own. For this is the glory of the Gospel to teach
20 us that *the end of the commandment is charity,* 1 *Tim.* 1. not
the drudging out a poore and worthlesse duty forc't from us
by the taxe, and taile of so many letters. This doctrine therefore can bee no command, but it must contradict the moral
law, the Gospel, and the Apostle himselfe both else where, and
25 heere also eevn in the act of speaking.

If then it be no command, it must remain to be a permission,
and that not absolute, for so it would be still contrary to the
law, but with such a caution as breaks not the law, but as the

manner of the Gospel is, fulfills it through charity. The law
had two reasons, the one was ceremonial, the pollution that
all Gentiles were to the Jewes; this the vision of *Peter* had
abolisht, Acts 10. and clens'd all creatures to the use of a
5 Christian. The *Corinthians* understood not this, but fear'd
lest dwelling in matrimony with an unbeleever, they were
defil'd. The Apostle discusses that scruple with an Evangelic
reason, shewing them that although God heretofore under
the law, not intending the conversion of the Gentiles, except
10 some special ones, held them as polluted things to the Jew, yet
now purposing to call them in, he hath purify'd them from
that legal uncleannesse wherein they stood, to use and to be
us'd in a pure manner.

For saith he, *The unbeleeving husband is sanctifi'd by the*
15 *wife, and the unbeleeving wife, is sanctifi'd by the husband,*
else were your children uncleane; but now they are holy. That
is, they are sanctify'd to you, from that legal impurity which
you so feare; and are brought into a neer capacity to be holy,
if they beleeve, and to have free accesse to holy things. In the
20 mean time, as being Gods creatures, a christian hath power
to use them according to their proper use; in as much as now,
all things to the pure are become pure. In this legal respect
therefore ye need not doubt to continue in mariage with an
unbeleever. Thus others also expound this place and *Cam-*
25 *eron* especially. This reason warrants us onely what wee may
doe without feare of pollution, does not binde us that we must.
But the other reason of the law to divorce an infidel was
moral, the avoiding of enticement from the true faith. This

cannot shrink; but remains in as full force as ever, to save the
actuall christian from the snare of a misbeleever. Yet if a
Christian full of grace and spirituall gifts finding the misbeleever not frowardly affected, feares not a seducing, but hopes
5 rather a gaining, who sees not that this morall reason is not
violated by not divorcing, which the law commanded to doe,
but better fulfill'd by the excellence of the Gospel working
through charity. For neither the faithfull is seduc't, and the
unfaithfull is either sav'd, or with all discharge of love, and
10 evangelic duty sought to be sav'd. But contrarywise if the in-
firme Christian shall bee commanded here against his minde,
against his hope, and against his strength, to dwell with all
the scandals, the houshold persecutions, or alluring temptations of an infidel, how is not the Gospel by this made harsher
15 then the law, and more yoaking? Therefore the Apostle ere
he deliver this other reason why wee need not in all hast put
away an infidel, his mind misgiving him least he should seem
to be the imposer of a new command, staies not for method,
but with an abrupt speed inserts the declaration of their liberty
20 in this matter.

But if the unbeleeving depart, let him depart; a brother or
a sister is not under bondage in such cases: but God hath
called us to peace.

[But if the unbeleeving depart.] This cannot be restrain'd
25 to locall departure only; for who knows not that an offencive
society is worse then a forsaking. If his purpose of cohabitation be to endanger the life or the conscience, Beza himselfe
is halfe perswaded, that this may purchase to the faithfull

person the same freedome that a desertion may; and so *Ge-rard* and others whom he cites. If therefore he depart in affection, if hee depart from giving hope of his conversion, if he disturb, or scoffe at religion, seduce, or tempt, if he rage,
5 doubtlesse not the weake only, but the strong may leave him, if not for feare, yet for the dignities sake of religion, which cannot be liable to all base affronts, meerely for the worshiping of a civil mariage. I take therefore *departing* to bee as large as the negative of being well pleas'd: that is, if he be not
10 pleas'd for the present to live lovingly, quietly, inoffensively, so as may give good hope; which appeares well by that which followes.

[*A brother or a sister is not under bondage in such cases.*]
If Saint *Paul* provide seriously against the bondage of a chris-
15 tian, it is not the only bondage to live unmaried for a deserting infidel, but to endure his presence intolerably, to beare indignities against his religion in words or deedes, to be wearied with seducements, to have idolatries and superstitions ever before his eyes, to be tormented with impure and prophane
20 conversation, this must needs be bondage to a christian; is this left all unprovided for, without remedy, or freedom granted? undoubtedly no, for, the Apostle leavs it furder to be consider'd with prudence, what bondage a brother or sister is not under, not onely in this case, but as hee speaks himselfe
25 plurally, *in such cases.*

[*But God hath called us to peace.*] To peace, not to bondage, not to brabbles and contentions with him who is not pleas'd to live peaceably, as mariage and christianity requires.

And where strife arises from a cause hopelesse to be allayd, what better way to peace then by separating that which is ill joyn'd. It is not divorce, that first breaks the peace of family, as som fondly comment on this place, but it is peace already
5 brok'n, which, when other cures fail, can only be restor'd to the faultles person by a necessary divorce. And Saint *Paul* heer warrants us to seeke peace, rather then to remain in bondage. If God hath call'd us to peace, why should we not follow him, why should we miserably stay in perpetual discord
10 under a servitude not requir'd?

[*For what knowest thou O wife, whether thou shalt save thy husband, &c.*] St. *Paul* having thus clear'd himselfe, not to goe about the mining of our christian liberty, not *to cast a snare upon us,* which to doe hee so much hated, returnes now
15 to the second reason of that law to put away an infidel, for feare of seducement, which hee does not heer contradict with a command now to venture that; but if neither the infirmity of the Christian, nor the strength of the unbeleever be fear'd, but hopes appearing that he may be won, he judges it no
20 breaking of that law, though the beleever be permitted to forbeare divorce, and can abide, without the peril of seducement, to offer the charity of a salvation to wife or husband, which is the fulfilling, not the transgressing of that law; and well worth the undertaking with much hazard and patience. For
25 what knowest thou whether thou shalt save thy wife, that is, till all meanes convenient and possible with discretion and probability, as human things are, have bin us'd. For Christ himselfe sends not our hope on pilgrimage to the worlds end;

but sets it bounds beyond which we need not wait on a brother, much lesse on an infidell. If after such a time we may count a professing Christian no better then a heathen, after less time perhaps wee may cease to hope of a heathen, that hee
5 will turne christian. Otherwise, to binde us harder then the law, and tell us wee are not under bondage, is meere mockery. If till the unbeleever please to part, we may not stirre from the house of our bondage, then certain this our liberty is not grounded in the purchas of Christ, but in the pleasure of a
10 miscreant. What knowes the loyal husband whether he may not save the adulteresse, he is not therfore bound to receive her. What knowes the wife but she may reclaim her husband who hath deserted her? yet the reformed Churches doe not enjoyn her to wait longer then after the contempt of an Ecclesiastical
15 Summons. *Beza* himselfe heer befriends us with a remark-able speech, *what could be firmly constituted in human mat-ters if under pretence of expecting grace from above, it should be never lawfull for us to seeke our right.* And yet in other cases not lesse reasonable to obtain a most just and needfull
20 remedy by divorce, he turnes the innocent party to a taske of prayers beyond the multitude of beads and *rosaries,* to beg the gift of chastity in recompence of an injurious mariage. But the Apostle is evident anough, *we are not under bondage,* trust-ing that he writes to those who are not ignorant what bond-
25 age is, to let supercilious determiners cheat them of their freedome. God hath call'd us to peace, and so doubtlesse hath left in our hands how to obtaine it seasonably; if it be not our own choise to sit ever like novices wretchedly servile.

Thus much the Apostle on this question between Christian
and Pagan, to us now of little use; yet supposing it written for
our instruction as it may be rightly apply'd, I doubt not but
that the difference between a true beleever and a heretic, or
5 any one truely religious either deserted or seeking divorce from
any one grossly erroneous or profane may be referr'd hither.
For St. *Paul* leaves us heer the solution not of this case only,
which little concernes us, but of *such like cases,* which may
occurr to us. For where the reasons directly square, who can
10 forbid why the verdit should not be the same? But this the
common writers allow us not. And yet from this text which
in plaine words gives liberty to none unlesse deserted by an
infidel, they collect the same freedom though the desertion
bee not for religion, which, as I conceive, they neede not doe;
15 but may without straining reduce it to the cause of fornication. For first they confesse that desertion is seldome without
a just suspition of adultery: next it is a breach of mariage in
the same kind, and in some sort worse: for adultery though it
give to another, yet it bereaves not al; but the deserter wholly
20 denies all right, and makes one flesh twain, which is counted
the absolutest breach of matrimony, and causes the other, as
much as in him lies, to commit sin, by being so left. Neverthelesse those reasons which they bring of establishing by this
place the like liberty from any desertion, are faire and solid:
25 and if the thing be lawfull, and can be prov'd so, more waies
then one, so much the safer. Their arguments I shall heer
recite, and that they may not com idle, shall use them to make
good the like freedome to divorce for other causes; and that

we are no more under bondage to any hainous default against the main ends of matrimony, then to a desertion: First they allege that to *Tim.* 1. 5. 8. *If any provide not for those of his own house, hee hath deny'd the faith, and is worse then an*
5 *Infidel.* But a deserter, say they, *can have no care of them who are most his owne, therefore the deserted party is not lesse to bee righted against such a one then against an infidel.* With the same evidence I argue, that man or wife who hates in wedloc, is perpetually unsociable, unpeacefull, or unduteous,
10 either not being able, or not willing to performe what the maine ends of mariage demand in helpe and solace, cannot bee said to care for who should bee dearest in the house; therefore is worse then an infidel in both regards, either in undertaking a duty which he cannot performe, to the undeserved
15 and unspeakable injury of the other party so defrauded and betrai'd, or not performing what he hath undertaken, whenas he may or might have, to the perjury of himselfe more irreligious then heathenisme. The blamelesse person therefore hath as good a plea to sue out his delivery from this bondage,
20 as from the desertion of an infidel. Since most writers cannot but grant that desertion is not only a local absence, but an intolerable society; or if they grant it not, the reasons of Saint *Paul* grant it, with all as much leave as they grant to enlarge a particular freedom from paganisme, into a general freedom
25 from any desertion. Secondly, they reason from the likenes of either fact, *the same losse redounds to the deserted by a christian, as by an infidel, the same peril of temptation.* And I in like manner affirme that if honest and free persons may be

allow'd to know what is most to their owne losse, the same
losse and discontent, but worse disquiet with continuall misery and temptation resides in the company, or better call'd
the persecution of an unfit, or an unpeaceable consort, then by
5 his desertion. For then the deserted may enjoy himselfe at
least. And he who deserts is more favourable to the party
whom his presence afflicts, then that importunat thing which
is and will be ever conversant before the eyes a loyal and individual vexation. As for those who still rudely urge it no loss
10 to mariage, no desertion, so long as the flesh is present and
offers a benevolence that hates, or is justly hated, I am not of
that vulgar and low perswasion, to thinke such forc'd em-
bracements as these worth the honour, or the humanity of
mariage, but farre beneath the soul of a rational and free-
15 borne man. Thirdly they say, *it is not the infidelity of the deserter, but the desertion of the infidel from which the Apostle
gives this freedom;* and I joyne that the Apostle could as little
require our subjection to an unfit and injurious bondage present, as to an infidel absent. To free us from that which is an
20 evil by being distant, and not from that which is an inmate,
and in the bosome evil, argues an improvident and careles deliverer. And thus all occasions, which way so ever they turn, are
not unofficious to administer somthing which may conduce to
explain, or to defend the assertion of this book touching di-
25 vorce. I complain of nothing, but that it is indeed too copious to
be the matter of a dispute, or a defence, rather to be yeelded, as
in the best ages, a thing of common reason, not of controversie.
What have I left to say? I fear to be more elaborat in such a

perspicuity as this; lest I should seem not to teach, but to upbraid the dulnes of an age; not to commun with reason in men,
but to deplore the loss of reason from among men: this only,
and not the want of more to say, is the limit of my discours.

5 *Who among the fathers have interpreted the words of Christ
concerning divorce, as is heer interpreted; and what the
civil law of Christian Emperors in the primitive Church
determin'd.*

Although testimony be in Logic an argument rightly call'd
10 *inartificial,* & doth not solidly fetch the truth by multiplicity
of Authors, nor argue a thing false by the few that hold so, yet
seeing most men from their youth so accustom, as not to
scanne reason, nor cleerly to apprehend it, but to trust for that
the names and numbers of such, as have got, and many times
15 undeservedly, the reputation among them to know much, and
because there is a vulgar also of teachers, who are as blind-
ly by whom they fancy led, as they lead the people, it will
not be amiss for them who had rather list themselves under
this weaker sort, and follow authorities, to take notice that
20 this opinion which I bring, hath bin favour'd, and by som of
those affirm'd, who in their time were able to carry what they
taught, had they urg'd it, through all Christendom; or to have
left it such a credit with all good men, as they who could not
bouldly use the opinion, would have fear'd to censure it. But
25 since by his appointment on whom the times and seasons wait,
every point of doctrin is not fatall to be throughly sifted out in
every age, it will be anough for me to find, that the thoughts

of wisest heads heertofore, and hearts no less reverenc't for
devotion have tended this way, and contributed their lot in
some good measure towards this which hath bin heer attain'd.
Others of them and modern especially, have bin as full in the
5 assertion, though not so full in the reason; so that either in
this regard, or in the former, I shall be manifest in a middle
fortune to meet the praise or dispraise of beeing somthing
first. But I deferr not what I undertooke to shew, that in the
Church both primitive and reformed, the words of Christ
10 have bin understood to grant divorce for other causes then
adultery; and that the word *fornication* in mariage hath a
larger sense then that commonly suppos'd.

Justin Martyr in his first Apology writt'n within 50. yeares
after St. *John* dy'd, relates a story which *Eusebius* transcribes,
15 that a certain matron of Rome, the wife of a vitious husband,
her selfe also formerly vitious, but converted to the faith, and
persuading the same to her husband, at lest the amendment
of his wicked life, upon his not yeilding to her daily entreaties
and persuasions in this behalf, procur'd by law to be divorc't
20 from him. This was neither for adultery, nor desertion, but
as the relation saies, *Esteeming it an ungodly thing to be the
consort of bed with him, Who against the law of nature and
of right sought out voluptuous waies.* Suppose he endeavour'd some unnaturall abuse, as the Greek admitts that mean-
25 ing, it cannot yet be call'd adultery; it therefore could be
thought worthy of divorce no otherwise then as equivalent,
or wors; and other vices will appear in other respects as much
divorsive. Next tis said her freinds advis'd her to stay a while;

and what reason gave they? not because they held unlawfull what she purpos'd, but because they thought she might longer yet hope his repentance. She obey'd, till the man going to *Alexandria*, and from thence reported to grow still more im-

5 penitent, not for any adultery or desertion, wherof neither can be gather'd, but, saith the *Martyr*, and speaks it like one approving, *lest she should be partaker of his unrighteous and ungodly deeds, remaining in wedloc, the communion of bed and board with such a person, she left him by a lawfull*

10 *divorce*. This cannot but give us the judgement of the Church in those pure and next to Apostolic times. For how els could the woman have bin permitted, or heer not reprehended; and if a wife might then doe this without reprooff, a husband certainly might no less, if not more.

15   *Tertullian* in the same age writing his 4. book against *Marcion* witnesses *that Christ by his answer to the Pharises protected the constitution of Moses as his own, and directed the institution of the creator,* for I alter not his *Carthaginian* phrase; *he excus'd rather then destroi'd the constitution of*

20 *Moses; I say he forbidd conditionally, if any one therefore put away that he may marry another: so that if he prohibited conditionally, then not wholly; and what he forbadd not wholly, he permitted otherwise, where the cause ceases for which he prohibited:* that is when a man makes it not the cause of

25 his putting away, meerely that he may marry again. *Christ teaches not contrary to Moses, the justice of divorce hath Christ the asserter: he would not have mariage separat, nor kept with ignominy, permitting then a divorce,* and guesses

that this vehemence of our Saviours sentence was cheifly bent
against *Herod,* as was cited before. Which leavs it evident
how *Tertullian* interpreted this prohibition of our Saviour:
for wheras the text is, *Whosoever putteth away and marieth*
5 *another,* wherfore should *Tertullian* explain it, *Whosoever*
putteth away that he may marry another, but to signify his
opinion that our Saviour did not forbidd divorce from an unworthy yoke, but forbidd the malice or the lust of a needles
change and cheifly those plotted divorces then in use.

10   *Origen* in the next century testifies to have known certain
who had the government of Churches in his time, who permitted som to marry, while yet their former husbands liv'd,
and excuses the deed, as don *not without cause, though with-*
out Scripture, which confirms that cause not to be adultery;
15 for how then was it against Scripture that they maried again.
And a little beneath, for I cite his 7. homily on *Matthew,* saith
he, *To endure faults wors then adultery and fornication,*
seems a thing unreasonable, and disputes therfore that Christ
did not speak by *way of precept, but as it were expounding.*
20 By which and the like speeches *Origen* declares his mind farre
from thinking that our Saviour confin'd all the causes of divorce to actual adultery.

    Lactantius of the age that succeeded speaking of this matter
in the 6. of his *institutions,* hath these words. *But lest any*
25 *think he may circumscribe divine precepts, let this be added,*
that all misinterpreting, and occasion of fraud, or death may
be remov'd, he commits adultery who marries the divorc't
wife, and, besides the crime of adultery, divorces a wife that

he may marry another. To divorce and marry another, and to divorce that he may marry another, are two different things; and imply that *Lactantius* thought not this place the forbidding of all necessary divorce, but such only as proceeded from the wanton desire of a future chois, not from the burden of a present affliction.

About this time the Councel of *Eliberis* in *Spain* decreed the husband excommunicat, *If he kept his wife being an adultress; but if he left her, he might after ten yeares be receav'd into communion, if he retain'd her any while in his house after the adultery known.* The councel of *Neocæsarea* in the year 314. decreed, that if the wife of any *Laic* were convicted of adultery, that man could not be admitted into the ministery: if after ordination it were committed, he was to divorce her; if not, he could not hold his ministery. The councel of *Nantes* condemn'd in 7. yeares penance the husband that would reconcile with an adultress. But how proves this that other causes may divorce? it proves thus; there can be but two causes why these councels enjoyn'd so strictly the divorsing of an adultress, either as an offender against God, or against the husband; in the latter respect they could not impose on him to divorce; for every man is the maister of his own forgivenes; who shal hinder him to pardon the injuries don against himself? It follows therfore that the divorce of an adultress was commanded by these three councels, as it was a sin against God; and by all consequence they could not but beleeve that other sins as hainous might with equal justice be the ground of a divorce.

Basil in his 73. rule, as *Chamier* numbers it, thus determins, that divorce ought not to be, unlesse for adultery, *or the*
hindrance to a godly life. What doth this but proclaime aloud
more causes of divorce then adultery, if by other sins besides
5 this, in wife or husband, the godlines of the better person may
be certainly hinder'd, and endanger'd.

Epiphanius no less ancient, writing against Heretics, &
therefore should himself be orthodoxal above others, ac-
quaints us in his second book *Tom.* 1, not that his private per-
10 suasion was, but that the whole Church in his time generally
thought other causes of divorce lawful besides adultery, as
comprehended under that name; If, saith he, *a divorce happ'n*
for any cause either fornication, or adultery, or any hainous
fault, the word of God blames not either the man or wife
15 *marrying again, nor cutts them off from the congregation, or*
from life, but beares with the infirmity; not that he may keep
both wives, but that leaving the former he may be lawfully
joyn'd to the latter, the holy word, and the holy Church of
God commiserates this man, especially, if he be otherwise of
20 *good conversation, and live according to Gods law.* This
place is cleerer then exposition, and needs no comment.

Ambrose on the 16. of *Luke*, teaches *that all wedloc is not*
Gods joyning and to the 19. of *Pro.* That a *wife is prepard of*
the Lord, as the old latin translates it, he answers that the
25 septuagint renders it, *a wife is fitted by the Lord, and temper'd*
to a kind of harmony; and where that harmony is there God
joyns; where it is not, there dissension reigns, which is not
from God, for God is love. This he brings to prove the marry-

ing of Christian with Gentile to be no mariage, and consequently divorc't without sin: but he who sees not this argument how plainly it serves to divorce any untunable, or un-
attonable matrimony, sees little. On the 1 to the *Cor.* 7, he
5 grants a woman may leave her husband not for only fornication, *but for Apostacy, and inverting nature, though not
marry again; but the man may:* heer are causes of divorce assign'd other then adultery. And going on he affirms, *that the
cause of God is greater then the cause of matrimony; that the*
10 *reverence of wedloc is not due to him who hates the author
thereof; that no matrimony is firm without devotion to God;
that dishonour don to God acquitts the other being deserted
from the bond of matrimony; that the faith of mariage is not
to be kept with such.* If these contorted sentences be ought
15 worth, it is not the desertion that breaks what is broken, but
the impiety; and who then may not for that cause better divorce, then tarry to be deserted? or these grave sayings of St.
Ambrose are but knacks.

Jerom on the 19. of *Matthew* explains, that for the cause of
20 fornication, or the *suspicion thereof a man may freely divorce.* What can breed that suspicion, but sundry faults leading that way? by *Jeroms* consent therfore divorce is free not
only for actuall adultery, but for any cause that may encline
a wise man to the just suspicion therof.

25 *Austin* also must be remember'd among those who hold
that this instance of fornication gives equal inference to other
faults equally hateful, for which to divorce: & therfore in his
books to *Pollentius* he disputes that *infidelity, as being a*

greater sin then adultery, ought so much the rather cause a divorce. And on the Sermon in the Mount, under the name of fornication will have *idolatry, or any harmfull superstition* contain'd, which are not thought to disturb matrimony so
5 directly as som other obstinacies and dissaffections, more against the daily duties of that cov'nant, & in the eastern tongues not unfrequently call'd fornication, as hath bin shew'n. *Hence is understood,* saith he, *that not only for bodily fornication, but for that which draws the mind from*
10 *Gods law, and fouly corrupts it, a man may without fault put away his wife, and a wife her husband, because the Lord excepts the cause of fornication, which fornication we are constrain'd to interpret in a general sense.* And in the first book of his *retractations* chap. 16. he retracts not this his opinion,
15 but commends it to serious consideration; and explains that he counted not there all sin to be fornication, but the more detestable sort of sins. The cause of fornication therefore is not in this discours newly interpreted to signify other faults infringing the duties of wedloc, besides adultery.
20   Lastly the council of *Agatha* in the year 506. can. 25. decreed, that *if lay men who divorc't without some great fault, or giving no probable cause, therfore divorc't, that they might marry som unlawfull person, or som other mans, if before the provinciall Bishops were made acquainted, or judge-*
25 *ment past, they presum'd this, excommunication was the penalty.* Whence it followes, that if the cause of divorce were som great offence, or that they gave probable causes for what they did, and did not therefore divorce that they might

presume with som unlawfull person, or what was another mans, the censure of Church in those daies did not touch them.

Thus having alleg'd anough to shew after what manner 5 the primitive Church for above 500. yeares understood our Saviours words touching divorce, I shall now with a labour less disperst, and sooner dispatcht, bring under view what the civil law of those times constituted about this matter: I say the civil law, which is the honour of every true Civilian to 10 stand for, rather then to count that for law, which the *pontificiall* Canon hath enthrall'd them to, and in stead of interpreting a generous and elegant law, made them the drudges of a blockish *Rubric*.

Theodosius and *Valentinian*, pious Emperors both, or- 15 dain'd that *as by consent lawfull mariages were made, so by consent, but not without the bill of divorce, they might be dissolv'd; and to dissolve was the more difficult, onely in favour of the children.* We see the wisedome and piety of that age one of the purest and learnedest since Christ, conceav'd 20 no hindrance in the words of our Saviour, but that a divorce mutually consented, might bee suffer'd by the law, especially if there were no children, or if there were, carefull provision was made. And further saith that law (supposing there wanted the consent of either) *wee designe the causes of di-* 25 *vorce by this most wholsom law; for as we forbid the dissolving of mariage without just cause, so we desire that a husband or a wife distrest by som advers necessity, should be freed, though by an unhappy, yet a necessary releefe.* What

dramm of wisedome, or religion (for charity is truest religion) could there be in that knowing age, which is not vir-
tually summ'd up in this most just law? As for those other
Christian Emperours, from *Constantine* the first of them,
5 finding the Roman law in this point so answerable to the
Mosaic, it might bee the likeliest cause why they alter'd nothing to restraint, but if ought, rather to liberty, for the helpe,
and consideration of the weaker sexe, according as the Gospel
seems to make the wife more equal to her husband in these
10 conjugal respects then the law of *Moses* doth. Therefore *if a
man were absent from his wife foure yeares, and in that space
not heard of, though gon to warre in the service of the Empire,* she might divorce, and mary another by the edict of
Constantine to *Dalmatius. Co. l. 5. tit.* 17. And this was an
15 age of the Church both antient, and cry'd up still for the most
flourishing in knowledge and pious government since the
Apostles. But to returne to this law of *Theodosius,* with this
observation by the way, that still as the Church corrupted, as
the Clergie grew more ignorant, and yet more usurping on
20 the Magistrate, who also now declin'd, so still divorce grew
more restrain'd; though certainly if better times permitted
the thing that worse times restrain'd, it would not weakly
argue that the permission was better, and the restraint worse.
This law therefore of *Theodosius* wiser in this then the most
25 of his successors, though not wiser then God and *Moses,*
reduc't the causes of divorce to a certain number which by the
judiciall law of God, and all recorded humanitie were left
before to the brest of each husband, provided that the dismisse

was not without reasonable conditions to the wife. But this
was a restraint not yet come to extreames. For besides adultery
and that not only actual, but suspected by many signes there
set down, any fault equally punishable with adultery, or
5 equally infamous might bee the cause of a divorce. Which
informes us how the wisest of those ages understood that place
in the Gospel, whereby, not the pilfering of a benevolence was
consider'd as the main and only breach of wedloc, as is now
thought, but the breach of love and peace, a more holy union
10 then that of the flesh; and the dignity of an honest person was
regarded, not to bee held in bondage with one whose ignominy was infectious. To this purpose was constituted *Cod. l.*
5. *tit.* 17. and *Authent. collat.* 4. *tit.* 1. *Novell.* 22. where
Justinian added three causes more. In the 117. *Novell.* most
15 of the same causes are allow'd, but the liberty of divorcing by
consent is repeal'd: but by whom? by *Justinian,* not a wiser,
not a more religious emperor then either of the former, but
noted by judicious writers for his fickle head in making and
unmaking lawes; and how *Procopius* a good historian, and
20 a counselor of state then living deciphers him in his other
actions, I willingly omitt. Nor was the Church then in better
case, but had the corruption of a 100. declining yeare swept
on it, when the statute of *consent* was call'd in; which as I
said, gives us every way more reason to suspect this restraint,
25 more then that liberty: which therfore in the reign of *Justin*
the succeeding Emperor was recall'd, *Novel.* 140. & establisht
with a preface more wise & christianly then for those times,
declaring the necessity to restore that *Theodosian* law, if no

other meanes of reconcilement could be found. And by whom
this law was abrogated, or how long after, I doe not finde; but
that those other causes remain'd in force, as long as the Greek
empire subsisted, and were assented by that Church, is to bee
5 read in the Canons and edicts compar'd by *Photius* the Patriarch, with the avertiments of *Balsamon,* and *Matthæus Monachus* thereon.

But long before those dayes *Leo* the son of *Basilius Macedo*
reigning about the yeare 886. and for his excellent wisdome
10 surnam'd the *Philosopher,* constituted *that in case of madnesse the husband might divorce after three yeares, the wife
after 5. Constitut. Leon.* 111. 112. This declares how hee
expounded our Saviour, and deriv'd his reasons from the
institution, which in his preface with great eloquence are
15 set downe; whereof a passage or two may give som proofe,
though better not divided from the rest. *There is not,* saith
he, *a thing more necessary to preserve mankind, then the
helpe giv'n him from his own rib; both God and nature so
teaching us: which being so, it was requisite that the provi-
20 dence of law, or if any other care be to the good of man, should
teach and ordaine those things which are to the helpe and
comfort of maried persons, and confirme the end of mariage
purpos'd in the beginning, not those things which afflict and
bring perpetuall misery to them.* Then answers the objection
25 that they are one flesh; *if Matrimony had held so as God
ordain'd it, he were wicked that would dissolve it. But if we
respect this in matrimony, that it be contracted to the good of
both, how shall he, who for some great evil feard, perswades*

not to marry though contracted, not perswade to unmarry, if
after marriage a calamity befall? should we bid beware least
any fall into an evil, and leave him helplesse who by humane
error is fall'n therein? This were as if we should use remedies
5 *to prevent a disease, but let the sick die without remedy.* The
rest will be worth reading in the author.

And thus we have the judgement first of primitive fathers;
next of the imperial law not disallow'd by the universal
Church in ages of her best authority; and lastly of the whole
10 Greeke Church and civil state, incorporating their Canons
and edicts together, that divorce was lawfull for other causes
equivalent to adultery, contain'd under the word fornication.
So that the exposition of our saviours sentence heer alleg'd
hath all these ancient and great asserters, is therefore neither
15 new nor licentious, as some now would perswade the com-
monalty; although it be neerer truth that nothing is more new
then those teachers themselves, & nothing more licentious
then some known to be, whose hypocrisie yet shames not to
take offence at this doctrine for licence; when as indeed they
20 feare it would remove licence, and leave them but few com-
panions.

That the Popes Canon law incroaching upon civil Magistracy
abolisht all divorce eevn for adultery. What the reformed
Divines have recover'd; and that the famousest of them
25 *have taught according to the assertion of this booke.*

But in these western parts of the empire it will appeare
almost unquestionable that the cited law of *Theodosius* and

Valentinian stood in force untill the blindest and corruptest times of Popedom displac't it. For that the volumes of *Justinian* never came into *Italy*, or beyond *Illiricum*, is the opinion of good Antiquaries. And that only manuscript thereof found in *Apulia* by *Lotharius* the *Saxon*, and giv'n to the state of *Pisa* for their aid at sea against the *Normans* of *Sicily*, was receav'd as a rarity not to bee matcht. And although the *Gothes*, and after them the *Lombards* and *Franks* who overrun the most of *Europ* except this *Island* (unlesse wee make our *Saxons* and *Normans* a limm of them) brought in their owne customes, yet that they follow'd the Roman laws in their contracts and mariages, *Agathias* the historian is alleg'd. And other testimonies relate that *Alaricus* & *Theodoric* their Kings writ their statutes out of this *Theodosian Code* which hath the recited law of Divorce. Neverthelesse while the Monarchs of Christendome were yet barbarous, and but halfe Christian, the Popes tooke this advantage of their weake superstition, to raise a corpulent law out of the canons and *decretals* of audacious preists; and presum'd also to set this in the front; *That the constitutions of princes are not above the constitutions of clergy, but beneath them.* Using this very instance of divorce as the first prop of their tyranny; by a false consequence drawn from a passage of *Ambrose* upon *Luke* where hee saith, though *Mans law grant it, yet Gods law prohibits it.* Whence *Gregory* the Pope writing to *Theoctista* inferrs the Ecclesiasticall Courts cannot be dissolv'd by the Magistrate. A faire conclusion from a double error. First in saying that the divine law prohibited divorce, for what will hee

make of *Moses;* next supposing that it did, how will it follow, that what ever Christ forbids in his Evangelic precepts, should be hal'd into a judicial constraint against the patterne of a divine law: Certainely the Gospel came not to enact such
5 compulsions. In the meane while wee may note heere that the restraint of divorce was one of the first faire seeming pleas which the Pope had, to step into secular authority, and with his Antichristian rigor to abolish the permissive law of Christian princes conforming to a sacred lawgiver. Which if we
10 consider, this papal and unjust restriction of divorce need not be so deere to us, since the plausible restraining of that, was in a manner the first loosning of Antichrist; and as it were the substance of his eldest horn. Nor doe we less remarkably ow the first meanes of his fall heer in *England* to the contemning
15 of that restraint by *Henry* 8. whose divorce he oppos'd. Yet was not that rigour executed anciently in spiritual Courts untill *Alexander* the third, who trod upon the neck of *Frederic Barbarossa* the Emperor, and summond our *Henry* 2. into *Normandy* about the death of *Becket.* He it was, that the
20 worthy author may be known, who first actually repeal'd the imperial law of divorce, and decreed this tyranous decree, that matrimony for no cause should be disolv'd, though for many causes it might separate; as may be seen *decret. Gregor. l.* 4. *tit.* 19. and in other places of the Canonicall Tomes. The main
25 good of which invention, wherein it consists who can tell? but that it hath one vertue incomparable, to fill all christendom with whordomes, and adulteries beyond the art of *Balaams* or of divells. Yet neither can these, though so perverse, but

acknowledge that the words of Christ under the name of fornication allow putting away for other causes then adultery
both from *bed and bord,* but not from the *bond;* their only
reason is, because mariage they beleeve to bee a Sacrament.
5 But our Divines who would seem long since to have renounc't
that reason, have so forgot them selves, as yet to hold the
absurdity, which but for that reason, unlesse there be some
mystery of Satan in it, perhaps the Papist would not hold.
Tis true, we grant divorce for actual & prov'd adultery, and
10 not for lesse then many tedious and unreparable yeares of
desertion, wherein a man shall loose all his hope of posterity,
which great and holy men have bewail'd, ere he can be
righted; and then perhaps on the confines of his old age,
when all is not worth the while. But grant this were season-
15 ably don; what are these two cases to many other, which
afflict the state of mariage as bad, and yet find no redresse?
What hath the soule of man deserv'd, if it be in the way of
salvation, that it should be morgag'd thus, and may not redeem it selfe according to conscience out of the hands of such
20 ignorant and slothfull teachers as these, who are neither able
nor mindful to give due tendance to that pretious cure which
they rashly undertake; nor have in them the noble goodnesse
to consider these distresses and accidents of mans life; but are
bent rather to fill their mouthes with Tithe and oblation. Yet
25 if they can learne to follow, as well as they can seeke to be
follow'd, I shall direct them to a faire number of renowned
men, worthy to be their leaders, who will commend to them
a doctrin in this point wiser then their own, and if they bee

not impatient, it will be the same doctrin which this treatis hath defended.

Wicklef that Englishman honor'd of God to be the first preacher of a general reformation to all *Europe,* was not in 5 this thing better taught of God, then to teach among his cheifest recoveries of truth, that divorce is lawfull to the christian for many other causes equall to adultery. This book indeed through the poverty of our Libraries I am forc't to cite from *Arnisæus* of *Halberstad on the right of mariage,* who 10 cites it from *Corasius* of *Tolouse, c. 4. Cent. Sct.* and he from *Wicklef, l. 4. Dial. c. 21.* So much the sorrier, for that I never lookt into author cited by his adversary upon this occasion, but found him more conducible to the question, then his quotation render'd him.

15 Next *Luther,* how great a servant of God, in his book of *conjugal life* quoted by *Gerard* out of the Dutch, allowes divorce for the obstinate denial of conjugal duty; and *that a man may send away a proud Vashti and marry an Esther in her stead.* It seemes, if this example shall not be impertinent, 20 that *Luther* meant not onely the refusall of benevolence, but a stubborn denial of any main conjugal duty; or if he did not, it will be evinc't from what he allowes. For out of question, with men that are not barbarous, love and peace, and fitnesse will be yeelded as essential to mariage, as corporal benevo- 25 lence. *Though I give my body to be burnt,* saith Saint *Paul, and have not charity, it profits me nothing.* So though the body prostitute it selfe to whom the mind affords no other love or peace, but constant malice and vexation, can this bod-

ily benevolence deserv to be call'd a mariage between Christians and rationall creatures.

    Melanchton, the third great luminary of reformation in his
book *concerning marriage* grants divorce for cruell usage, and
5 danger of life, urging the authority of that *Theodosian* law,
which he esteemes written with the grave deliberation of
godly men; *and that they who reject this law, and thinke it
disagreeing from the Gospel, understand not the difference of
law and Gospel; that the Magistrat ought not only to defend*
10 *life, but to succour the weake conscience, lest broke with greif
and indignation it relinquish praier, and turn to som unlawful thing.* What if this heavy plight of despaire arise from
other discontents in wedloc which may goe to the soule of a
good man more then the danger of his life, or cruel using,
15 which a man cannot bee liable to, suppose it be ingratefull
usage, suppose it be perpetuall spight and disobedience, suppose a hatred, shall not the Magistrat free him from this disquiet which interrupts his prayers, and disturbs the cours of
his service to God and his Country all as much, and brings
20 him such a misery, as that he more desires to leave his life then
feares to loose it: Shall not this equally concerne the office of
civil protection, and much more the charity of a true Church
to remedy?

    Erasmus who for learning was the wonder of his age, both
25 in his *notes* on *Matthew,* and on the first to the *Corinthians* in
a large and eloquent discourse, and in his answer to *Phimos-
tonus* a Papist, maintaines (and no protestant then living
contradicted him) that the words of Christ comprehend

many other causes of divorce under the name of fornication.

Bucer, whom our famous Dr *Rainolds* was wont to preferr before *Calvin,* in his comment on *Matthew,* and in his second booke *of the Kingdome of Christ,* treats of divorce at large to
5 the same effect, as is written in *the doctrine and discipline of divorce* lately publisht, and the translation is extant: whom lest I should be thought to have wrested to mine own purpose, take somthing more out of his 49. Chap. which I then for brevity omitted. *It will be the duty of pious princes, and all*
10 *who govern Church, or common wealth, if any, whether husband or wife, shall affirme their want of such who either will, or can tolerably performe the necessary duties of maried life, to grant that they may seeke them such, and marry them; if they make it appeare that such they have not.* This book he
15 wrote heer in *England,* where he liv'd the greatest admir'd man, and this hee dedicated to *Edward* the sixth.

Fagius rankt among the famous divines of *Germany,* whom *Frederic* at that time the *Palatine* sent for to be the reformer of his Dominion, and whom afterwards *England* sought to,
20 and obtain'd of him to come and teach her, differs not in this opinion from *Bucer,* as his notes on the *Chaldey paraphrast* well testify.

The whole Church of *Strasburgh* in her most flourishing time, when *Zellius, Hedio, Capito,* and other great Divines
25 taught there, and those two renouned magistrates *Farrerus* and *Sturmius* govern'd that common wealth and Academy to the admiration of all *Germany,* hath thus in the 21. Article. *We teach that if according to the word of God, yea or against*

it, divorces happen, to doe according to Gods word, Deut.
24. 1. Mat. 19. 1 Cor. 7. and the observation of the primitive
Church, and the Christian constitution of pious Cæsars.

    Peter Martyr seems in word our easy adversary, but is in
5 deed for us: toward which though it be somthing when he
saith of this opinion, *that it is not wicked, and can hardly be*
refuted, this which followes is much more, *I speake not heer*
saith he, *of natural impediments which may so happ'n, that*
the matrimony can no longer hold: but adding, *that he often*
10 *wonder'd, how the antient and most christian Emperors es-*
tablisht those lawes of divorce, and neither Ambrose, *who had*
such influence upon the lawes of Theodosius, *nor any of those*
holy fathers found fault, nor any of the Churches, why the
Magistrats of this day should be so loth to constitute the same.
15 *Perhaps they feare an inundation of divorces, which is not*
likely, whenas we reade not either among the Ebrews, Greeks,
or Romans *that they were much frequent where they were*
most permitted. If they judge christian men worse then Jewes
or Pagans, they both injure that name, and by this reason will
20 *bee constrain'd to grant divorces the rather; because it was*
permitted as a remedy of evil, for who would remove the
medcin, while the disease is yet so rife? This being read both
in *his common places,* & on the first *to the Corinthians,* with
what we shall relate more of him yet ere the end, sets him ab-
25 solutely on this side. Not to insist that in both these, & other
places of his commentaries hee grants divorce not onely for
desertion, but for the seducement and scandalous demeanour
of a heretical consort.

Musculus a divine of no obscure fame distinguishes betweene the religious and the civil determination of divorce;
and leaving the civil wholly to the lawyers, pronounces a conscionable divorce for impotence not only natural, but acci-
5 dental, if it be durable. His equity it seems, can enlarge the
words of Christ to one cause more then adultery; why may
not the reason of another man as wise, enlarge them to another
cause.

Gualter of *Zuric* a well known judicious commentator in
10 his Homilies on *Matthew,* allows divorce for *Leprosie, or any
other cause which renders unfit for wedloc,* and calls this
rather *a nullity of mariage then a divorce,* and who, that is not
himselfe a meer body, can restrain all the unfitnes of mariage
only to a corporal defect.

15 *Hemingius* an Author highly esteem'd, and his works
printed at *Geneva,* writing of divorce, confesses that lerned
men *vary in this question, some granting three causes thereof,
some five, others many more;* he himselfe gives us sixe, *adultery, desertion, inability, error, evill usage, and impiety,* using
20 argument *that Christ under one special containes the whole
kind, & under the name & example of fornication* he includes *other causes equipollent.* This discours he wrote at the
request of many who had the judging of these causes in *Denmark and Norway,* who by all likelyhood follow'd his advice.

25 *Hunnius* a Doctor of *Wittenberg,* well known both in
Divinity & other arts, on the 19. of *Matt.* affirmes *that the
exception of fornication exprest by our Saviour excludes not
other causes equalling adultery, or destructive to the substan-*

tials of matrimony; but was oppos'd to the custom of the Jewes who made divorce for every light cause.

Felix Bidenbachius an eminent Divine in the Dutchy of *Wirtemberg* affirmes *that the obstinat refusal of conjugal due*
5 *is a lawful cause of divorce,* and gives an instance *that the consistory of that state so judg'd.*

Gerard cites *Harbardus* an author not unknown, and *Arnisæus* cites *Wigandus,* both yeelding divorce *in case of cruel usage;* and another author who testifies *to have seen in a duke-*
10 *dom of Germany mariages disjoynd for some implacable enmities arising.*

Beza one of the strictest against divorce, denies it not *for danger of life from a Heretic,* or *importunat solicitation to doe ought against religion:* and counts it *all one whether the*
15 *heretic desert, or would stay upon intolerable conditions.* But this decision well examin'd will be found of no solidity. For *Beza* would be askt why, if God so strictly exact our stay in any kind of wedloc, wee had not better stay and hazard a murdering for Religion at the hand of a wife, or husband, as
20 he and others enjoyn us to stay and venture it for all other causes but that? and why a mans life is not as well and warrantably sav'd by divorcing from an orthodox murderer, as a heretical? Againe, if desertion be confest by him to consist not only in the forsaking, but in the unsufferable conditions of
25 staying, a man may as well deduce the lawfulnesse of divorcing from any intolerable conditions (if his grant bee good that wee may divorce thereupon from a heretic) as he can deduce it lawfull to divorce from any deserter, by finding it lawful to

divorce from a deserting infidel. For this is plaine, if Saint
Pauls permission to divorce an infidel deserter, inferre it lawfull for any malicious desertion, then doth *Beza*'s definition
of a deserter transferr it selfe with like facility from the cause
5 of religion to the cause of malice, and proves it as good to
divorce from him who intolerably stayes as from him who
purposely departs; and leaves it as lawfull to depart from him
who urgently requires a wicked thing, though professing the
same religion, as from him who urges a heathenish or super-
10 stitious compliance in a different faith. For if there be such
necessity of our abiding, wee ought rather to abide the utmost
for religion then for any other cause; seeing both the cause of
our stay is pretended our religion to mariage, and the cause of
our suffering is suppos'd our constant mariage to religion.
15 *Beza* therfore by his owne definition of a deserter justifies a
divorce from any wicked or intolerable conditions rather in
the same religion then in a different.

   Aretius a famous Divine of *Bern* approves many causes of
divorce in his *Problemes,* and adds *that the lawes and consis-*
20 *tories of Swizzerland approve them also.* As first, *adultery,*
and that not actual only, but intentional, alleging *Matthew*
the fifth, *Whosoever looketh to lust, hath committed adultery*
already in his heart. Wherby saith he, *our Saviour shewes that*
the breach of matrimony may be not only by outward act, but
25 *by the heart and desire; when that hath once possest, it renders*
the conversation intolerable, and commonly the fact followes.
Other causes to the number of 9. or 10. consenting in most
with the imperial lawes, may bee read in the author himselfe,

who averrs them *to be grave and weighty*. All these are men
of name in Divinity, and to these if need were, might be
added more. Nor have the Civilians bin all so blinded by the
Canon, as not to avouch the justice of those old permissions
5 touching divorce.

  Alciat of *Millain,* a man of extraordinary wisedome and
learning, in the sixt book of his *Parerga* defends those imperial
lawes, *not repugnant to the Gospel, as the Church then interpreted.* For saith hee, *the antients understood him separat by*
10 *man,whom passions and corrupt affections divorc't,not,if the*
provincial Bishops first heard the matter, and judg'd, as the
councel of Agatha declares; and on some part of the Code hee
names *Isidorus Hispalensis* the first computer of Canons, *to
be in the same minde.* And in the former place gives his opinion
15 *that divorce might be more lawfully permitted then usury.*

  Corasius recorded by *Helvicus* among the famous Lawyers
hath been already cited of the same judgement.

  Wesembechius a much nam'd Civilian in his comment on
this law defends it, and affirms *that our Saviour excluded not*
20 *other faults equall to adultery; and that the word fornication*
*signifies larger among the Hebrewes then with us, compre-
hending every fault which alienates from him to whom obedience is due, and that the primitive Church interpreted so.*

  Grotius yet living, and of prime note among learned men
25 retires plainly from the Canon to the antient civility, yea to
the Mosaic law, *as being most just and undecevable.* On the
fifth of *Matt.* he saith, *that Christ made no civil lawes, but
taught us how to use law: that the law sent not a husband to*

the Judge about this matter of divorce, but left him to his owne
conscience; that Christ therfore cannot be thought to send
him; that adultery may be judg'd by a vehement suspition;
that the exception of adultery seems an example of other like
5 *offences;* proves it *from the manner of speech, the maxims of*
law, the reason of charity, and common equity.

These authorities without long search I had to produce, all
excellent men, som of them such as many ages had brought
forth none greater: almost the meanest of them might deserve
10 to obtain credit in a singularity; what might not then all of
them joyn'd in an opinion so consonant to reason? For although som speak of this cause, others of that, why divorce
may be, yet all agreeing in the necessary enlargement of that
textual straitnes, leave the matter to equity, not to literal
15 bondage, and so the opinion closes. Nor could I have wanted
more testimonies, had the cause needed a more sollicitous en-
quiry. But herein the satisfaction of others hath bin studied,
not the gaining of more assurance to mine own perswasion:
although authorities contributing reason withall, bee a good
20 confirmation and a welcom. But God, I solemnly attest him,
withheld from my knowledge the consenting judgement of
these men so late, untill they could not bee my instructers,
but only my unexpected witnesses to partial men, that in this
work I had not given the worst experiment of an industry
25 joyn'd with integrity and the free utterance though of an un-
popular truth. Which yet to the people of *England* may, if
God so please, prove a memorable informing; certainly a benefit which was intended them long since by men of highest

repute for wisedome & piety, *Bucer & Erasmus.* Only this one autority more, whether in place or out of place, I am not to omitt; which if any can think a small one, I must bee patient it is no smaller then the whole assembl'd autority of *England*
5 both Church and State; and in those times which are on record for the purest and sincerest that ever shon yet on the reformation of this Iland, the time of *Edward* the 6th. That worthy Prince having utterly abolisht the Canon Law out of his Dominions, as his Father did before him, appointed
10 by full vote of Parlament, a Committy of two and thirty chosen men, Divines and Lawyers, of whom *Cranmer* the Archbishop, *Peter Martyr,* and *Walter Haddon,* (not without the assistance of Sir *John Cheeke* the Kings Tutor, a man at that time counted the learnedest of Englishmen, & for piety
15 not inferior) were the chief, to frame anew som Ecclesiastical Laws, that might be instead of what was abrogated. The work with great diligence was finisht, and with as great approbation of that reforming age was receav'd; and had bin doubtlesse, as the learned Preface thereof testifies, establisht
20 by Act of Parlament, had not the good Kings death so soon ensuing, arrested the furder growth of Religion also, from that season to this. Those laws, thus founded on the memorable wisedome and piety of that religious Parlament and Synod, allow divorce and second mariage *not only for adul-*
25 *tery or desertion, but for any capital enmity or plot laid against the others life, and likewise for evil and fierce usage;* nay the 12. Chap. of that title by plaine consequence declares, *that lesser contentions, if they be perpetual, may obtaine di-*

vorce: which is all one really with the position by me held in
the former treatise publisht on this argument, herein only differing that there the cause of perpetual strife was put for example in the unchangeable discord of som natures; but in
5 these lawes intended us by the best of our ancestors, the effect
of continual strife is determin'd no unjust plea of divorce,
whether the cause be naturall or wilfull. Wherby the warinesse and deliberation from which that discourse proceeded,
will appeare, & that God hath aided us to make no bad con-
10 clusion of this point; seeing the opinion which of late hath
undergon ill censures among the vulgar, hath now prov'd to
have don no violence to Scripture, unlesse all these famous
Authors alleg'd have done the like, nor hath affirm'd ought
more then what indeed the most nominated Fathers of the
15 Church both ancient and modern are unexpectedly found affirming, the lawes of Gods peculiar people, & of primitive
Christendom found to have practis'd, reformed Churches and
states to have imitated, and especially the most pious Church-
times of this Kingdom to have fram'd and publisht, and, but
20 for sad hindrances in the sudden change of religion, had
enacted by Parlament. Hence forth let them who condemn
the assertion of this book for new and licentious, be sorry; lest,
while they think to be of the graver sort, and take on them to
be teachers, they expose themselves rather to be pledg'd up
25 and down by men who intimatly know them, to the discovery
and contempt of their ignorance and presumption.

The End.

COLASTERION

A REPLY TO A NAMELESS ANSWER AGAINST
THE DOCTRINE AND DISCIPLINE OF DIVORCE

COLASTERION:

A

REPLY TO

A

NAMELES ANSVVER

AGAINST

The Doctrine and Discipline of Divorce.

WHEREIN.

The trivial Author of that Answer is discover'd, the Licencer conferr'd with, and the
Opinion which they traduce defended.

By the former Author, *J. M.*

PROV. 26. 5.

*Answer a Fool according to his folly, leß bee bee wise in his
own conceit.*

Printed in the Year, 1645.

COLASTERION:

A Reply to a nameless Answer against the
Doctrine and Discipline of Divorce.

AFTER many rumors of confutations and convictions forth comming against *The Doctrine and Discipline of Divorce,* and now and then a by-blow from the Pulpit, featherd with a censure strict indeed, but
5 how true, more beholding to the autority of that devout place which it borrowd to bee utterd in, then to any sound reason which it could oracle, while I still hop'd as for a blessing to see som peece of diligence, or lerned discretion come from them, it was my hap at length lighting on a certain parcel of
10 *Quæries,* that seek and finde not, to finde not seeking, at the taile of *Anabaptistical, Antinomian, Heretical, Atheistical* epithets, a jolly slander, call'd *Divorce at pleasure*: I stood a while and wonder'd, what wee might doe to a mans heart, or what anatomie use, to finde in it sincerity; for all our wonted
15 marks every day fail us, and where wee thought it was, wee see it is not, for alter and change residence it cannot sure. And yet I see no good of body or of minde secure to a man for all his past labours without perpetual watchfulnes, and perseverance. When as one above others who hath suffer'd
20 much and long in the defence of Truth, shall after all this, give her cause to leav him so destitute and so vacant of her

defence, as to yeild his mouth to bee the common road of
Truth and Falshood, and such falshood as is joyn'd with the
rash and heedles calumny of his neighbour. For what book
hath hee ever met with, as his complaint is, *Printed in the*
5 *City,* maintaining either in the title, or in the whole persuance, *Divorce at pleasure?* Tis true, that to divorce upon extreme necessity, when through the perversnes, or the apparent unfitnes of either, the continuance can bee to both no
good at all, but an intolerable injury and temptation to the
10 wronged and the defrauded, to divorce then, there is a book
that writes it lawfull. And that this Law is a pure and wholsom national Law, not to be with-held from good men, because others likely anough may abuse it to thir pleasure, can
not bee charg'd upon that book, but must bee enterd a bold
15 and impious accusation against God himself; who did not
for this abuse withhold it from his own people. It will bee
just therfore, and best for the reputation of him who in his
Subitanes hath thus censur'd, to recall his sentence. And if,
out of the abundance of his volumes, and the readiness of his
20 quill, and the vastness of his other imploiments, especially in
the great audit for accounts, hee can spare us ought to the
better understanding of this point, hee shall bee thankt in
public, and what hath offended in the book, shall willingly
submitt to his correction. Provided he bee sure not to come
25 with those old and stale suppositions, unless hee can take
away cleerly what that discours hath urg'd against them, by
one who will expect other arguments to bee perswaded the
good health of a sound answer, then the gout and dropsy of

a big margent, litter'd and overlaid with crude and huddl'd
quotations. But as I still was waiting, when these light arm'd
refuters would have don pelting at thir three lines utterd with
a sage delivery of no reason, but an impotent and wors then
5 *Bonner*-like censure to burn that which provokes them to a
fair dispute, at length a book was brought to my hands, entitl'd *An Answer to the Doctrine and Discipline of Divorce.*
Gladly I receiv'd it, and very attentively compos'd my self to
read; hoping that now som good man had voutsaft the pains
10 to instruct mee better, then I could yet learn out of all the
volumes which for this purpos I had visited. Only this I
marvel'd, and other men have since, when as I, in a Subject
so new to this age, and so hazardous to please, conceal'd not
my name, why this Author defending that part which is so
15 creeded by the people, would conceal his? But ere I could
enter three leaves into the Pamflet, (for I deferr the peasantly
rudenes, which by the Licencers leav, I met with afterwards)
my satisfaction came in abundantly, that it could bee nothing
why hee durst not name himself, but the guilt of his own
20 wretchednes. For first, not to speak of his abrupt and bald
beginning, his very first page notoriously bewraies him an
illiterat, and arrogant presumer in that which hee understands not; bearing us in hand as if hee knew both Greek and
Ebrew, and is not able to spell it; which had hee bin, it had
25 bin either writt'n as it ought, or scor'd upon the Printer. If it
bee excus'd as the carelesnes of his deputy, bee it known, the
lerned Author himself is inventoried, and summ'd up, to the
utmost value of his Livery cloak. Who ever hee bee, though

this to som may seem a slight contest, I shall yet continue to
think that man full of other secret injustice, and deceitfull
pride, who shall offer in public to assume the skill, though it bee
but of a tongue which hee hath not, and would catch his read-
5 ers to beleeve of his ability, that which is not in him. The Licencer indeed, as his autority now stands, may licence much;
but if these Greek *Orthographies* were of his licencing; the
boyes at School might reck'n with him at his Grammar. Nor
did I finde this his want of the pretended Languages alone,
10 but accompanied with such a low and home-spun expression
of his Mother *English* all along, without joynt or frame, as
made mee, ere I knew furder of him, often stop, and conclude, that this Author could for certain bee no other then
som mechanic. Nor was the stile flat and rude, and the mat-
15 ter grave and solid, for then ther had bin pardon, but so shallow and so unwary was that also, as gave sufficiently the
character of a gross and sluggish, yet a contentious and over-
weening pretender. For first, it behooving him to shew, as
hee promises, what divorce is, and what the true doctrine and
20 Discipline therof, and this beeing to doe by such principles
and prooffs as are receav'd on both sides, hee performes neither of these; but shews it first from the *Judaical* practice,
which hee himself disallows, and next from the practice of
Canon Law, which the Book hee would confute, utterly re-
25 jects, and all Laws depending theron; which this puny
Clark calls *The Laws of England,* and yet pronounces them
by an Ecclesiastical judge: as if that were to bee accounted the
Law of *England,* which depended on the Popery of *England*;

or if it were, this Parlament hee might know hath now
damn'd that judicature. So that whether his meaning were
to inform his own party, or to confute his adversary, instead
of shewing us the true Doctrin and Discipline of Divorce,
5 hee shews us nothing but his own contemptible ignorance.
For what is the *Mosaic* Law to his opinion, and what is the
Canon utterly now antiquated, either to that or to mine? Yee
see already what a faithfull definer wee have him. From such
a wind-egg of definition as this, they who expect any of his
10 other arguments to bee well hatcht, let them enjoy the vertu
of thir worthy Champion. But one thing more I observ'd, a
singular note of his stupidity, and that his Trade is not to
meddle with Books, much less with Confutations. When as
the Doctrin of Divorce had now a whole year bin publisht
15 the second time, with many Arguments added, and the
former ones better'd and confirm'd, this idle pamflet comes
reeling forth against the first Edition only; as may appear to
any by the pages quoted. Which put me in minde of what by
chance I had notice of to this purpos the last Summer, as
20 nothing so serious, but happns oft times to bee attended with
a ridiculous accident, it was then told mee that *the Doctrin
of divorce* was answerd, and the answer half printed against
the first Edition; not by one, but by a pack of heads; of
whom the cheif, by circumstance, was intimated to mee, and
25 since ratifi'd to bee no other, if any can hold laughter, and I
am sure none will guess him lower, then an actual Serving-
man. This creature, for the Story must on, (and what though
hee bee the lowest person of an interlude, hee may deserv a

canvasing,) transplanted himself, and to the improvment of
his wages, and your better notice of his capacity, turn'd Solliciter. And having convers'd much with a stripling Divine
or two of those newly fledge Probationers, that usually come
5 scouting from the University, and ly heer no lame legers to
pop into the Bethesda of som Knights Chaplainship, where
they bring grace to his good cheer, but no peace or benediction els to his house; these made the Champarty, hee contributed the Law, and both joynd in the Divinity. Which made
10 mee intend, following the advice also of freinds, to lay aside
the thought of mis-spending a Reply to the buzze of such a
Drones nest. But finding that it lay, what ever was the matter, half a year after unfinisht in the press, and hearing for
certain that a Divine of note, out of his good will to the opin-
15 ion, had takn it into his revise, and somthing had put out,
somthing put in, and stuck it heer and there with a clove of
his own Calligraphy, to keep it from tainting, and furder
when I saw the stuff, though very cours and thred-bare, gar-
nisht and trimly fac't with the commendations of a Licencer,
20 I resolv'd, so soon, as leisure granted mee the recreation, that
my man of Law should not altogether loose his solliciting.
Although I impute a share of the making to him whose name
I find in the approbation, who may take, as his mind servs
him, this Reply. In the mean while it shall bee seen, I refuse
25 no occasion, and avoid no adversary, either to maintane what
I have begun, or to give it up for better reason.

To begin then with the Licencer and his censure. For a
Licencer is not contented now to give his single Imprimatur,

but brings his chair into the Title leaf; there sits and judges
up or judges down what book hee pleases; if this bee suffer'd,
what worthles Author, or what cunning Printer will not bee
ambitious of such a Stale to put off the heaviest gear; which
5 may in time bring in round fees to the Licencer, and
wretched mis-leading to the People. But to the matter: he
approves *the publishing of this Book, to preserv the strength
and honour of Mariage against those sad breaches and dangerous abuses of it.* Belike then the wrongfull suffering of all
10 those sad breaches and abuses in Mariage to a remediless
thraldom, is *the strength and honour of Mariage*; a boistrous
and bestial strength, a dis-honourable honour, an infatuated
Doctrine, wors then the *salvo jure* of tyrannizing, which wee
all fight against. Next hee saith that *common discontents
15 make these breaches in unstaid mindes, and men givn to
change.* His words may be apprehended, as if they disallow'd
only to divorce for *common discontents in unstaid mindes,*
having no cause, but a *desire of change,* and then wee agree.
But if hee take all discontents *on this side adultery,* to bee
20 common, that is to say, not difficult to endure, and to affect
only *unstaid mindes,* it might administer just cause to think
him the unfittest man that could bee, to offer at a comment
upon *Job*; as seeming by this to have no more true sense of a
good man in his afflictions, then those *Edomitish* Freinds
25 had, of whom *Job* complains, and against whom God testifies his anger. Shall a man of your own coat, who hath es-
pous'd his flock; and represents Christ more, in beeing the
true husband of his Congregation, then an ordnary man doth

in beeing the husband of his wife, and yet this representment is thought a cheif cause why Mariage must bee inseparable, shall this spiritual man ordnarily for the increase of his maintenance, or any slight cause forsake that wedded cure of
5 souls, that should bee dearest to him, and marry another, and another, and shall not a person wrongfully afflicted, and persecuted eevn to extremity, forsake an unfit, injurious, and pestilent mate, ty'd only by a civil and fleshly covnant? If you bee a man so much hating change, hate that other
10 change; if your self bee not guilty, counsel your brethren to hate it; and leav to bee the supercilious judge of other mens miseries and changes, that your own bee not judg'd. The reasons of your licen't pamflet, you say *are good;* they must bee better then your own then. I shall wonder els how such a
15 trivial fellow was accepted and commended, to bee the confuter of so dangerous an opinion as yee give out mine.

Now therfore to your *Atturney,* since no worthier an adversary makes his appearance, nor this neither his appearance, but lurking under the safety of his nameles obscurity:
20 such as yee turn him forth at the Postern, I must accept him; and in a better temper then *Ajax,* doe mean to scourge this *Ramme* for yee, till I meet with his *Ulysses.*

Hee begins with Law, and wee have it of him as good cheap, as any hucster at Law, newly set up, can possibly
25 afford, and as impertinent; but for that hee hath receiv'd his hansel. Hee presumes also to cite the Civil Law, which, I perceav by his citing never came within his *dormitory,* yet what hee cites makes but against himself.

His second thing therfore is to refute the advers position,
and very methodically, three pages before hee sets it down;
and sets his own in the place, *that disagreement of minde or
disposition, though shewing it self in much sharpnes is not*
5 *by the Law of God, or man, a just cause of divorce.*

To this position I answer, that it lays no battery against
mine, no, nor so much as faces it, but tacks about, long ere it
come neer, like a harmles and respectfull confutement. For I
confess that disagreement of minde or disposition, though in
10 much sharpnes, is not alwaies a just cause of divorce; for
much may bee endur'd. But what if the sharpnes bee much
more then his much? To that point it is our mis-hap wee
have not heer his grave decision. Hee that will contradict the
positive which I alleg'd, must hold that no disagreement of
15 minde, or disposition, can divorce, though shewn in most
sharpnes; otherwise hee leaves a place for equity to appoint
limits, and so his following arguments will either not prove
his own position, or not disprove mine.

His first Argument, all but what hobbles to no purpos is
20 this. *Wher the Scripture commands a thing to bee don, it
appoints when, how, and for what, as in the case of death or
excommunication. But the Scripture directs not what measure of disagreement or contrariety may divorce; Therfore,
the Scripture allows not any divorce for disagreement.*

25 *Answer;* First I deny your *major,* the Scripture appoints
many things, and yet leaves the circumstance to mans discretion, particularly, in your own examples; Excommunication is not taught when, and for what to bee, but left to the

Church. How could the Licencer let pass this childish ignorance and call it *good*. Next, in matter of death, the Laws of
England, wherof you have intruded to bee an opiniastrous
Sub advocate, and are bound to defend them, conceave it not
5 enjoyn'd in Scripture, when or for what cause they shall put
to death, as in adultery, theft, and the like; your *minor* also
is fals, for the Scripture plainly sets down for what measure
of disagreement a man may divorce, *Deut.* 24. 1. Learn better what that phrase means, *if shee finde no favour in his*
10 *eyes.*

Your second Argument, without more tedious fumbling is
breifly thus. *If diversity in Religion, which breeds a greater*
dislike then any natural disagreement may not cause a di-
vorce, then may not the lesser disagreement: but diversity of
15 *Religion may not; Ergo.*

Answer, First, I deny in the *major,* that diversity of Religion, breeds a greater dislike to mariage duties, then natural
disagreement. For between *Israelite,* or Christian and Infidel
more often hath bin seen too much love: but between them
20 who perpetually clash in natural contrarieties, it is repugnant
that ther should bee ever any maried love or concord. Next, I
deny your *minor,* that it is commanded not to divorce in
diversity of Religion, if the Infidel will stay: for that place in
St. *Paul,* commands nothing, as *that book* at large affirm'd,
25 though you over-skipt it.

Secondly, if it doe command, it is but with condition, that
the Infidel bee content, and well pleas'd to stay, which cuts
off the supposal of any great hatred or disquiet between

them; seeing the Infidel had liberty to depart at pleasure; and so this comparison avails nothing.

Your third Argument is from Deut. 22. *If a man hate his wife, and raise an ill report, that hee found her no virgin,* if
5 this were fals, *he might not put her away,* though hated never so much.

Answer, This was a malicious hatred bent against her life, or to send her out of dores without her portion. Such a hater looses by due punishment that privilege, Deut. 24. 1. to di-
10 vorce for a natural dislike, which though it could not love conjugally, yet sent away civilly, and with just conditions. But doubtles the Wife in that former case had liberty to depart from her fals accuser, lest his hatred should prove mortal; els that Law peculiarly made to right the woman, had
15 turn'd to her greatest mischeif.

Your fourth Argument, *One Christian ought to bear the infirmities of another, but cheifly of his Wife.*

Answer, I grant, infirmities, but not outrages, not perpetual defraudments of truest conjugal society, not injuries and
20 vexations as importunat as fire. Yet to endure very much, might doe well an exhortation, but not a compulsive Law. For the Spirit of God himself by *Solomon* declares that such a consort *the earth cannot bear, and better dwell in a corner on the house top, or in the Wildernes.* Burdens may bee born,
25 but still with consideration to the strength of an honest man complaining. Charity indeed bids us forgive our enemies, yet doth not force us to continue freindship and familiarity with those freinds who have bin fals or unworthy toward us:

but is contented in our peace with them, at a fair distance. Charity commands not the husband to receav again into his bosom the adulterous Wife, but thinks it anough, if hee dismiss her with a beneficent and peacefull dismission. No more
5 doth Charity command, nor can her rule compell, to retain in neerest union of wedloc, one whose other grossest faults, or disabilities to perform what was covnanted, are the just causes of as much greevance and dissention in a Family, as the private act of adultery. Let not therfore under the name
10 of fulfilling Charity, such an unmercifull, and more then legal yoke, bee padlockt upon the neck of any Christian.

Your fifth Argument, *If the husband ought love his Wife, as Christ his Church, then ought shee not to bee put away for contrariety of minde.*
15 *Answer,* This similitude turnes against him. For if the husband must bee as Christ to the Wife, then must the wife bee as the Church to her husband. If ther bee a perpetual contrariety of minde in the Church toward Christ, Christ himselfe threat'ns to divorce such a Spouse, and hath often don
20 it. If they urge, this was no true Church, I urge again, that was no true Wife.

His sixth Argument is from the 5 of *Matthew* 32. which hee expounds after the old fashion, and never takes notice of what I brought against that exposition; Let him therfore seek
25 his answer there. Yet can hee not leav this Argument, but hee must needs first shew us a curvett of his madnes, holding out an objection, and running himself upon the point. *For,* saith hee, *if Christ except no cause but adultery, then all other*

causes as frigidity, incestuous mariage, &c. are no causes of
divorce; and answers *that the speech of Christ holds univer-*
sally, as hee intended it namely to condemn such divorce, as
was groundlesly practiz'd among the Jews, for every cause
5 *which they thought sufficient; not checking the law of con-*
sanguinities or affinities, or forbidding other cause which
makes mariage void, Ipso facto.

Answ. Look to it now you be not found taking fees on
both sides, for if you once bring limitations to the universal
10 words of Christ, another will doe as much with as good autority, and affirm, that neither did hee check the Law Deut.
24. 1. nor forbid the causes that make mariage void actually;
which if any thing in the world doth, unfitnes doth, and contrariety of minde; yea, more then adultery, for that makes
15 not the mariage void, nor much more unfit, but for the time,
if the offended party forgive; but unfitnes and contrariety
frustrates and nullifies for ever, unless it bee a rare chance,
all the good and peace of wedded conversation; and leaves
nothing between them enjoyable, but a prone and savage
20 necessity, not worth the name of mariage, unaccompanied
with love. Thus much his own objection hath don against
himself.

Argu. 7. Hee insists, *that man and wife are one flesh, ther-*
fore must not separat. But must bee sent to look again upon
25 the 35. pag. of that book, where hee might have read an
answer, which hee stirrs not. Yet can hee not abstain, but hee
must doe us another pleasure ere hee goes; Although I call
the Common Pleas to witness, I have not hir'd his tongue,

whatever men may think by his arguing. For besides adultery, hee excepts *other causes which dissolv the union of
beeing one flesh, either directly, or by consequence.* If only
adultery bee excepted by our Saviour, and hee voluntarily can
5 adde other exceptions that dissolv that union *both directly
and by consequence,* these words of Christ, the main obstacle
of divorce, are open to us by his own invitation to include
what ever causes dissolv that union of flesh, *either directly or
by consequence.* Which, till hee name other causes more
10 likely, I affirm to bee don soonest by unfitness and contrariety
of minde. For that induces hatred, which is the greatest dis-
solver, both of spiritual and corporal union, turning the
minde and consequently the body to other objects. Thus our
doubty adversary, *either directly, or by consequence* yeilds us
15 the question with his own mouth, and the next thing hee
does, recants it again.

His eighth Argument shivers in the uttering, and hee confesses *to bee not over confident of it,* but of the rest it may bee
sworn hee is. St. *Paul,* 1 *Cor.* 7. saith, that *the married have
20 trouble in the flesh,* therfore wee must bear it, though never
so intolerable.

I Answer, if this bee a true consequence, why are not all
troubles to bee born alike? why are wee suffer'd to divorce
adulteries, desertions, or frigidities? Who knows not that
25 trouble and affliction is the decree of God upon every state of
life? follows it therfore, that though they grow excessive, and
insupportable, wee must not avoid them? if wee may in all
other conditions, and not in mariage, the doom of our suffer-

ing ties us not by the trouble, but by the bond of mariage;
and that must bee prov'd inseparable from other reasons, not
from this place. And his own confession declares the weaknes
of this Argument, yet his ungovern'd arrogance could not
5 bee disswaded from venting it.

His ninth Argument is, *That a husband must love his wife
as himself, therfore hee may not divorce for any disagreement, no more then hee may separat his soul from his body.*

I Answer, if hee love his wife as himself, hee must love her
10 so farre as hee may preserv himself to her in a cherfull and
comfortable manner, and not so as to ruin himself by anguish
and sorrow, without any benefit to her. Next, if the husband
must love his wife as himself, shee must bee understood a
wife in som reasonable measure, willing, and sufficient to
15 perform the cheif duties of her Covnant, els by the hold of
this argument, it would bee his great sin to divorce either for
adultery, or desertion. The rest of this will run circuit with
the union of one flesh, which was answer'd before. And that
to divorce a relative and *Metaphorical* union of two bodies
20 into one flesh, cannot bee likn'd in all things to the dividing
of that natural union of soul and body into one person, is
apparent of it self.

His last Argument hee fetches *from the inconveniences
that would follow upon this freedom of divorce, to the cor-*
25 *rupting of mens mindes, and the overturning of all human
society.*

But for mee, let God and *Moses* answer this blasphemer,
who dares bring in such a foul endightment against the di-

vine Law. Why did God permit this to his people the Jewes,
but that the right and good which came directly therby, was
more in his esteem, then the wrong and evil which came by
accident. And for those weak supposes of Infants that would
5 be left in their mothers belly, (which must needs bee good
news for Chamber-maids, to hear a Serving-man grown so
provident for great bellies) and portions, and joyntures likely
to incurr imbezlement heerby, the ancient civil Law instructs
us plentifully how to award, which our profound opposite
10 knew not, for it was not in his Tenures.

His Arguments are spun, now follows the Chaplain with
his Antiquities, wiser if hee had refrain'd, for his very touching ought that is lerned, soiles it, and lays him still more and
more open a conspicuous gull. There beeing both Fathers
15 and Councels more ancient, wherwith to have serv'd his purpos better then with what hee cites, how may we doe to know
the suttle drift that mov'd him to begin first with the *twelfth
Councel of Toledo?* I would not undervalue the depth of his
notion, but perhaps he had heard that the men of *Toledo*
20 had store of good blade-mettle, and were excellent at cut-
tling; who can tell but it might bee the reach of his policy,
that these able men of decision, would doe best to have the
prime stroke among his testimonies in deciding this cause.
But all this craft avails him not; for seeing they allow no
25 cause of divorce but fornication, what doe these keen Doctors
heer but cut him over the sinews with thir Toledo's, for holding in the precedent page other causes of divorce besides, *both
directly, and by consequence.* As evil doth that *Saxon* Coun-

cel, next quoted, bestead him. For if it allow divorce precisely
for no cause but fornication, it thwarts his own Exposition:
and if it understand fornication largely, it sides with whom
hee would confute. However the autority of that Synod can
5 bee but small, beeing under *Theodorus,* the *Canterbury*
Bishop, a Grecian Monk of *Tarsus,* revolted from his own
Church to the Pope. What have wee next? The Civil Law
stufft in between two Councels, as if the *Code* had bin som
Synod; for that hee understood himself in this quotation is
10 incredible; where the Law, *Cod. l. 3. tit. 38. leg.* 11. speaks
not of divorce, but against the dividing of possessions to
divers heires, wherby the maried servants of a great family
were divided perhaps into distant Countries, and Colonies,
Father from Son, Wife from Husband, sore against thir will.
15 Somwhat lower hee confesses, *that the Civill Law allows
many reasons of divorce, but the Cannon Law decrees otherwise.* A fair credit to his Cause; and I amaze me, though the
fancy of this doult bee as obtuse and sad as any mallet, how
the Licencer could sleep out all this, and suffer him to uphold
20 his opinion, by Canons, & *Gregorian decretals,* a Law which
not only his adversary, but the whole reformation of this
Church and state hath branded and rejected. As ignorantly,
and too ignorantly to deceav any Reader but an unlerned, hee
talks of *Justin Martyrs* Apology, not telling us which of the
25 twain; for that passage in the beginning of his first, which I
have cited els-where, plainly makes against him: So doth
Tertullian, cited next, and next *Erasmus,* the one against
Marcion, the other in his Annotations on *Matthew,* and to

the *Corinthians*. And thus yee have the List of his choice Antiquities, as pleasantly chosen as yee would wish from a man of his handy Vocation, puft up with no luck at all, above the stint of his capacity.

5   Now hee comes to the Position, which I sett down whole; and like an able text man slits it into fowr, that hee may the better come at it with his Barbar Surgery, and his sleevs turn'd up. Wherin first hee denies *that any disposition, unfitness, or contrariety of minde is unchangeable in nature, but* 10 *that by the help of diet and physic it may be alter'd.*

I mean not to dispute Philosophy with this Pork, who never read any. But I appeal to all experience, though there bee many drugs to purge those redundant humors, and circulations that commonly impair health, and are not natural, 15 whether any man can with the safety of his life bring a healthy constitution into physic with this designe, to alter his natural temperament, and disposition of minde. How much more vain, and ridiculous would it bee, by altering and rooting up the grounds of nature, which is most likely to produce 20 death or madnes, to hope the reducing of a minde to this or that fitnes, or two disagreeing mindes to a mutual sympathy. Suppose they might, and that with great danger of thir lives and right senses, alter one temperament, how can they know that the succeeding disposition will not bee as farre from 25 fitnes and agreement? They would perhaps change Melancholy into Sanguin, but what if fleam, and choler in as great a measure come instead, the unfitnes will be still as difficult and troublesom. But lastly, whether these things bee changeable,

or not, experience teacheth us, and our Position supposes that
they seldom doe change in any time commensurable to the
necessities of man, or convenient to the ends of mariage. And
if the fault bee in the one, shall the other live all his daies in
5 bondage and misery for anothers perversnes, or immedicable
disaffection? To my friends, of which may fewest bee so
unhappy, I have a remedy, as they know, more wise and
manly to prescribe: but for his friends and followers (of
which many may deserv justly to feel themselvs the unhap-
10 pines which they consider not in others) I send them by his
advice to sit upon the stool and strain, till their cross dispositions and contrarieties of minde shall change to a better correspondence, and to a quicker apprehension of common
sense, and thir own good.

15   His second Reason is as heedles, *because that grace may*
change the disposition, therfore no indisposition may cause
divorce.

   Answ. First, it will not bee deniable that many persons,
gracious both, may yet happn to bee very unfitly marryed, to
20 the great disturbance of either. Secondly, what if one have
grace, the other not, and will not alter, as the Scripture testifies ther bee of those, in whom wee may expect a change,
when *the Blackamore changes his colour, or the Leopard his*
spots, Jer. 13. 23. shall the gracious therfore dwell in torment
25 all his life, for the ungracious? Wee see that holiest precepts,
then which ther can no better physic bee administerd to the
minde of man, and set on with powerfull preaching, cannot
work this cure, no not in the family, not in the wife of him

that preaches day and night to her. What an unreasonable thing it is that men, and Clergy-men especially, should exact such wondrous changes in another mans house, and are seen to work so little in thir own?

5   To the second point of the position, that this *unfitnes* hinders the main ends, and benefits of mariage, hee answers, *if I mean the unfitnes of choler, or sullen disposition, that soft words according to Solomon, pacify wrath.*

But I reply, that the saying of *Salomon,* is a Proverb fre-
10 quently true, not universally, as both the event shews, and many other sentences writtn by the same Author particularly of an evill woman, *Prov.* 21. 9. 19. and in other Chapters, that shee is better shun'd then dwelt with, and a desert is preferr'd before her society. What need the Spirit of God put
15 this chois into our heads, if soft words could alwaies take effect with her? How frivolous is, not only this disputer, but hee that taught him thus, and let him come abroad.

To his second answer I return this, that although there bee not easily found such an *antipathy, as to hate one another like*
20 *a toad or poison,* yet that there is oft such a dislike in both, or either, to conjugal love, as hinders all the comfort of Matrimony, scars any can bee so simple, as not to apprehend. And what can be *that favour, found* or not found *in the eyes of the Husband,* but a natural liking or disliking, wherof the Law
25 of God, *Deut.* 24. beares witnes, as of an ordnary accident, and determins wisely, and divinely therafter. And this disaffection happning to bee in the one, not without the unspeakable discomfort of the other, must hee bee left like a thing

consecrated to calamity, and despair without redemption?

Against the third branch of the position hee denies *that solace, and peace, which is contrary to discord and variance, is the main end of mariage.* What then? Hee will have it 5 *the solace of male, and female.* Came this doctrin out of som School, or som stie? Who but one forsak'n of all sense and civil nature, and cheifly of Christianity, will deny that peace contrary to discord, is the calling and the general end of every Christian, and of all his actions, and more especially of 10 mariage, which is the dearest league of love, and the dearest resemblance of that love which in Christ is dearest to his Church; how then can peace and comfort, as it is contrary to discord, which God hates to dwell with, not bee the main end of mariage? Discord then wee ought to fly, and to pursue 15 peace, farre above the observance of a civil covnant, already brokn, and the breaking dayly iterated on the other side. And what better testimony then the words of the institution it self, to prove, that a conversing solace, & peacefull society is the prime end of mariage, without which no other help, or 20 office can bee mutual, beseeming the dignity of reasonable creatures, that such as they should be coupl'd in the rites of nature by the meer compulsion of lust, without love, or peace, wors then wild beasts. Nor was it half so wisely spokn, as some deem, though *Austin* spake it, that if God had intended 25 other then copulation in Mariage, he would for *Adam* have created a freind, rather then a wife, to convers with; and our own writers blame him for this opinion; for which and the like passages, concerning mariage, hee might bee justly taxt

of rusticity in these affairs. For this cannot but bee with ease conceav'd, that there is one society of grave freindship, and another amiable and attractive society of conjugal love, besides the deed of procreation, which of it self soon cloies, and
5 is despis'd, unless it bee cherisht and re-incited with a pleasing conversation. Which if ignoble and swainish mindes cannot apprehend, shall such merit therfore to be the censurers of more generous and vertuous Spirits?

Against the last point of the position, to prove that con-
10 trariety of minde is not a greater cause of divorce, then corporal frigidity, hee enters into such a tedious and drawling tale of *burning, and burning, and lust and burning,* that the dull argument it self burnes to, for want of stirring; and yet all this burning is not able to expell the frigidity of his brain.
15 So long therfore, as that cause in the position shall bee prov'd a sufficient cause of divorce, rather then spend words with this fleamy clodd of an *Antagonist,* more then of necessity, and a little merriment, I will not now contend whether it bee a greater cause then frigidity, or no.

20 His next attempt is upon the Arguments which I brought to prove the position. And for the first, not finding it of that structure, as to bee scal'd with his short ladder, hee retreats with a bravado, that it deservs no answer. And I as much wonder what the whole book deserv'd to bee thus troubl'd
25 and sollicited by such a paltry Solliciter. I would hee had not cast the gracious eye of his duncery upon the small deserts of a pampflet, whose every line meddl'd with, uncases him to scorn and laughter.

That which hee takes for the second Argument, if hee
look better, is no argument, but an induction to those that
follow. Then hee stumbles that I should say, the gentlest ends
of Mariage, confessing that hee understands it not. And I
5 beleev him heartily: for how should hee, a Servingman both
by nature and by function, an Idiot by breeding, and a Solliciter by presumption, ever come to know, or feel within
himself, what the meaning is of gentle? Hee blames it for
a neat phrase, for nothing angers him more then his own
10 proper contrary. Yet altogether without art sure hee is not;
for who could have devis'd to give us more breifly a better
description of his own Servility?

But what will become now of the busines I know not; for
the man is suddenly takn with a lunacy of Law, and speaks
15 revelations out of the *Atturneys Academy,* only from a lying
spirit: for hee saies that *where a thing is void,* ipso facto, *there
needs no legal proceeding to make it void.* Which is fals, for
mariage is void by adultery, or frigidity, yet not made void
without legal proceeding. Then asks my opinion of *John a
20 Nokes,* and *John a Stiles;* and I answer him, that I for my part
think *John Dory,* was a better man then both of them: for
certainly, they were the greatest wranglers that ever liv'd, and
have fill'd all our Law-books with the obtunding story of thir
suits and trials.

25   After this hee tells us a miraculous peece of antiquity, how
two *Romans, Titus, and Sempronius made feoffments,* at
Rome sure, and *levied Fines* by the Common Law. But now
his fit of Law past, yet hardly come to himself, hee maintains,

that if Mariage bee void, as beeing neither of God nor nature, *there needs no legal proceeding to part it,* and I tell him, that offends not mee; *Then,* quoth hee, *this is no thing to your book, beeing the Doctrin and Disciplin of Divorce.* But that 5 I deny him; for all Discipline is not legal, that is to say jurid-ical, but som is personal, som Economical, and som Eccle-siastical. Lastly, if I prove that contrary dispositions are joyn'd neither of God nor nature, and so the mariage void, *hee will give mee the controversy.* I have prov'd it in that 10 book to any wise man, and without more a doe the Institu-tion proves it.

Where I answer an Objection usually made, that the dis-position ought to bee known before mariage, and shew how difficult it is to choose a fit consort, and how easie to mistake, 15 the Servitor would know what I mean by conversation, de-claring his capacity nothing refin'd since his Law-puddering, but still the same it was in the Pantry, and at the Dresser. Shall I argue of conversation with this hoyd'n to goe and practice at his opportunities in the Larder? To men of qual-20 ity I have said anough, and experience confirms by daily ex-ample, that wisest, sobrest, justest men are somtimes mis-erably mistak'n in thir chois. Whom to leav thus without remedy, tost and tempested in a most unquiet sea of afflic-tions and temptations, I say is most unchristianly.

25 But hee goes on to untruss my Arguments, imagining them his Maisters points. Only in the passage following, I cannot but admire the ripenes, and the pregnance of his native trechery, endeavouring to bee more a Fox then his wit

will suffer him. Wheras I breifly mention'd certain heads of
Discours, which I referr'd to a place more proper according
to my method, to bee treated there at full with all thir Reasons
about them, this Brain-worm against all the Laws of Dispute,
5 will needs deal with them heer. And as a Country Hinde
somtimes ambitious to shew his betters that hee is not so
simple as you take him, and that hee knows his advantages,
will teach us a new trick to confute by. And would you think
to what a pride hee swels in the contemplation of his rare
10 stratagem, offring to carp at the language of a book, which
yet hee confesses to bee generally commended; while himself
will bee acknowledg'd by all that read him, the basest and
the hungriest endighter, that could take the boldnes to look
abroad. Observ now the arrogance of a groom, how it will
15 mount. I had writt'n, that common adultery is a thing which
the rankest Politician would think it shame and disworship
that his Law should countenance. First, it offends him that
rankest should signify ought, but his own smell; who, that
knows *English,* would not understand mee, when I say a
20 rank Serving-man, a rank petti-fogger, to mean a meer Serv-
ingman, a meer and arrant petti-fogger, who lately was so
hardy, as to lay aside his buckram wallet, and make himself
a fool in Print, with confuting books, which are above him.
Next the word Politician is not us'd to his maw, and ther-
25 upon hee plaies the most notorious hobbihors, jesting and
frisking in the luxury of his non-sense with such poor fetches
to cog a laughter from us, that no antic hobnaile at a Morris,
but is more hansomly facetious.

Concerning that place Deut. 24. 1. which hee saith to bee *the main pillar of my opinion,* though I rely more on the institution then on that. These two pillars I doe indeed confess are to mee as those two in the porch of the Temple,
5 *Jachin* and *Boaz,* which names import establishment, and strength; nor doe I fear, who can shake them. The exposition of *Deut.* which I brought, is the receav'd Exposition both ancient and modern, by all lerned men, unless it bee a Monk-ish Papist heer and there: and the gloss which hee and his
10 obscure assistant would perswade us to, is meerly new, and absurd, presuming out of his utter ignorance in the Ebrew, to interpret those words of the Text, first in a mistakn sense of *uncleanness,* against all approved Writers. Secondly, in a limited sense, when as the original speaks without limitation,
15 *some uncleannes, or any;* and it had bin a wise Law indeed to mean it self particular, and not to express the case which this acute Rabbie hath all this while bin hooking for. Wherby they who are most partial to him, may guess that somthing is in this doctrin which I allege, that forces the adversary to
20 such a new & strain'd Exposition, wherin hee does nothing for above foure pages, but founder himself to and fro in his own objections, one while denying *that divorce was permit-ted,* another while affirming, *that it was permitted for the wives sake,* and after all distrusts himself. And for his surest
25 retirement, betakes him to those old suppositions, *that Christ abolisht the Mosaic Law of divorce; that the Jews had not sufficient knowledge in this point, through the darknes of the dispensation of heavenly things; that under the plen-*

teous grace of the Gospel, wee are ty'd by cruellest compul-
sion, to live in mariage till death, with the wickedest, the
worst, the most persecuting mate. These ignorant and doting
surmises, he might have read confuted at large, eevn in the
5 first Edition; but found it safer to pass that part over in
silence. So that they who see not the sottishnes of this his
new and tedious Exposition, are worthy to love it dearly.

His Explanation don, hee charges mee with a *wicked*
gloss, and almost blasphemy, for saying that Christ in teach-
10 ing meant not always to bee tak'n word for word; but like a
wise Physician administring one excess against another, to
reduce us to a perfet mean. Certainly to teach thus, were no
dishonest method: Christ himself hath often us'd *hyperbolies*
in his teaching; and gravest Authors, both *Aristotle* in the
15 second of his *Ethics* to *Nichomachus,* and *Seneca* in his seventh *De Beneficiis,* advise us to stretch out the line of precept
oft times beyond measure, that while wee tend furder, the
mean might bee the easier attain'd. And who-ever comments
that fifth of *Matthew,* when hee comes to the *turning of*
20 *cheek after cheek to blows,* and the *parting both with cloak*
and coat, if any please to bee the rifler, will bee forc't to rec-
ommend himself to the same Exposition, though this cater-
ing Law-monger bee bold to call it *wicked.* Now note another pretious peece of him; *Christ,* saith hee, *doth not say*
25 *that an unchast look is adultery, but the lusting after her;* as
if the looking unchastly, could bee without lusting. This
gear is Licenc't for good reason: *Imprimatur.*

Next hee would prove that the speech of Christ is not

utter'd in excess against the Pharises, First, *Because hee speaks it to his Disciples, Matth.* 5. which is fals, for hee spake it to the multitude, as by the first *vers.* is evident, among which in all likelihood were many Pharises, but out
5 of doubt, all of them Pharisæan disciples, and bred up in their Doctrin; from which extremes of error and falsity, Christ throughout his whole Sermon labours to reclaim the people. Secondly, saith hee, *Because Christ forbidds not only putting away, but marrying her who is put away.* Acutely,
10 as if the Pharises might not have offended as much in marrying the divorc'd, as in divorcing the maried. The precept may bind all, rightly understood; and yet the vehement manner of giving it, may bee occasion'd only by the Pharises.

Finally, hee windes up his Text with much doubt and
15 trepidation; for it may bee his trenchers were not scrap't, and that which never yet afforded corn of savour to his noddle, the Salt-seller was not rubb'd: and therfore in this *hast easily granting, that his answers fall foule upon each other,* and praying, you would not think *hee writes as a*
20 *profet, but as a man,* hee runns to the black jack, fills his flagon, spreds the table, and servs up dinner.

After waiting and voiding, hee thinks to void my second Argument, and the contradictions that will follow, both in the Law and Gospel, if the *Mosaic* Law were abrogated by
25 our Saviour, and a compulsive prohibition fixt instead: and sings his old song, *that the Gospel counts unlawfull that which the Law allow'd,* instancing in *Circumcision, Sacrifices, Washings.* But what are these Ceremonial things to

the changing of a morall point in houshold dutie, equally
belonging to Jew and Gentile; divorce was then right, now
wrong; then permitted in the rigorous time of Law, now forbidd'n by Law eevn to the most extremely afflicted in the
5 favourable time of grace and freedom. But this is not for an
unbutton'd fellow to discuss in the Garret, at his tressle, and
dimension of candle by the snuffe; which brought forth his
cullionly paraphrase on St. *Paul,* whom he brings in, discoursing such idle stuff to the *Maids, and Widdows,* as his
10 own servile inurbanity forbeares not to put into the Apostles
mouth, *of the soules conversing:* and this hee presumes to
doe beeing a bayard, who never had the soul to know, what
conversing means, but as his provender, and the familiarity
of the Kitchin school'd his conceptions.

15   Hee passes to the third Argument, like a Boar in a Vin-
yard, doing nought els, but still as hee goes, champing and
chewing over, what I could mean by this *Chimera* of a fit
conversing Soul, notions and words never made for those
chopps; but like a generous Wine, only by overworking the
20 settl'd mudd of his fancy, to make him drunk, and disgorge
his vileness the more openly. All persons of gentle breeding
(I say gentle, though this Barrow grunt at the word) I know
will apprehend and bee satisfy'd in what I spake, how unpleasing and discontenting the society of body must needs
25 be between those whose mindes cannot bee sociable. But
what should a man say more to a snout in this pickle, what
language can be low and degenerat anough?

     The fourth Argument which I had, was, that Mariage

beeing a Covnant, the very beeing wherof consists in the
performance of unfained love and peace, if that were not
tolerably perform'd, the Covnant became broke and rev-
ocable. Which how can any in whose minde the principles
of right reason and justice are not cancell'd, deny; for how
can a thing subsist, when the true essence therof is dissolv'd?
yet this hee denies, and yet in such a manner as alters my
assertion, for hee puts in, *though the main end bee not attain'd in full measure:* but my position is, if it be not tolerably attain'd, as throughout the whole Discours is apparent.

Now for his Reasons; *Heman found not that peace and
solace, which is the main end of communion with God,
should hee therfore break off that communion?*

I answer, that if *Heman* found it not, the fault was certainly his own: but in Mariage it happns farre otherwise:
Somtimes the fault is plainly not his who seeks Divorce:
Somtimes it cannot bee discern'd, whose fault it is: and therfore cannot in reason or equity bee the matter of an absolute
prohibition.

His other instance declares, what a right handicrafts man
hee is of petty cases, and how unfitt to bee ought els at highest, but a hacney of the Law. *I change houses with a man;
it is suppos'd I doe it for mine own ends; I attain them not in
this house; I shall not therfore goe from my bargain.* How
without fear might the young *Charinus* in *Andria* now cry
out, *what likenes can bee heer to a Mariage?* In this bargain
was no capitulation, but the yeilding of possession to one
another, wherin each of them had his several end apart: in

Mariage there is a solemn vow of love and fidelity each to other: this bargain is fully accomplisht in the change; In Mariage the covnant still is in performing. If one of them perform nothing tolerably, but instead of love, abound in
5 disaffection, disobedience, fraud, and hatred, what thing in the nature of a covnant shall bind the other to such a perdurable mischeif? Keep to your Problemes of ten groats, these matters are not for pragmatics, and folkmooters to babble in.

Concerning the place of *Paul,* that *God hath call'd us to*
10 *peace,* 1 Cor. 7. and therfore certainly, if any where in this world, wee have a right to claim it reasonably in mariage, tis plain anough in the sense which I gave, and confess'd by *Paræus,* and other Orthodox Divines, to bee a good sense, and this Answerer, doth not weak'n it. The other place, *that*
15 *hee who hateth, may put away,* which, if I shew him, he promises to yeeld the whole controversie, is, besides, *Deut.* 24. 1. *Deut.* 21. 14. and before this, *Exod.* 21. 8. Of *Malachy* I have spok'n more in another place; and say again that the best interpreters, all the ancient, and most of the modern
20 translate it, as I cited, and very few otherwise, wherof perhaps *Junius* is the cheif.

Another thing troubles him, that mariage is call'd the mystery of Joy. Let it still trouble him; for what hath hee to doe either with joy, or with mystery? He thinks it *frantic*
25 *divinity* to say, It is not the outward continuance of mariage, that keeps the covnant of mariage whole, but whosoever doth most according to peace and love, whether in mariage or divorce, hee breaks mariage lest. If I shall spell it to him, *Hee*

breaks mariage lest, is to say, hee dishonours not mariage; for *least* is tak'n in the Bible, and other good Authors, for, *not at all.* And a particular mariage a man may break, if for a lawfull cause, and yet not break, that is, not violate, or dis-
5 honour the Ordnance of Mariage. Hence those two questions that follow, are left ridiculous; and the *Maids at Algate,* whom hee flouts, are likely to have more witt then the Serv-ingman at Addlegate.

Whereas hee taxes mee of adding to the Scripture in that
10 I said, Love only is the fulfilling of every Commandment, I cited no particular Scripture, but spake a general sense, which might bee collected from many places. For seeing love includes Faith, what is ther that can fulfill every command-ment but only love? And I meant, as any intelligent Reader
15 might apprehend, every positive, and civil commandment, wherof Christ hath taught us that *man is the Lord.* It is not the formal duty of worship, or the sitting still, that keeps the holy rest of Sabbath; but whosoever doth most according to charity, whether hee work, or work not; hee breaks the holy
20 rest of Sabbath least. So Mariage beeing a civil Ordinance made for man, not man for it; hee who doth that which most accords with charity, first to himself, next to whom hee next ows it, whether in mariage or divorce, hee breaks the Ordi-nance of mariage least. And what in Religious prudence, can
25 bee charity to himself, and what to his Wife, either in con-tinuing, or in dissolving the mariage knot, hath bin already oft anough discours'd. So that what St. *Paul* saith of circum-cision, the same I stick not to say of a civil ordinance, made

to the good, and comfort of man, not to his ruin; mariage is
nothing, and divorce is nothing, *but faith, which worketh by
love*. And this I trust none can mistake.

Against the fifth Argument, That a Christian in a higher
5 order of Preist-hood, then that Levitical, is a person dedicat to
joy and peace; and therfore needs not in Subjection to a civil
Ordinance, made to no other end but for his good (when
without his fault hee findes it impossible to bee decently or
tolerably observ'd) to plunge himself into immeasurable dis-
10 tractions and temptations, above his strength; against this
hee proves nothing, but gadds into silly conjectures of what
abuses would follow, and with as good reason might declaim
against the best things that are.

Against the sixt Argument, that to force the continuance
15 of mariage between mindes found utterly unfit, and dispro-
portional, is against nature, and seems forbidd under that
allegorical precept of *Moses, Not to sow a field with divers
seed, lest both bee defil'd, not to plough with an Oxe and an
Ass together,* which I deduc'd by the pattern of St. *Pauls*
20 reasoning what was meant *by not muzzling the Oxe,* hee
rambles over a long narration, to tell us that by *the Oxen are
meant the Preachers:* which is not doubted. Then hee de-
mands, *if this my reasoning bee like St. Pauls,* and I answer
him, yes. Hee replies that *sure St. Paul would bee asham'd
25 to reason thus.* And I tell him, No. Hee grants that place
which I alleg'd, 2 *Cor.* 6. of unequal yoking, *may allude to
that of Moses,* but saies, *I cannot prove it makes to my purpos,* and shews not first, how hee can disprove it. Waigh,

Gentlemen, and consider, whether my affirmations, backt
with reason, may hold ballance against the bare denials of this
ponderous confuter, elected by his ghostly Patrons to bee my
copes-mate.

5   Proceeding on to speak of mysterious things in nature, I
had occasion to fit the language therafter, matters not for the
reading of this odious fool, who thus ever when hee meets
with ought above the cogitation of his breeding, leavs the
noysom stench of his rude slot behind him, maligning that
10 any thing should bee spoke or understood, above his own
genuine basenes; and gives sentence that his confuting hath
bin imploy'd about *a frothy, immeritous and undeserving
discours.* Who could have beleevd so much insolence durst
vent it self from out the hide of a varlet, as thus to censure
15 that which men of mature judgement have applauded to bee
writ with good reason. But this contents him not, hee falls
now to rave in his barbarous abusivenes; and why? a reason
befitting such an Artificer, because he saith *the Book is contrary to all human lerning;* When as the world knows that
20 all, both human and divine lerning, till the Canon Law,
allow'd divorce by consent, and for many causes without
consent. Next he dooms it, *as contrary to Truth;* when as it
hath bin disputable among lerned men, ever since it was
prohibited: and is by *Peter Martyr* thought an *opinion not
25 impious, but hard to bee refuted;* and by *Erasmus* deem'd
a Doctrin *so charitable and pious, as, if it cannot bee us'd,
were to bee wisht it could;* but is by *Martin Bucer,* a man of
dearest and most religious memory in the Church, taught

and maintan'd to bee either most lawfully us'd, or most lawfully permitted. And for this, for I affirm no more then
Bucer, what censure doe you think, Readers he hath condemn'd the book to? To a death no less infamous then *to be*
5 *burnt by the hangman.* Mr. Licencer, for I deal not now
with this caitif, never worth my earnest, & now not seasonable for my jest, you are reputed a man discreet anough,
religious anough, honest anough, that is, to an ordnary com-
petence in all these. But now your turn is, to hear what your
10 own hand hath earn'd ye, that when you suffer'd this nameles hangman to cast into public such a despightfull con-
tumely upon a name and person deserving of the Church
and State equally to your self, and one who hath don more
to the present advancement of your own Tribe, then you or
15 many of them have don for themselvs, you forgot to bee
either honest, Religious, or discreet. What ever the State
might doe concerning it, suppos'd a matter to expect evill
from, I should not doubt to meet among them with wise, and
honourable, and knowing men. But as to this brute Libel,
20 so much the more impudent and lawless for the abus'd autority which it bears, I say again, that I abominat the censure
of Rascalls and their Licencers.

   With difficulty I return to what remains of this ignoble
task, for the disdain I have to change a period more with the
25 filth and venom of this gourmand, swell'd into a confuter.
Yet for the satisfaction of others, I endure all this.

   Against the seventh Argument, that if the Canon Law and
Divines allow divorce for conspiracy of death, they may as

well allow it to avoid the same consequence from the likelihood of naturall causes;

First, hee denies that the Canon so decrees.

I Answer, that it decrees for danger of life, as much as for
5 adultery. *Decret. Gregor. l. 4. tit.* 19. and in other places:
and the best Civilians who cite the Canon Law, so collect, as
Schneidewin in institut. tit. 10. *p.* 4. *de divort.* and indeed
who would have deny'd it, but one of a reprobate ignorance
in all hee meddles with.

10   Secondly, hee saith, the case alters, for there the offender
who seeks the life, doth implicitly at least act a divorce.

And I answer, that heer nature though no offender, doth
the same. But if an offender *by acting a divorce,* shall release
the offended, this is an ample grant against himself. Hee
15 saith, *nature teacheth to save life from one who seeks it.* And
I say she teaches no less to save it from any other cause that
endangers it. Hee saith, *that heer they are both actors.* Admit they were, it would not be uncharitable to part them; yet
somtimes they are not both actors, but the one of them most
20 lamentedly passive. So hee concludes, *Wee must not take
advantage of our own faults and corruptions to release us
from our duties.* But shall wee take no advantage to save our
selvs from the faults of another, who hath anull'd his right
to our duty? No, saith hee, *Let them die of the sullens, and
25 try who will pitty them.* Barbarian, the shame of all honest
Atturneys, why doe they not hoiss him over the barre, and
blanket him?

Against the eighth Argument, that they who are destitute

of all mariageable guifts, except a body not plainly unfit, have
not the calling to marry, and consequently married and so
found, may bee divorc'd, this, hee saith, *is nothing to the
purpose,* and not fit to bee answer'd. I leav it therfore to the
judgement of his Maisters.

Against the ninth Argument, that mariage is a human
society, and so cheifly seated in agreement and unity of
minde: If therfore the minde cannot have that due society by
mariage, that it may reasonably and humanly desire, it can
bee no human society, and so not without reason divorcible,
here hee falsifies, and turnes what the position requir'd of a
reasonable agreement in the main matters of society, into *an
agreement in all things,* which makes the opinion not mine,
and so hee leavs it.

At last, and in good howr we are com to his farewell,
which is to bee a concluding taste of his jabberment at in Law,
the flashiest and the fustiest that ever corrupted in such an
unswill'd hogshead.

Against my tenth Argument, as he calls it, but as I intended it, my other position, that Divorce is not a thing de-
terminable by a compulsive Law, for that all Law is for som
good that may be frequently attain'd without the admixture
of a wors inconvenience; but the Law forbidding divorce,
never attains to any good end of such prohibition, but rather
multiplies evill; therfore, the prohibition of divorce is no
good Law. Now for his Atturneys prise: but first, like a
right cunning and sturdy Logician, hee denies my Argument
not mattering whether in the *major* or *minor:* and saith,

there are many Laws made for good, and yet that good is not
attain'd, through the defaults of the party, but a greater in-
convenience follows.

But I reply that this Answer builds upon a shallow foun-
5 dation, and most unjustly supposes every one in default, who
seeks divorce from the most injurious wedloc. The default
therfore will bee found in the Law it self; which is neither
able to punish the offender, but the innocent must withall
suffer; nor can right the innocent, in what is cheifly sought,
10 the obtainment of love or quietnes. His instances out of the
Common Law, are all so quite beside the matter which hee
would prove, as may bee a warning to all clients how they
venture thir busines with such a cock-braind Solliciter. For
beeing to shew som Law of *England,* attaining to no good
15 end, and yet through no default of the party, who is therby
debarr'd all remedy, hee shews us only how som doe loos the
benefit of good Laws through their own default. His first
example saith, *It is a just Law that every one shall peaceably*
enjoy his estate in Lands or otherwise. Does this Law attain
20 to no good end? the Barr will blush at this most incogitant
woodcock. But see if a draft of *Littleton* will recover him to
his senses. *If this man having Fee simple in his Lands, yet*
will take a Leas of his own Lands, from another, this shall
bee an Estoppel to him in an Assise from the recovering of
25 *his own Land.* Mark now, and register him. How many are
there of ten thousand who have such a Fee simple in their
sconse, as to take a Leas of their own Lands from another?
So that this inconvenience lights upon scars one in an age,

and by his own default; and the Law of enjoying each man
his own, is good to all others. But on the contrary, this prohibition of divorce is good to none, and brings inconvenience
to numbers, who lie under intolerable greevances, without
5 thir own default, through the wickednes or folly of another;
and all this iniquity the Law remedies not, but in a manner
maintains. His other cases are directly to the same purpos,
and might have bin spar'd, but that hee is a tradsman of the
Law, and must be born with at his first setting up, to lay
10 forth his best ware, which is only gibbrish.

I have now don that, which for many causes I might have
thought, could not likely have bin my fortune, to bee put to
this under-work of scowring and unrubbishing the low and
sordid ignorance of such a presumptuous lozel. Yet *Hercu-*
15 *les* had the labour once impos'd upon him to carry dung out
of the *Augean* stable. At any hand I would bee ridd of him:
for I had rather, since the life of man is likn'd to a Scene, that
all my entrances and *exits* might mixe with such persons
only, whose worth erects them and their actions to a grave
20 and *tragic* deportment, and not to have to doe with *Clowns*
and *Vices*. But if a man cannot peaceably walk into the
world, but must bee infested, somtimes at his face, with
dorrs and horsflies, somtimes beneath, with bauling whip-
pets, and shin-barkers, and these to bee set on by plot and
25 consultation with a *Junto* of Clergy men and Licencers, commended also and rejoyc't in by those whose partiality cannot yet forgoe old papisticall principles, have I not cause to
bee in such a manner defensive, as may procure mee freedom

to pass more unmolested heerafter by these incumbrances, not so much regarded for themselvs, as for those who incite them. And what defence can properly bee us'd in such a despicable encounter as this, but either the flap or the spurn?
5 If they can afford mee none but a ridiculous adversary, the blame belongs not to mee, though the whole Dispute bee strew'd and scatter'd with ridiculous. And if hee have such an ambition to know no better who are his mates, but among those needy thoughts, which though his two faculties of Serv-
10 ingman and Solliciter, should compound into one mongrel, would bee but thin and meager, if in this penury of Soul hee can bee possible to have the lustiness to think of fame, let him but send mee how hee calls himself, and I may chance not fail to endorse him on the backside of posterity, not a *golden,*
15 but a brazen Asse. Since my fate extorts from mee a talent of sport, which I had thought to hide in a napkin, hee shall bee my *Batrachomuomachia,* my *Bavius,* my *Calandrino,* the common adagy of ignorance and over-weening. Nay perhaps, as the provocation may bee, I may bee driv'n to curle
20 up this gliding prose into a rough *Sotadic,* that shall rime him into such a condition, as instead of judging good Books to bee burnt by the executioner, hee shall be readier to be his own hangman. Thus much to this *Nuisance.*

But as for the Subject it self which I have writt, and now
25 defend, according as the opposition beares, if any man equal to the matter shall think it appertains him to take in hand this controversy, either excepting against ought writt'n, or perswaded hee can shew better how this question of such

moment to bee throughly known may receav a true determination, not leaning on the old and rott'n suggestions
wheron it yet leanes, if his intents bee sincere to the public,
and shall carry him on without bitternes to the opinion, or to
5 the person dissenting, let him not, I entreate him, guess by
the handling, which meritoriously hath bin bestowd on this
object of contempt and laughter, that I account it any displeasure don mee to bee contradicted in Print: but as it leads
to the attainment of any thing more true, shall esteem it a
10 benefit; and shall know how to return his civility and faire
Argument in such a sort, as hee shall confess that to doe so
is my choise, and to have don thus was my chance.

The End.

OF EDUCATION

TO MASTER SAMUEL HARTLIB

OF EDUCATION.

To Master *Samuel Hartlib.*

Written above twenty Years since.

Mr. *Hartlib,*

I AM long since perswaded, that to say, or do ought worth memory and imitation, no purpose or respect should sooner move us, then simply the love of God, and of
5 mankind. Nevertheless to write now the reforming of Education, though it be one of the greatest and noblest designs that can be thought on, and for the want whereof this Nation perishes, I had not yet at this time been induc't, but by your earnest entreaties, and serious conjurements; as having my
10 mind for the present half diverted in the pursuance of some other assertions, the knowledge and the use of which, cannot but be a great furtherance both to the enlargement of truth, and honest living, with much more peace. Nor should the laws of any private friendship have prevail'd with me to
15 divide thus, or transpose my former thoughts, but that I see those aims, those actions which have won you with me the esteem of a person sent hither by some good providence from a far country to be the occasion and the incitement of great good to this Island. And, as I hear, you have obtain'd the
20 same repute with men of most approved wisdom, and some of highest authority among us. Not to mention the learned correspondence which you hold in forreign parts, and the ex-

traordinary pains and diligence which you have us'd in this
matter both here, and beyond the Seas; either by the definite
will of God so ruling, or the peculiar sway of nature, which
also is Gods working. Neither can I think that so reputed,
5 and so valu'd as you are, you would to the forfeit of your own
discerning ability, impose upon me an unfit and over-pon-
derous argument, but that the satisfaction which you profess
to have receiv'd from those incidental Discourses which we
have wander'd into, hath prest and almost constrain'd you
10 into a perswasion, that what you require from me in this point,
I neither ought, nor can in conscience deferre beyond this
time both of so much need at once, and so much opportunity
to try what God hath determin'd. I will not resist therefore,
whatever it is either of divine, or humane obligement that you
15 lay upon me; but will forthwith set down in writing, as you
request me, that voluntary *Idea,* which hath long in silence
presented it self to me, of a better Education, in extent and
comprehension far more large, and yet of time far shorter,
and of attainment far more certain, then hath been yet in prac-
20 tice. Brief I shall endeavour to be; for that which I have to
say, assuredly this Nation hath extream need should be done
sooner then spoken. To tell you therefore what I have bene-
fited herein among old renowned Authors, I shall spare; and
to search what many modern *Janua's* and *Didactics* more
25 then ever I shall read, have projected, my inclination leads me
not. But if you can accept of these few observations which
have flowr'd off, and are, as it were, the burnishing of many
studious and contemplative years altogether spent in the

search of religious and civil knowledge, and such as pleas'd
you so well in the relating, I here give you them to dispose of.

The end then of Learning is to repair the ruines of our first
Parents by regaining to know God aright, and out of that
5 knowledge to love him, to imitate him, to be like him, as we
may the neerest by possessing our souls of true vertue, which
being united to the heavenly grace of faith makes up the highest perfection. But because our understanding cannot in this
body found it self but on sensible things, nor arrive so clearly
10 to the knowledge of God and things invisible, as by orderly
conning over the visible and inferior creature, the same
method is necessarily to be follow'd in all discreet teaching.
And seeing every Nation affords not experience and tradition
enough for all kind of Learning, therefore we are chiefly
15 taught the Languages of those people who have at any time
been most industrious after Wisdom; so that Language is but
the Instrument conveying to us things usefull to be known.
And though a Linguist should pride himself to have all the
Tongues that *Babel* cleft the world into, yet, if he have not
20 studied the solid things in them as well as the Words & Lexicons, he were nothing so much to be esteem'd a learned man,
as any Yeoman or Tradesman competently wise in his Mother
Dialect only. Hence appear the many mistakes which have
made Learning generally so unpleasing and so unsuccessful;
25 first we do amiss to spend seven or eight years meerly in scrap-
ing together so much miserable Latine and Greek, as might
be learnt otherwise easily and delightfully in one year. And
that which casts our proficiency therein so much behind, is

our time lost partly in too oft idle vacancies given both to
Schools and Universities, partly in a preposterous exaction,
forcing the empty wits of Children to compose Theams,
Verses and Orations, which are the acts of ripest judgment
5 and the final work of a head fill'd by long reading and observing, with elegant maxims, and copious invention. These are
not matters to be wrung from poor striplings, like blood out
of the Nose, or the plucking of untimely fruit: besides the ill
habit which they get of wretched barbarizing against the
10 Latin and Greek *idiom,* with their untutor'd *Anglicisms,*
odious to be read, yet not to be avoided without a well continu'd and judicious conversing among pure Authors di-
gested, which they scarce taste, whereas, if after some pre-
paratory grounds of speech by their certain forms got into
15 memory, they were led to the praxis thereof in some chosen
short book lesson'd throughly to them, they might then forthwith proceed to learn the substance of good things, and Arts
in due order, which would bring the whole language quickly
into their power. This I take to be the most rational and most
20 profitable way of learning Languages, and whereby we may
best hope to give account to God of our youth spent herein:
And for the usual method of teaching Arts, I deem it to be an
old errour of Universities not yet well recover'd from the Scho-
lastick grossness of barbarous ages, that in stead of beginning
25 with Arts most easie, and those be such as are most obvious
to the sence, they present their young unmatriculated Novices
at first comming with the most intellective abstractions of
Logick and Metaphysicks: So that they having but newly left

those Grammatick flats and shallows where they stuck un-
reasonably to learn a few words with lamentable construction,
and now on the sudden transported under another climate to
be tost and turmoil'd with their unballasted wits in fadomless
5 and unquiet deeps of controversie, do for the most part grow
into hatred and contempt of Learning, mockt and deluded all
this while with ragged Notions and Babblements, while they
expected worthy and delightful knowledge; till poverty or
youthful years call them importunately their several wayes,
10 and hasten them with the sway of friends either to an ambitious and mercenary, or ignorantly zealous Divinity; Some
allur'd to the trade of Law, grounding their purposes not on
the prudent and heavenly contemplation of justice and equity
which was never taught them, but on the promising and pleas-
15 ing thoughts of litigious terms, fat contentions, and flowing
fees; others betake them to State affairs, with souls so unprincipl'd in vertue, and true generous breeding, that flattery, and
Court shifts and tyrannous Aphorisms appear to them the
highest points of wisdom; instilling their barren hearts with a
20 conscientious slavery, if, as I rather think, it be not fain'd.
Others lastly of a more delicious and airie spirit, retire themselves knowing no better, to the enjoyments of ease and luxury, living out their daies in feast and jollity; which indeed is
the wisest and the safest course of all these, unless they were
25 with more integrity undertaken. And these are the fruits of
mispending our prime youth at the Schools and Universities
as we do, either in learning meer words or such things chiefly,
as were better unlearnt.

I shall detain you no longer in the demonstration of what we should not do, but strait conduct ye to a hill side, where I will point ye out the right path of a vertuous and noble Education; laborious indeed at the first ascent, but else so smooth, 5 so green, so full of goodly prospect, and melodious sounds on every side, that the Harp of *Orpheus* was not more charming. I doubt not but ye shall have more adoe to drive our dullest and laziest youth, our stocks and stubbs from the infinite desire of such a happy nurture, then we have now to hale and 10 drag our choisest and hopefullest Wits to that asinine feast of sowthistles and brambles which is commonly set before them, as all the food and entertainment of their tenderest and most docible age. I call therefore a compleat and generous Education that which fits a man to perform justly, skilfully and 15 magnanimously all the offices both private and publick of Peace and War. And how all this may be done between twelve, and one and twenty, less time then is now bestow'd in pure trifling at Grammar and *Sophistry,* is to be thus order'd.

20   First to find out a spatious house and ground about it fit for an *Academy,* and big enough to lodge a hundred and fifty persons, whereof twenty or thereabout may be attendants, all under the government of one, who shall be thought of desert sufficient, and ability either to do all, or wisely to direct, and 25 oversee it done. This place should be at once both School and University, not needing a remove to any other house of Schollership, except it be some peculiar Colledge of Law, or Physick, where they mean to be practitioners; but as for those

general studies which take up all our time from *Lilly* to the commencing, as they term it, Master of Art, it should be absolute. After this pattern, as many Edifices may be converted to this use, as shall be needful in every City throughout this

5 Land, which would tend much to the encrease of Learning and Civility every where. This number, less or more thus collected, to the convenience of a foot Company, or interchangeably two Troops of Cavalry, should divide their daies work into three parts, as it lies orderly. Their Studies, their Exer-

10 cise, and their Diet.

For their Studies, First they should begin with the chief and necessary rules of some good Grammar, either that now us'd, or any better: and while this is doing, their speech is to be fashion'd to a distinct and clear pronuntiation, as near as

15 may be to the *Italian,* especially in the Vowels. For we *Englishmen* being far Northerly, do not open our mouths in the cold air, wide enough to grace a Southern Tongue; but are observ'd by all other Nations to speak exceeding close and inward: So that to smatter Latine with an English mouth, is

20 as ill a hearing as Law-French. Next to make them expert in the usefullest points of Grammar, and withall to season them, and win them early to the love of vertue and true labour, ere any flattering seducement, or vain principle seise them wandering, some easie and delightful Book of Education would

25 be read to them; whereof the Greeks have store, as *Cebes, Plutarch,* and other Socratic discourses. But in Latin we have none of classic authority extant, except the two or three first Books of *Quintilian,* and some select pieces elsewhere. But

here the main skill and groundwork will be, to temper them
such Lectures and Explanations upon every opportunity, as
may lead and draw them in willing obedience, enflam'd with
the study of Learning, and the admiration of Vertue; stirr'd
5 up with high hopes of living to be brave men, and worthy
Patriots, dear to God, and famous to all ages. That they may
despise and scorn all their childish, and ill-taught qualities,
to delight in manly, and liberal Exercises: which he who hath
the Art, and proper Eloquence to catch them with, what with
10 mild and effectual perswasions, and what with the intima-
tion of some fear, if need be, but chiefly by his own example,
might in a short space gain them to an incredible diligence
and courage: infusing into their young brests such an ingenuous and noble ardor, as would not fail to make many of them
15 renowned and matchless men. At the same time, some other
hour of the day, might be taught them the rules of Arithmetick, and soon after the Elements of Geometry even playing,
as the old manner was. After evening repast, till bed-time
their thoughts will be best taken up in the easie grounds of
20 Religion, and the story of Scripture. The next step would be
to the Authors *Agriculture, Cato, Varro,* and *Columella,* for
the matter is most easie, and if the language be difficult, so
much the better, it is not a difficulty above their years. And
here will be an occasion of inciting and inabling them here-
25 after to improve the tillage of their Country, to recover the
bad Soil, and to remedy the waste that is made of good: for
this was one of *Hercules* praises. Ere half these Authors be
read (which will soon be with plying hard, and daily) they

cannot chuse but be masters of any ordinary prose. So that
it will be then seasonable for them to learn in any modern
Author, the use of the Globes, and all the Maps; first with
the old names, and then with the new: or they might be
5 then capable to read any compendious method of natural
Philosophy. And at the same time might be entring into
the Greek tongue, after the same manner as was before prescrib'd in the Latin; whereby the difficulties of Grammar
being soon overcome, all the Historical Physiology of *Aris-*
10 *totle* and *Theophrastus* are open before them, and as I may
say, under contribution. The like access will be to *Vitruvius,*
to *Seneca's* natural questions, to *Mela, Celsus, Pliny,* or *So-*
linus. And having thus past the principles of *Arithmetick,*
Geometry, Astronomy, and *Geography* with a general com-
15 pact of Physicks, they may descend in *Mathematicks* to the
instrumental science of *Trigonometry,* and from thence to
Fortification, Architecture, Enginry, or Navigation. And in
natural Philosophy they may proceed leisurely from the History of Meteors, Minerals, plants and living Creatures as far
20 as Anatomy. Then also in course might be read to them out
of some not tedious Writer the Institution of Physick; that
they may know the tempers, the humours, the seasons, and
how to manage a crudity: which he who can wisely and timely
do, is not only a great Physitian to himself, and to his friends,
25 but also may at some time or other, save an Army by this
frugal and expenseless means only; and not let the healthy
and stout bodies of young men rot away under him for want
of this discipline; which is a great pity, and no less a shame to

the Commander. To set forward all these proceedings in Nature and Mathematicks, what hinders, but that they may procure, as oft as shal be needful, the helpful experiences of Hunters, Fowlers, Fishermen, Shepherds, Gardeners, Apoth-
5 ecaries; and in the other sciences, Architects, Engineers, Mariners, Anatomists; who doubtless would be ready some for reward, and some to favour such a hopeful Seminary. And this will give them such a real tincture of natural knowledge, as they shall never forget, but daily augment with delight.
10 Then also those Poets which are now counted most hard, will be both facil and pleasant, *Orpheus, Hesiod, Theocritus, Aratus, Nicander, Oppian, Dionysius,* and in Latin *Lucretius, Manilius,* and the rural part of *Virgil.*

By this time, years and good general precepts will have
15 furnisht them more distinctly with that act of reason which in *Ethics* is call'd *Proairesis:* that they may with some judgement contemplate upon moral good and evil. Then will be requir'd a special reinforcement of constant and sound endoctrinating to set them right and firm, instructing them more
20 amply in the knowledge of Vertue and the hatred of Vice: while their young and pliant affections are led through all the moral works of *Plato, Xenophon, Cicero, Plutarch, Laertius,* and those *Locrian* remnants; but still to be reduc't in their nightward studies wherewith they close the dayes work, under
25 the determinate sentence of *David* or *Salomon,* or the Evanges and Apostolic Scriptures. Being perfect in the knowledge of personal duty, they may then begin the study of Economics. And either now, or before this, they may have easily learnt at

any odd hour the *Italian* Tongue. And soon after, but with
wariness and good antidote, it would be wholsome enough to
let them taste some choice Comedies, Greek, Latin, or *Italian:*
Those Tragedies also that treat of Houshold matters, as *Tra-*
5 *chiniæ, Alcestis,* and the like. The next remove must be to the
study of *Politicks;* to know the beginning, end, and reasons
of Political Societies; that they may not in a dangerous fit of
the Common-wealth be such poor, shaken, uncertain Reeds,
of such a tottering Conscience, as many of our great Coun-
10 sellers have lately shewn themselves, but stedfast pillars of the
State. After this they are to dive into the grounds of Law, and
legal Justice; deliver'd first, and with best warrant by *Moses;*
and as far as humane prudence can be trusted, in those extoll'd
remains of Grecian Law-givers, *Licurgus, Solon, Zaleucus,*
15 *Charondas,* and thence to all the Roman *Edicts* and Tables
with their *Justinian;* and so down to the *Saxon* and common
Laws of *England,* and the Statutes. Sundayes also and every
evening may be now understandingly spent in the highest
matters of *Theology,* and Church History ancient and mod-
20 ern: and ere this time the Hebrew Tongue at a set hour might
have been gain'd, that the Scriptures may be now read in their
own original; whereto it would be no impossibility to add the
Chaldey, and the *Syrian* Dialect. When all these employments are well conquer'd, then will the choise Histories,
25 *Heroic Poems,* and *Attic* Tragedies of stateliest and most
regal argument, with all the famous Political Orations offer
themselves; which if they were not only read; but some of
them got by memory, and solemnly pronounc't with right

accent, and grace, as might be taught, would endue them even
with the spirit and vigor of *Demosthenes* or *Cicero, Euripides,*
or *Sophocles*. And now lastly will be the time to read with
them those organic arts which inable men to discourse and
5 write perspicuously, elegantly, and according to the fitted
stile of lofty, mean, or lowly. Logic therefore so much as is
useful, is to be referr'd to this due place withall her well
coucht Heads and Topics, untill it be time to open her contracted palm into a gracefull and ornate Rhetorick taught
10 out of the rule of *Plato, Aristotle, Phalereus, Cicero, Hermo-
genes, Longinus*. To which Poetry would be made subse-
quent, or indeed rather precedent, as being less suttle and fine,
but more simple, sensuous and passionate. I mean not here
the prosody of a verse, which they could not but have hit on
15 before among the rudiments of Grammar; but that sublime
Art which in *Aristotles Poetics,* in *Horace,* and the *Italian*
Commentaries of *Castelvetro, Tasso, Mazzoni,* and others,
teaches what the laws are of a true *Epic* Poem, what of a *Dra-
matic,* what of a *Lyric,* what Decorum is, which is the grand
20 master-piece to observe. This would make them soon perceive what despicable creatures our common Rimers and Play-
writers be, and shew them, what religious, what glorious and
magnificent use might be made of Poetry both in divine and
humane things. From hence and not till now will be the right
25 season of forming them to be able Writers and Composers in
every excellent matter, when they shall be thus fraught with
an universal insight into things. Or whether they be to speak
in Parliament or Counsel, honour and attention would be

waiting on their lips. There would then also appear in Pulpits other Visages, other gestures, and stuff otherwise wrought then what we now sit under, oft times to as great a trial of our patience as any other that they preach to us. These are the
5 Studies wherein our noble and our gentle Youth ought to bestow their time in a disciplinary way from twelve to one and twenty; unless they rely more upon their ancestors dead, then upon themselves living. In which methodical course it is so suppos'd they must proceed by the steddy pace of learning
10 onward, as at convenient times for memories sake to retire back into the middle ward, and sometimes into the rear of what they have been taught, untill they have confirm'd, and solidly united the whole body of their perfeted knowledge, like the last embattelling of a Roman Legion. Now will be
15 worth the seeing what Exercises and Recreations may best agree, and become these Studies.

Their Exercise.

The course of Study hitherto briefly describ'd, is, what I can guess by reading, likest to those ancient and famous
20 Schools of *Pythagoras, Plato, Isocrates, Aristotle* and such others, out of which were bred up such a number of renowned Philosophers, Orators, Historians, Poets and Princes all over *Greece, Italy,* and *Asia,* besides the flourishing Studies of *Cyrene* and *Alexandria.* But herein it shall exceed them, and
25 supply a defect as great as that which *Plato* noted in the Common-wealth of *Sparta;* whereas that City train'd up their Youth most for War, and these in their Academies and

Lycæum, all for the Gown, this institution of breeding which
I here delineate, shall be equally good both for Peace and War.
Therefore about an hour and a half ere they eat at Noon
should be allow'd them for exercise and due rest afterwards:
5 But the time for this may be enlarg'd at pleasure, according
as their rising in the morning shall be early. The Exercise
which I commend first, is the exact use of their Weapon, to
guard and to strike safely with edge, or point; this will keep
them healthy, nimble, strong, and well in breath, is also the
10 likeliest means to make them grow large and tall, and to
inspire them with a gallant and fearless courage, which being
temper'd with seasonable Lectures and Precepts to them of
true Fortitude and Patience, will turn into a native and
heroick valour, and make them hate the cowardise of doing
15 wrong. They must be also practiz'd in all the Locks and
Gripes of Wrastling, wherein English men were wont to
excell, as need may often be in fight to tugg or grapple, and to
close. And this perhaps will be enough, wherein to prove and
heat their single strength. The interim of unsweating them-
20 selves regularly, and convenient rest before meat may both
with profit and delight be taken up in recreating and composing their travail'd spirits with the solemn and divine har-
monies of Musick heard or learnt; either while the skilful
Organist plies his grave and fancied descant, in lofty fugues,
25 or the whole Symphony with artful and unimaginable touches
adorn and grace the well studied chords of some choice Composer; sometimes the Lute, or soft Organ stop waiting on
elegant Voices either to Religious, martial, or civil Ditties;

which if wise men and Prophets be not extreamly out, have a
great power over dispositions and manners, to smooth and
make them gentle from rustick harshness and distemper'd
passions. The like also would not be unexpedient after Meat
5 to assist and cherish Nature in her first concoction, and send
their minds back to study in good tune and satisfaction.
Where having follow'd it close under vigilant eyes till about
two hours before supper, they are by a sudden alarum or
watch word, to be call'd out to their military motions, under
10 skie or covert, according to the season, as was the Roman
wont; first on foot, then as their age permits, on Horseback,
to all the Art of Cavalry; That having in sport, but with much
exactness, and daily muster, serv'd out the rudiments of their
Souldiership in all the skill of Embattelling, Marching, En-
15 camping, Fortifying, Besieging and Battering, with all the
helps of ancient and modern stratagems, *Tacticks* and war-
like maxims, they may as it were out of a long War come forth
renowned and perfect Commanders in the service of their
Country. They would not then, if they were trusted with fair
20 and hopeful armies, suffer them for want of just and wise
discipline to shed away from about them like sick feathers,
though they be never so oft suppli'd: they would not suffer
their empty and unrecrutible Colonels of twenty men in a
Company to quaff out, or convey into secret hoards, the wages
25 of a delusive list, and a miserable remnant: yet in the mean
while to be over-master'd with a score or two of drunkards,
the only souldery left about them, or else to comply with all
rapines and violences. No certainly, if they knew ought of

that knowledge that belongs to good men or good Governours, they would not suffer these things. But to return to our
own institute, besides these constant exercises at home, there
is another opportunity of gaining experience to be won from
5 pleasure it self abroad; In those vernal seasons of the year,
when the air is calm and pleasant, it were an injury and sullen-
ness against nature not to go out, and see her riches, and partake in her rejoycing with Heaven and Earth. I should not
therefore be a perswader to them of studying much then, after
10 two or three year that they have well laid their grounds, but
to ride out in Companies with prudent and staid Guides, to
all the quarters of the Land: learning and observing all places
of strength, all commodities of building and of soil, for Towns
and Tillage, Harbours and Ports for Trade. Sometimes taking
15 Sea as far as to our Navy, to learn there also what they can in
the practical knowledge of sailing and of Sea-fight. These
ways would try all their peculiar gifts of Nature, and if there
were any secret excellence among them, would fetch it out,
and give it fair opportunities to advance it self by, which could
20 not but mightily redound to the good of this Nation, and
bring into fashion again those old admired Vertues and Excellencies, with far more advantage now in this purity of
Christian knowledge. Nor shall we then need the *Monsieurs*
of *Paris* to take our hopefull Youth into their slight and prod-
25 igal custodies and send them over back again transform'd
into Mimicks, Apes and Kicshoes. But if they desire to see
other Countries at three or four and twenty years of age, not
to learn Principles but to enlarge Experience, and make wise

observation, they will by that time be such as shall deserve the
regard and honour of all men where they pass, and the society
and friendship of those in all places who are best and most
eminent. And perhaps then other Nations will be glad to
5 visit us for their Breeding, or else to imitate us in their own
Country.

Now lastly for their Diet there cannot be much to say, save
only that it would be best in the same House; for much time
else would be lost abroad, and many ill habits got; and that it
10 should be plain, healthful, and moderate I suppose is out of
controversie. Thus Mr. *Hartlib,* you have a general view in
writing, as your desire was, of that which at several times I
had discourst with you concerning the best and Noblest way
of Education; not beginning as some have done from the
15 Cradle, which yet might be worth many considerations, if
brevity had not been my scope, many other circumstances also
I could have mention'd, but this to such as have the worth in
them to make trial, for light and direction may be enough.
Only I believe that this is not a Bow for every man to shoot in
20 that counts himself a Teacher; but will require sinews almost
equal to those which *Homer* gave *Ulysses,* yet I am withall
perswaded that it may prove much more easie in the assay,
then it now seems at distance, and much more illustrious:
howbeit not more difficult then I imagine, and that imagina-
25 tion presents me with nothing but very happy and very possible according to best wishes; if God have so decreed, and this
age have spirit and capacity enough to apprehend.

The End.

AREOPAGITICA

A SPEECH OF MR. JOHN MILTON FOR THE
LIBERTY OF UNLICENC'D PRINTING, TO THE
PARLIAMENT OF ENGLAND

AREOPAGITICA;

A

SPEECH

OF

Mr. JOHN MILTON

For the Liberty of Vnlicenc'd PRINTING,

To the Parlament of ENGLAND.

Τὐλδίθερον δ' ἐκεῖνο, εἴ τις θέλҁ πόλҁ
Χρησόν τι βέλҁ μ' εἰς μέσον φέρειν, ἔχҁν·
Καὶ ταῦθ' ὁ χρήζων, λαμπρός ἐσθ', ὁ μὴ θέλων,
Σιγᾷ, τί τέτων ἐστὶν ἰσαίτερον πόλҁ;

Euripid. Hicetid.

This is true Liberty when free born men
Having to advise the public may speak free,
Which he who can, and will, deserv's high praise,
Who neither can nor will, may hold his peace;
What can be juster in a State then this?

Euripid. Hicetid.

LONDON,
Printed in the Yeare, 1644.

For the Liberty of unlicenc'd Printing.

THEY who to States and Governours of the Common-
wealth direct their Speech, High Court of Parlament,
or wanting such accesse in a private condition, write
that which they foresee may advance the publick good; I
5 suppose them as at the beginning of no meane endeavour, not
a little alter'd and mov'd inwardly in their mindes: Some
with doubt of what will be the successe, others with feare of
what will be the censure; some with hope, others with confidence of what they have to speake. And me perhaps each of
10 these dispositions, as the subject was whereon I enter'd, may
have at other times variously affected; and likely might in
these formost expressions now also disclose which of them
sway'd most, but that the very attempt of this addresse thus
made, and the thought of whom it hath recourse to, hath got
15 the power within me to a passion, farre more welcome then
incidentall to a Preface. Which though I stay not to confesse
ere any aske, I shall be blamelesse, if it be no other, then the
joy and gratulation which it brings to all who wish and promote their Countries liberty; whereof this whole Discourse
20 propos'd will be a certaine testimony, if not a Trophey. For
this is not the liberty which wee can hope, that no grievance
ever should arise in the Commonwealth, that let no man in
this World expect; but when complaints are freely heard,
deeply consider'd, and speedily reform'd, then is the utmost
25 bound of civill liberty attain'd, that wise men looke for. To

which if I now manifest by the very sound of this which I
shall utter, that wee are already in good part arriv'd, and yet
from such a steepe disadvantage of tyranny and superstition
grounded into our principles as was beyond the manhood of a
5 *Roman* recovery, it will bee attributed first, as is most due,
to the strong assistance of God our deliverer, next to your
faithfull guidance and undaunted Wisdome, Lords and Commons of *England*. Neither is it in Gods esteeme the diminu-
tion of his glory, when honourable things are spoken of good
10 men and worthy Magistrates; which if I now first should begin to doe, after so fair a progresse of your laudable deeds,
and such a long obligement upon the whole Realme to your
indefatigable vertues, I might be justly reckn'd among the
tardiest, and the unwillingest of them that praise yee. Never-
15 thelesse there being three principall things, without which
all praising is but Courtship and flattery, First, when that
only is prais'd which is solidly worth praise: next when greatest likelihoods are brought that such things are truly and
really in those persons to whom they are ascrib'd, the other,
20 when he who praises, by shewing that such his actuall perswasion is of whom he writes, can demonstrate that he flat-
ters not; the former two of these I have heretofore endeavour'd, rescuing the employment from him who went about
to impaire your merits with a triviall and malignant *Encom-*
25 *ium;* the latter as belonging chiefly to mine owne acquittall,
that whom I so extoll'd I did not flatter, hath been reserv'd
opportunely to this occasion. For he who freely magnifies
what hath been nobly done, and fears not to declare as freely

what might be done better, gives ye the best cov'nant of his
fidelity; and that his loyalest affection and his hope waits on
your proceedings. His highest praising is not flattery, and
his plainest advice is a kinde of praising; for though I should
5 affirme and hold by argument, that it would fare better with
truth, with learning, and the Commonwealth, if one of your
publisht Orders which I should name, were call'd in, yet at
the same time it could not but much redound to the lustre of
your milde and equall Government, when as private persons
10 are hereby animated to thinke ye better pleas'd with publick
advice, then other statists have been delighted heretofore with
publicke flattery. And men will then see what difference
there is between the magnanimity of a trienniall Parlament,
and that jealous hautinesse of Prelates and cabin Counsel-
15 lours that usurpt of late, when as they shall observe yee in the
midd'st of your Victories and successes more gently brooking
writt'n exceptions against a voted Order, then other Courts,
which had produc't nothing worth memory but the weake
ostentation of wealth, would have endur'd the least signifi'd
20 dislike at any sudden Proclamation. If I should thus farre
presume upon the meek demeanour of your civill and gentle
greatnesse, Lords and Commons, as what your publisht Order
hath directly said, that to gainsay, I might defend my selfe
with ease, if any should accuse me of being new or insolent,
25 did they but know how much better I find ye esteem it to
imitate the old and elegant humanity of Greece, then the bar-
barick pride of a *Hunnish* and *Norwegian* statelines. And
out of those ages, to whose polite wisdom and letters we ow

that we are not yet *Gothes* and *Jutlanders,* I could name him who from his private house wrote that discourse to the Parlament of *Athens,* that perswades them to change the forme of *Democraty* which was then establisht. Such honour was 5 done in those dayes to men who profest the study of wisdome and eloquence, not only in their own Country, but in other Lands, that Cities and Siniories heard them gladly, and with great respect, if they had ought in publick to admonish the State. Thus did *Dion Prusæus* a stranger and a privat Orator 10 counsell the *Rhodians* against a former Edict: and I abound with other like examples, which to set heer would be superfluous. But if from the industry of a life wholly dedicated to studious labours, and those naturall endowments haply not the worst for two and fifty degrees of northern latitude, so 15 much must be derogated, as to count me not equall to any of those who had this priviledge, I would obtain to be thought not so inferior, as your selves are superior to the most of them who receiv'd their counsell: and how farre you excell them, be assur'd, Lords and Commons, there can no greater testi- 20 mony appear, then when your prudent spirit acknowledges and obeyes the voice of reason from what quarter soever it be heard speaking; and renders ye as willing to repeal any Act of your own setting forth, as any set forth by your Predecessors.

25 If ye be thus resolv'd, as it were injury to thinke ye were not, I know not what should withhold me from presenting ye with a fit instance wherein to shew both that love of truth which ye eminently professe, and that uprightnesse of your

judgement which is not wont to be partiall to your selves; by
judging over again that Order which ye have ordain'd *to
regulate Printing. That no Book, pamphlet, or paper shall be
henceforth Printed, unlesse the same be first approv'd and*
5 *licenc't by such,* or at least one of such as shall be thereto appointed. For that part which preserves justly every mans
Copy to himselfe, or provides for the poor, I touch not, only
wish they be not made pretenses to abuse and persecute honest and painfull Men, who offend not in either of these par-
10 ticulars. But that other clause of Licencing Books, which we
thought had dy'd with his brother *quadragesimal* and *matrimonial* when the Prelats expir'd, I shall now attend with such
a Homily, as shall lay before ye, first the inventors of it to bee
those whom ye will be loath to own; next what is to be
15 thought in generall of reading, what ever sort the Books be;
and that this Order avails nothing to the suppressing of scandalous, seditious, and libellous Books, which were mainly
intended to be supprest. Last, that it will be primely to the
discouragement of all learning, and the stop of Truth, not
20 only by disexercising and blunting our abilities in what we
know already, but by hindring and cropping the discovery
that might bee yet further made both in religious and civill
Wisdome.

I deny not, but that it is of greatest concernment in the
25 Church and Commonwealth, to have a vigilant eye how
Bookes demeane themselves as well as men; and thereafter to
confine, imprison, and do sharpest justice on them as male-
factors: For Books are not absolutely dead things, but doe

contain a potencie of life in them to be as active as that soule was whose progeny they are; nay they do preserve as in a violl the purest efficacie and extraction of that living intellect that bred them. I know they are as lively, and as vigorously
5 productive, as those fabulous Dragons teeth; and being sown up and down, may chance to spring up armed men. And yet on the other hand unlesse warinesse be us'd, as good almost kill a Man as kill a good Book; who kills a Man kills a reasonable creature, Gods Image; but hee who destroyes a good
10 Booke, kills reason it selfe, kills the Image of God, as it were in the eye. Many a man lives a burden to the Earth; but a good Booke is the pretious life-blood of a master spirit, imbalm'd and treasur'd up on purpose to a life beyond life. 'Tis true, no age can restore a life, whereof perhaps there is no
15 great losse; and revolutions of ages doe not oft recover the losse of a rejected truth, for the want of which whole Nations fare the worse. We should be wary therefore what persecution we raise against the living labours of publick men, how we spill that season'd life of man preserv'd and stor'd up in
20 Books; since we see a kinde of homicide may be thus committed, sometimes a martyrdome, and if it extend to the whole impression, a kinde of massacre, whereof the execution ends not in the slaying of an elementall life, but strikes at that ethereall and fift essence, the breath of reason it selfe,
25 slaies an immortality rather then a life. But lest I should be condemn'd of introducing licence, while I oppose Licencing, I refuse not the paines to be so much Historicall, as will serve to shew what hath been done by ancient and famous Com-

monwealths, against this disorder, till the very time that this
project of licencing crept out of the *Inquisition,* was catcht
up by our Prelates, and hath caught some of our Presbyters.

In *Athens* where Books and Wits were ever busier then in
5 any other part of *Greece,* I finde but only two sorts of writings which the Magistrate car'd to take notice of; those either
blasphemous and Atheisticall, or Libellous. Thus the Books
of *Protagoras* were by the Judges of *Areopagus* commanded
to be burnt, and himselfe banisht the territory for a discourse
10 begun with his confessing not to know *whether there were
gods, or whether not:* And against defaming, it was decreed
that none should be traduc'd by name, as was the manner of
Vetus Comœdia, whereby we may guesse how they censur'd
libelling: And this course was quick enough, as *Cicero* writes,
15 to quell both the desperate wits of other Atheists, and the
open way of defaming, as the event shew'd. Of other sects
and opinions though tending to voluptuousnesse, and the
denying of divine providence they tooke no heed. Therefore
we do not read that either *Epicurus,* or that libertine school
20 of *Cyrene,* or what the *Cynick* impudence utter'd, was ever
question'd by the Laws. Neither is it recorded that the writings of those old Comedians were supprest, though the acting
of them were forbid; and that *Plato* commended the reading
of *Aristophanes* the loosest of them all, to his royall scholler
25 *Dionysius,* is commonly known, and may be excus'd, if holy
Chrysostome, as is reported, nightly studied so much the
same Author and had the art to cleanse a scurrilous vehemence
into the stile of a rousing Sermon. That other leading City

of *Greece, Lacedæmon,* considering that *Lycurgus* their Law-giver was so addicted to elegant learning, as to have been the first that brought out of *Ionia* the scatter'd workes of *Homer,* and sent the Poet *Thales* from *Creet* to prepare and mollifie 5 the *Spartan* surlinesse with his smooth songs and odes, the better to plant among them law and civility, it is to be won-der'd how muselesse and unbookish they were, minding nought but the feats of Warre. There needed no licencing of Books among them for they dislik'd all, but their owne *La-* 10 *conick Apothegms,* and took a slight occasion to chase *Ar-chilochus* out of their City, perhaps for composing in a higher straine then their owne souldierly ballats and roundels could reach to: Or if it were for his broad verses, they were not therein so cautious, but they were as dissolute in their pro-15 miscuous conversing; whence *Euripides* affirmes in *Andro-mache,* that their women were all unchaste. Thus much may give us light after what sort Bookes were prohibited among the Greeks. The Romans also for many ages train'd up only to a military roughnes, resembling most the *Lacedæmonian* 20 guise, knew of learning little but what their twelve Tables, and the *Pontifick* College with their *Augurs* and *Flamins* taught them in Religion and Law, so unacquainted with other learning, that when *Carneades* and *Critolaus,* with the *Stoick Diogenes* comming Embassadors to *Rome,* tooke 25 thereby occasion to give the City a tast of their Philosophy, they were suspected for seducers by no lesse a man then *Cato* the Censor, who mov'd it in the Senat to dismisse them speed-ily, and to banish all such *Attick* bablers out of *Italy.* But

Scipio and others of the noblest Senators withstood him and
his old *Sabin* austerity; honour'd and admir'd the men; and
the Censor himself at last in his old age fell to the study of
that whereof before hee was so scrupulous. And yet at the
5 same time *Nævius* and *Plautus* the first Latine comedians
had fill'd the City with all the borrow'd Scenes of *Menander*
and *Philemon*. Then began to be consider'd there also what
was to be don to libellous books and Authors; for *Nævius*
was quickly cast into prison for his unbridl'd pen, and re-
10 leas'd by the *Tribunes* upon his recantation: We read also
that libels were burnt, and the makers punisht by *Augustus*.
The like severity no doubt was us'd if ought were impiously
writt'n against their esteemed gods. Except in these two
points, how the world went in Books, the Magistrat kept no
15 reckning. And therefore *Lucretius* without impeachment
versifies his Epicurism to *Memmius,* and had the honour to
be set forth the second time by *Cicero* so great a father of the
Commonwealth; although himselfe disputes against that
opinion in his own writings. Nor was the Satyricall sharp-
20 nesse, or naked plainnes of *Lucilius,* or *Catullus,* or *Flaccus,*
by any order prohibited. And for matters of State, the story
of *Titus Livius,* though it extoll'd that part which *Pompey*
held, was not therefore supprest by *Octavius Cæsar* of the
other Faction. But that *Naso* was by him banisht in his old
25 age, for the wanton Poems of his youth, was but a meer covert of State over some secret cause: and besides, the Books
were neither banisht nor call'd in. From hence we shall meet
with little else but tyranny in the Roman Empire, that we

may not marvell, if not so often bad, as good Books were silenc't. I shall therefore deem to have bin large anough in producing what among the ancients was punishable to write, save only which, all other arguments were free to treat on.

5 By this time the Emperors were become Christians, whose discipline in this point I doe not finde to have bin more severe then what was formerly in practice. The Books of those whom they took to be grand Hereticks were examin'd, refuted, and condemn'd in the generall Councels; and not till
10 then were prohibited, or burnt by autority of the Emperor. As for the writings of Heathen authors, unlesse they were plaine invectives against Christianity, as those of *Porphyrius* and *Proclus,* they met with no interdict that can be cited, till about the year 400. in a *Carthaginian* Councel, wherein Bish-
15 ops themselves were forbid to read the Books of Gentiles, but Heresies they might read: while others long before them on the contrary scrupl'd more the Books of Hereticks, then of Gentiles. And that the primitive Councels and Bishops were wont only to declare what Books were not commendable,
20 passing no furder, but leaving it to each ones conscience to read or to lay by, till after the yeare 800. is observ'd already by *Padre Paolo* the great unmasker of the *Trentine* Councel. After which time the Popes of *Rome* engrossing what they pleas'd of Politicall rule into their owne hands, extended their
25 dominion over mens eyes, as they had before over their judgements, burning and prohibiting to be read, what they fansied not; yet sparing in their censures, and the Books not many which they so dealt with: till *Martin* the 5. by his Bull not

only prohibited, but was the first that excommunicated the
reading of hereticall Books; for about that time *Wicklef* and
Husse growing terrible, were they who first drove the Papall
Court to a stricter policy of prohibiting. Which cours *Leo* the
5 10, and his successors follow'd, untill the Councell of Trent,
and the Spanish Inquisition engendring together brought
forth, or perfeted those Catalogues, and expurging Indexes
that rake through the entralls of many an old good Author,
with a violation wors then any could be offer'd to his tomb.
10 Nor did they stay in matters Hereticall, but any subject that
was not to their palat, they either condemn'd in a prohibition,
or had it strait into the new Purgatory of an Index. To fill up
the measure of encroachment, their last invention was to ordain that no Book, pamphlet, or paper should be Printed (as
15 if S. *Peter* had bequeath'd them the keys of the Presse also
out of Paradise) unlesse it were approv'd and licenc't under
the hands of 2 or 3 glutton Friers. For example:

Let the Chancellor *Cini* be pleas'd to see if in this present
    work be contain'd ought that may withstand the Print-
20   ing,

Vincent Rabatta Vicar of *Florence.*

I have seen this present work, and finde nothing athwart
    the Catholick faith and good manners: In witnesse
    whereof I have given, &c.

25   *Nicolò Cini* Chancellor of *Florence.*

Attending the precedent relation, it is allow'd that this
    present work of *Davanzati* may be Printed,

Vincent Rabatta, &c.

It may be Printed, *July* 15.

  Friar *Simon Mompei d' Amelia* Chancellor of the
   holy office in *Florence.*

Sure they have a conceit, if he of the bottomlesse pit had not
5 long since broke prison, that this quadruple exorcism would
barre him down. I feare their next designe will be to get into
their custody the licencing of that which they say *Claudius*
intended, but went not through with. Voutsafe to see another
of their forms the Roman stamp:

10   *Imprimatur,* If it seem good to the reverend Master of the
   holy Palace,   *Belcastro* Vicegerent.
  Imprimatur

   Friar *Nicolò Rodolphi* Master of the holy Palace.

Sometimes 5 *Imprimaturs* are seen together dialogue-wise in
15 the Piatza of one Title page, complementing and ducking
each to other with their shav'n reverences, whether the Author, who stands by in perplexity at the foot of his Epistle,
shall to the Presse or to the spunge. These are the prety re-
sponsories, these are the deare Antiphonies that so bewitcht
20 of late our Prelats, and their Chaplaines with the goodly
Eccho they made; and besotted us to the gay imitation of a
lordly *Imprimatur,* one from Lambeth house, another from
the West end of *Pauls;* so apishly Romanizing, that the word
of command still was set downe in Latine; as if the learned
25 Grammaticall pen that wrote it, would cast no ink without
Latine: or perhaps, as they thought, because no vulgar tongue

*Quo veniam daret flatum crepitumque ventris in convivio emittendi.
Sueton. in Claudio.

was worthy to expresse the pure conceit of an *Imprimatur;* but rather, as I hope, for that our English, the language of men ever famous, and formost in the atchievements of liberty, will not easily finde servile letters anow to spell such a dicta-
5 torie presumption English. And thus ye have the Inventors and the originall of Book-licencing ript up, and drawn as lineally as any pedigree. We have it not, that can be heard of, from any ancient State, or politie, or Church, nor by any Statute left us by our Ancestors elder or later; nor from the
10 moderne custom of any reformed Citty, or Church abroad; but from the most Antichristian Councel, and the most tyran-nous Inquisition that ever inquir'd. Till then Books were ever as freely admitted into the World as any other birth; the issue of the brain was no more stifl'd then the issue of the
15 womb: no envious *Juno* sate cros-leg'd over the nativity of any mans intellectuall off-spring; but if it prov'd a Monster, who denies, but that it was justly burnt, or sunk into the Sea. But that a Book in wors condition then a peccant soul, should be to stand before a Jury ere it be borne to the World, and
20 undergo yet in darknesse the judgement of *Radamanth* and his Collegues, ere it can passe the ferry backward into light, was never heard before, till that mysterious iniquity provokt and troubl'd at the first entrance of Reformation, sought out new limbo's and new hells wherein they might include our
25 Books also within the number of their damned. And this was the rare morsell so officiously snatcht up, and so ilfavourdly imitated by our inquisiturient Bishops, and the attendant mi-norites their Chaplains. That ye like not now these most cer-

tain Authors of this licencing order, and that all sinister intention was farre distant from your thoughts, when ye were importun'd the passing it, all men who know the integrity of your
actions, and how ye honour Truth, will clear yee readily.

5 But some will say, What though the Inventors were bad,
the thing for all that may be good? It may so; yet if that
thing be no such deep invention, but obvious, and easie for
any man to light on, and yet best and wisest Commonwealths
through all ages, and occasions have forborne to use it, and
10 falsest seducers, and oppressors of men were the first who
tooke it up, and to no other purpose but to obstruct and hinder the first approach of Reformation; I am of those who beleeve, it will be a harder alchymy then *Lullius* ever knew, to
sublimat any good use out of such an invention. Yet this only
15 is what I request to gain from this reason, that it may be held
a dangerous and suspicious fruit, as certainly it deserves, for
the tree that bore it, untill I can dissect one by one the properties it has. But I have first to finish, as was propounded,
what is to be thought in generall of reading Books, what ever
20 sort they be, and whether be more the benefit, or the harm
that thence proceeds?

Not to insist upon the examples of *Moses, Daniel* & *Paul*,
who were skilfull in all the learning of the Ægyptians, Cal-
deans, and Greeks, which could not probably be without
25 reading their Books of all sorts, in *Paul* especially, who
thought it no defilement to insert into holy Scripture the sentences of three Greek Poets, and one of them a Tragedian,
the question was, notwithstanding sometimes controverted

among the Primitive Doctors, but with great odds on that
side which affirm'd it both lawfull and profitable, as was
then evidently perceiv'd, when *Julian* the Apostat, and sut-
tlest enemy to our faith, made a decree forbidding Christians
5 the study of heathen learning: for, said he, they wound us
with our own weapons, and with our owne arts and sciences
they overcome us. And indeed the Christians were put so to
their shifts by this crafty means, and so much in danger to
decline into all ignorance, that the two *Apollinarii* were fain
10 as a man may say, to coin all the seven liberall Sciences out of
the Bible, reducing it into divers forms of Orations, Poems,
Dialogues, ev'n to the calculating of a new Christian Grammar. But saith the Historian *Socrates,* The providence of God
provided better then the industry of *Apollinarius* and his son,
15 by taking away that illiterat law with the life of him who devis'd it. So great an injury they then held it to be depriv'd of
Hellenick learning; and thought it a persecution more un-
dermining, and secretly decaying the Church, then the open
cruelty of *Decius* or *Dioclesian*. And perhaps it was the same
20 politick drift that the Divell whipt St. *Jerom* in a lenten
dream, for reading *Cicero;* or else it was a fantasm bred by
the feaver which had then seis'd him. For had an Angel bin
his discipliner, unlesse it were for dwelling too much upon
Ciceronianisms, & had chastiz'd the reading, not the vanity,
25 it had bin plainly partiall; first to correct him for grave
Cicero, and not for scurrill *Plautus* whom he confesses to
have bin reading not long before; next to correct him only,
and let so many more ancient Fathers wax old in those pleas-

ant and florid studies without the lash of such a tutoring ap-
parition; insomuch that *Basil* teaches how some good use
may be made of *Margites* a sportfull Poem, not now extant,
writ by *Homer;* and why not then of *Morgante* an Italian
5 Romanze much to the same purpose. But if it be agreed we
shall be try'd by visions, there is a vision recorded by *Euse-*
bius far ancienter then this tale of *Jerom* to the Nun *Eusto-*
chium, and besides has nothing of a feavor in it. *Dionysius*
Alexandrinus was about the year 240, a person of great name
10 in the Church for piety and learning, who had wont to avail
himself much against hereticks by being conversant in their
Books; untill a certain Presbyter laid it scrupulously to his
conscience, how he durst venture himselfe among those defil-
ing volumes. The worthy man loath to give offence fell into
15 a new debate with himselfe what was to be thought; when
suddenly a vision sent from God, it is his own Epistle that so
averrs it, confirm'd him in these words: Read any books what
ever come to thy hands, for thou art sufficient both to judge
aright, and to examine each matter. To this revelation he as-
20 sented the sooner, as he confesses, because it was answerable
to that of the Apostle to the Thessalonians, Prove all things,
hold fast that which is good. And he might have added another remarkable saying of the same Author; To the pure
all things are pure, not only meats and drinks, but all kinde
25 of knowledge whether of good or evill; the knowledge cannot defile, nor consequently the books, if the will and conscience be not defil'd. For books are as meats and viands are;
some of good, some of evill substance; and yet God in that

unapocryphall vision, said without exception, Rise *Peter,* kill
and eat, leaving the choice to each mans discretion. Whole-
some meats to a vitiated stomack differ little or nothing from
unwholesome; and best books to a naughty mind are not un-
5 appliable to occasions of evill. Bad meats will scarce breed
good nourishment in the healthiest concoction; but herein
the difference is of bad books, that they to a discreet and judicious Reader serve in many respects to discover, to confute,
to forewarn, and to illustrate. Wherof what better witnes can
10 ye expect I should produce, then one of your own now sitting
in Parlament, the chief of learned men reputed in this Land,
Mr. *Selden,* whose volume of naturall & national laws
proves, not only by great autorities brought together, but by
exquisite reasons and theorems almost mathematically de-
15 monstrative, that all opinions, yea errors, known, read, and
collated, are of main service & assistance toward the speedy
attainment of what is truest. I conceive therefore, that when
God did enlarge the universall diet of mans body, saving
ever the rules of temperance, he then also, as before, left ar-
20 bitrary the dyeting and repasting of our minds; as wherein
every mature man might have to exercise his owne leading
capacity. How great a vertue is temperance, how much of
moment through the whole life of man? yet God committs
the managing so great a trust, without particular Law or pre-
25 scription, wholly to the demeanour of every grown man.
And therefore when he himself tabl'd the Jews from heaven,
that Omer which was every mans daily portion of Manna, is
computed to have bin more then might have well suffic'd the

heartiest feeder thrice as many meals. For those actions which enter into a man, rather then issue out of him, and therefore defile not, God uses not to captivat under a perpetuall childhood of prescription, but trusts him with the
5 gift of reason to be his own chooser; there were but little work left for preaching, if law and compulsion should grow so fast upon those things which hertofore were govern'd only by exhortation. *Salomon* informs us that much reading is a wearines to the flesh; but neither he, nor other inspir'd
10 author tells us that such, or such reading is unlawfull: yet certainly had God thought good to limit us herein, it had bin much more expedient to have told us what was unlawfull, then what was wearisome. As for the burning of those Ephesian books by St. *Pauls* converts, tis reply'd the books were
15 magick, the Syriack so renders them. It was a privat act, a voluntary act, and leaves us to a voluntary imitation: the men in remorse burnt those books which were their own; the Magistrat by this example is not appointed: these men practiz'd the books, another might perhaps have read them
20 in some sort usefully. Good and evill we know in the field of this World grow up together almost inseparably; and the knowledge of good is so involv'd and interwoven with the knowledge of evill, and in so many cunning resemblances hardly to be discern'd, that those confused seeds which were
25 impos'd on *Psyche* as an incessant labour to cull out, and sort asunder, were not more intermixt. It was from out the rinde of one apple tasted, that the knowledge of good and evill as two twins cleaving together leapt forth into the World. And

perhaps this is that doom which *Adam* fell into of knowing good and evill, that is to say of knowing good by evill.
As therefore the state of man now is; what wisdome can
there be to choose, what continence to forbeare without the
5 knowledge of evill? He that can apprehend and consider
vice with all her baits and seeming pleasures, and yet abstain,
and yet distinguish, and yet prefer that which is truly better,
he is the true wayfaring Christian. I cannot praise a fugitive
and cloister'd vertue, unexercis'd & unbreath'd, that never
10 sallies out and sees her adversary, but slinks out of the race,
where that immortall garland is to be run for, not without
dust and heat. Assuredly we bring not innocence into the
world, we bring impurity much rather: that which purifies
us is triall, and triall is by what is contrary. That vertue
15 therefore which is but a youngling in the contemplation of
evill, and knows not the utmost that vice promises to her followers, and rejects it, is but a blank vertue, not a pure; her
whitenesse is but an excrementall whitenesse; Which was
the reason why our sage and serious Poet *Spencer*, whom I
20 dare be known to think a better teacher then *Scotus* or
Aquinas, describing true temperance under the person of
Guion, brings him in with his palmer through the cave of
Mammon, and the bowr of earthly blisse that he might see
and know, and yet abstain. Since therefore the knowledge
25 and survay of vice is in this world so necessary to the constituting of human vertue, and the scanning of error to the confirmation of truth, how can we more safely, and with lesse
danger scout into the regions of sin and falsity then by read-

ing all manner of tractats, and hearing all manner of reason?
And this is the benefit which may be had of books promis-
cuously read. But of the harm that may result hence three
kinds are usually reckn'd. First, is fear'd the infection that
5 may spread; but then all human learning and controversie in
religious points must remove out of the world, yea the Bible
it selfe; for that oftimes relates blasphemy not nicely, it describes the carnall sense of wicked men not unelegantly, it
brings in holiest men passionately murmuring against provi-
10 dence through all the arguments of *Epicurus:* in other great
disputes it answers dubiously and darkly to the common
reader: And ask a Talmudist what ails the modesty of his
marginall Keri, that *Moses* and all the Prophets cannot perswade him to pronounce the textuall Chetiv. For these causes
15 we all know the Bible it selfe put by the Papist into the first
rank of prohibited books. The ancientest Fathers must be
next remov'd, as *Clement* of *Alexandria,* and that *Eusebian*
book of Evangelick preparation, transmitting our ears
through a hoard of heathenish obscenities to receive the Gos-
20 pel. Who finds not that *Irenæus, Epiphanius, Jerom,* and
others discover more heresies then they well confute, and
that oft for heresie which is the truer opinion. Nor boots it
to say for these, and all the heathen Writers of greatest infection, if it must be thought so, with whom is bound up the
25 life of human learning, that they writ in an unknown tongue,
so long as we are sure those languages are known as well to
the worst of men, who are both most able, and most diligent
to instill the poison they suck, first into the Courts of Princes,

acquainting them with the choicest delights, and criticisms
of sin. As perhaps did that *Petronius* whom *Nero* call'd his
Arbiter, the Master of his revels; and that notorious ribald
of *Arezzo,* dreaded, and yet dear to the Italian Courtiers.
5 I name not him for posterities sake, whom *Harry* the 8.
nam'd in merriment his Vicar of hell. By which compendious way all the contagion that foreine books can infuse,
will finde a passage to the people farre easier and shorter then
an Indian voyage, though it could be sail'd either by the
10 North of *Cataio* Eastward, or of *Canada* Westward, while
our Spanish licencing gags the English Presse never so severely. But on the other side that infection which is from
books of controversie in Religion, is more doubtfull and
dangerous to the learned, then to the ignorant; and yet those
15 books must be permitted untoucht by the licencer. It will be
hard to instance where any ignorant man hath bin ever seduc't by Papisticall book in English, unlesse it were commended and expounded to him by some of that Clergy: and
indeed all such tractats whether false or true are as the
20 Prophesie of *Isaiah* was to the *Eunuch,* not to be *understood
without a guide.* But of our Priests and Doctors how many
have bin corrupted by studying the comments of Jesuits and
Sorbonists, and how fast they could transfuse that corruption into the people, our experience is both late and sad. It
25 is not forgot, since the acute and distinct *Arminius* was per-
verted meerly by the perusing of a namelesse discours writt'n
at *Delf,* which at first he took in hand to confute. Seeing
therefore that those books, & those in great abundance which

are likeliest to taint both life and doctrine, cannot be supprest
without the fall of learning, and of all ability in disputation,
and that these books of either sort are most and soonest
catching to the learned, from whom to the common people
5 what ever is hereticall or dissolute may quickly be convey'd,
and that evill manners are as perfectly learnt without books
a thousand other ways which cannot be stopt, and evill doctrine not with books can propagate, except a teacher guide,
which he might also doe without writing, and so beyond
10 prohibiting, I am not able to unfold, how this cautelous enterprise of licencing can be exempted from the number of
vain and impossible attempts. And he who were pleasantly
dispos'd, could not well avoid to lik'n it to the exploit of
that gallant man who thought to pound up the crows by
15 shutting his Parkgate. Besides another inconvenience, if
learned men be the first receivers out of books, & dispredders
both of vice and error, how shall the licencers themselves be
confided in, unlesse we can conferr upon them, or they assume to themselves above all others in the Land, the grace of
20 infallibility, and uncorruptednesse? And again, if it be true,
that a wise man like a good refiner can gather gold out of
the drossiest volume, and that a fool will be a fool with the
best book, yea or without book, there is no reason that we
should deprive a wise man of any advantage to his wisdome,
25 while we seek to restrain from a fool, that which being restrain'd will be no hindrance to his folly. For if there should
be so much exactnesse always us'd to keep that from him
which is unfit for his reading, we should in the judgement of

Aristotle not only, but of *Salomon,* and of our Saviour, not
voutsafe him good precepts, and by consequence not willingly admit him to good books; as being certain that a wise
man will make better use of an idle pamphlet, then a fool
5 will do of sacred Scripture. 'Tis next alleg'd we must not
expose our selves to temptations without necessity, and next
to that, not imploy our time in vain things. To both these
objections one answer will serve, out of the grounds already
laid, that to all men such books are not temptations, nor
10 vanities; but usefull drugs and materialls wherewith to
temper and compose effective and strong med'cins, which
mans life cannot want. The rest, as children and childish
men, who have not the art to qualifie and prepare these
working minerals, well may be exhorted to forbear, but
15 hinder'd forcibly they cannot be by all the licencing that
Sainted Inquisition could ever yet contrive; which is what
I promis'd to deliver next, That this order of licencing con-
duces nothing to the end for which it was fram'd; and hath
almost prevented me by being clear already while thus
20 much hath bin explaining. See the ingenuity of Truth, who
when she gets a free and willing hand, opens her self faster,
then the pace of method and discours can overtake her. It
was the task which I began with, To shew that no Nation,
or well instituted State, if they valu'd books at all, did ever
25 use this way of licencing; and it might be answer'd, that this
is a piece of prudence lately discover'd. To which I return,
that as it was a thing slight and obvious to think on, so if it
had bin difficult to finde out, there wanted not among them

long since, who suggested such a cours; which they not following, leave us a pattern of their judgement, that it was not
the not knowing, but the not approving, which was the
cause of their not using it. *Plato,* a man of high autority
5 indeed, but least of all for his Commonwealth, in the book
of his laws, which no City ever yet receiv'd, fed his fancie
with making many edicts to his ayrie Burgomasters, which
they who otherwise admire him, wish had bin rather buried
and excus'd in the *genial* cups of an *Academick* night-
10 sitting. By which laws he seems to tolerat no kind of learning, but by unalterable decree, consisting most of practicall
traditions, to the attainment whereof a Library of smaller
bulk then his own dialogues would be abundant. And there
also enacts that no Poet should so much as read to any privat
15 man, what he had writt'n, untill the Judges and Law-keep-
ers had seen it, and allow'd it: But that *Plato* meant this Law
peculiarly to that Commonwealth which he had imagin'd,
and to no other, is evident. Why was he not else a Law-giver
to himself, but a transgressor, and to be expell'd by his own
20 Magistrats; both for the wanton epigrams and dialogues
which he made, and his perpetuall reading of *Sophron
Mimus,* and *Aristophanes,* books of grossest infamy, and also
for commending the latter of them though he were the malicious libeller of his chief friends, to be read by the Tyrant
25 *Dionysius,* who had little need of such trash to spend his time
on? But that he knew this licencing of Poems had reference
and dependence to many other proviso's there set down in
his fancied republic, which in this world could have no place:

and so neither he himself, nor any Magistrat, or City ever
imitated that cours, which tak'n apart from those other col-
laterall injunctions must needs be vain and fruitlesse. For if
they fell upon one kind of strictnesse, unlesse their care were
5 equall to regulat all other things of like aptnes to corrupt the
mind, that single endeavour they knew would be but a fond
labour; to shut and fortifie one gate against corruption, and
be necessitated to leave others round about wide open. If
we think to regulat Printing, thereby to rectifie manners,
10 we must regulat all recreations and pastimes, all that is delightfull to man. No musick must be heard, no song be set or
sung, but what is grave and *Dorick*. There must be licencing
dancers, that no gesture, motion, or deportment be taught
our youth but what by their allowance shall be thought
15 honest; for such *Plato* was provided of; It will ask more then
the work of twenty licencers to examin all the lutes, the vio-
lins, and the ghittarrs in every house; they must not be
suffer'd to prattle as they doe, but must be licenc'd what they
may say. And who shall silence all the airs and madrigalls,
20 that whisper softnes in chambers? The Windows also, and
the *Balcone's* must be thought on, there are shrewd books,
with dangerous Frontispices set to sale; who shall prohibit
them, shall twenty licencers? The villages also must have
their visitors to enquire what lectures the bagpipe and the
25 rebbeck reads ev'n to the ballatry, and the gammuth of every
municipal fidler, for these are the Countrymans *Arcadia's*
and his *Monte Mayors*. Next, what more Nationall corruption, for which England hears ill abroad, then houshold

gluttony; who shall be the rectors of our daily rioting? and
what shall be done to inhibit the multitudes that frequent
those houses where drunk'nes is sold and harbour'd? Our
garments also should be referr'd to the licencing of some
5 more sober work-masters to see them cut into a lesse wanton
garb. Who shall regulat all the mixt conversation of our
youth, male and female together, as is the fashion of this
Country, who shall still appoint what shall be discours'd,
what presum'd, and no furder? Lastly, who shall forbid and
10 separat all idle resort, all evill company? These things will
be, and must be; but how they shall be lest hurtfull, how lest
enticing, herein consists the grave and governing wisdom of
a State. To sequester out of the world into *Atlantick* and
Eutopian polities, which never can be drawn into use, will
15 not mend our condition; but to ordain wisely as in this world
of evill, in the midd'st whereof God hath plac't us unavoidably. Nor is it *Plato's* licencing of books will doe this, which
necessarily pulls along with it so many other kinds of licencing, as will make us all both ridiculous and weary, and yet
20 frustrat; but those unwritt'n, or at least unconstraining laws
of vertuous education, religious and civill nurture, which
Plato there mentions, as the bonds and ligaments of the
Commonwealth, the pillars and the sustainers of every
writt'n Statute; these they be which will bear chief sway
25 in such matters as these, when all licencing will be easily
eluded. Impunity and remissenes, for certain are the bane of
a Commonwealth, but here the great art lyes to discern in
what the law is to bid restraint and punishment, and in what

things perswasion only is to work. If every action which is
good, or evill in man at ripe years, were to be under pittance,
and prescription, and compulsion, what were vertue but a
name, what praise could be then due to well-doing, what
5 grammercy to be sober, just or continent? many there be
that complain of divin Providence for suffering *Adam* to
transgresse, foolish tongues! when God gave him reason, he
gave him freedom to choose, for reason is but choosing; he
had bin else a meer artificiall *Adam,* such an *Adam* as he is
10 in the motions. We our selves esteem not of that obedience,
or love, or gift, which is of force: God therefore left him free,
set before him a provoking object, ever almost in his eyes;
herein consisted his merit, herein the right of his reward, the
praise of his abstinence. Wherefore did he creat passions
15 within us, pleasures round about us, but that these rightly
temper'd are the very ingredients of vertu? They are not
skilfull considerers of human things, who imagin to remove
sin by removing the matter of sin; for, besides that it is a
huge heap increasing under the very act of diminishing,
20 though some part of it may for a time be withdrawn from
some persons, it cannot from all, in such a universall thing
as books are; and when this is done, yet the sin remains
entire. Though ye take from a covetous man all his treasure,
he has yet one jewell left, ye cannot bereave him of his covet-
25 ousnesse. Banish all objects of lust, shut up all youth into
the severest discipline that can be exercis'd in any hermitage,
ye cannot make them chaste, that came not thither so: such
great care and wisdom is requir'd to the right managing of

this point. Suppose we could expell sin by this means; look
how much we thus expell of sin, so much we expell of vertue: for the matter of them both is the same; remove that,
and ye remove them both alike. This justifies the high prov-
5 idence of God, who though he command us temperance,
justice, continence, yet powrs out before us ev'n to a pro-
fusenes all desirable things, and gives us minds that can
wander beyond all limit and satiety. Why should we then
affect a rigor contrary to the manner of God and of nature,
10 by abridging or scanting those means, which books freely
permitted are, both to the triall of vertue, and the exercise of
truth. It would be better done to learn that the law must
needs be frivolous which goes to restrain things, uncertainly
and yet equally working to good, and to evill. And were I
15 the chooser, a dram of well-doing should be preferr'd before
many times as much the forcible hindrance of evill-doing.
For God sure esteems the growth and compleating of one
vertuous person, more then the restraint of ten vitious. And
albeit what ever thing we hear or see, sitting, walking, trav-
20 elling, or conversing may be fitly call'd our book, and is of
the same effect that writings are, yet grant the thing to be
prohibited were only books, it appears that this order hitherto is far insufficient to the end which it intends. Do we not
see, not once or oftner, but weekly that continu'd Court-
25 libell against the Parlament and City, Printed, as the wet
sheets can witnes, and dispers't among us, for all that licencing can doe? yet this is the prime service a man would think,
wherein this order should give proof of it self. If it were ex-

ecuted, you'l say. But certain, if execution be remisse or
blindfold now, and in this particular, what will it be hereafter, and in other books. If then the order shall not be vain
and frustrat, behold a new labour, Lords and Commons, ye
5 must repeal and proscribe all scandalous and unlicenc't
books already printed and divulg'd; after ye have drawn
them up into a list, that all may know which are condemn'd,
and which not; and ordain that no forrein books be deliver'd
out of custody, till they have bin read over. This office will
10 require the whole time of not a few overseers, and those no
vulgar men. There be also books which are partly usefull
and excellent, partly culpable and pernicious; this work will
ask as many more officials, to make expurgations, and ex-
punctions, that the Commonwealth of learning be not dam-
15 nify'd. In fine, when the multitude of books encrease upon
their hands, ye must be fain to catalogue all those Printers
who are found frequently offending, and forbidd the importation of their whole suspected *typography*. In a word, that
this your order may be exact, and not deficient, ye must re-
20 form it perfectly according to the model of *Trent* and *Sevil,*
which I know ye abhorre to doe. Yet though ye should con-
discend to this, which God forbid, the order still would be
but fruitlesse and defective to that end whereto ye meant it.
If to prevent sects and schisms, who is so unread or so un-
25 catechis'd in story, that hath not heard of many sects refus-
ing books as a hindrance, and preserving their doctrine
unmixt for many ages, only by unwritt'n traditions. The
Christian faith, for that was once a schism, is not unknown

to have spread all over *Asia,* ere any Gospel or Epistle was
seen in writing. If the amendment of manners be aym'd at,
look into Italy and Spain, whether those places be one scruple
the better, the honester, the wiser, the chaster, since all the
5 inquisitionall rigor that hath bin executed upon books.

Another reason, whereby to make it plain that this order
will misse the end it seeks, consider by the quality which
ought to be in every licencer. It cannot be deny'd but that
he who is made judge to sit upon the birth, or death of books
10 whether they may be wafted into this world, or not, had
need to be a man above the common measure, both studious,
learned, and judicious; there may be else no mean mistakes
in the censure of what is passable or not; which is also no
mean injury. If he be of such worth as behoovs him, there
15 cannot be a more tedious and unpleasing journey-work, a
greater losse of time levied upon his head, then to be made
the perpetuall reader of unchosen books and pamphlets,
oftimes huge volumes. There is no book that is acceptable
unlesse at certain seasons; but to be enjoyn'd the reading of
20 that at all times, and in a hand scars legible, whereof three
pages would not down at any time in the fairest Print, is an
imposition which I cannot beleeve how he that values time,
and his own studies, or is but of a sensible nostrill should be
able to endure. In this one thing I crave leave of the present
25 licencers to be pardon'd for so thinking: who doubtlesse took
this office up, looking on it through their obedience to the
Parlament, whose command perhaps made all things seem
easie and unlaborious to them; but that this short triall hath

wearied them out already, their own expressions and excuses
to them who make so many journeys to sollicit their licence,
are testimony anough. Seeing therefore those who now pos-
sesse the imployment, by all evident signs wish themselves
5 well ridd of it, and that no man of worth, none that is not a
plain unthrift of his own hours is ever likely to succeed them,
except he mean to put himself to the salary of a Presse-cor-
rector, we may easily foresee what kind of licencers we are to
expect hereafter, either ignorant, imperious, and remisse, or
10 basely pecuniary. This is what I had to shew wherein this
order cannot conduce to that end, whereof it bears the intention.

I lastly proceed from the no good it can do, to the manifest
hurt it causes, in being first the greatest discouragement and
15 affront, that can be offer'd to learning and to learned men.
It was the complaint and lamentation of Prelats, upon every
least breath of a motion to remove pluralities, and distribute
more equally Church revennu's, that then all learning would
be for ever dasht and discourag'd. But as for that opinion, I
20 never found cause to think that the tenth part of learning
stood or fell with the Clergy: nor could I ever but hold it for
a sordid and unworthy speech of any Churchman who had a
competency left him. If therefore ye be loath to dishearten
utterly and discontent, not the mercenary crew of false pre-
25 tenders to learning, but the free and ingenuous sort of such
as evidently were born to study, and love lerning for it self,
not for lucre, or any other end, but the service of God and of
truth, and perhaps that lasting fame and perpetuity of praise

which God and good men have consented shall be the reward
of those whose publisht labours advance the good of mankind, then know, that so far to distrust the judgement & the
honesty of one who hath but a common repute in learning,
5 and never yet offended, as not to count him fit to print his
mind without a tutor and examiner, lest he should drop a
scism, or something of corruption, is the greatest displeasure
and indignity to a free and knowing spirit that can be put
upon him. What advantage is it to be a man over it is to be
10 a boy at school, if we have only scapt the ferular, to come
under the fescu of an *Imprimatur?* if serious and elaborat
writings, as if they were no more then the theam of a Grammar lad under his Pedagogue must not be utter'd without the
cursory eyes of a temporizing and extemporizing licencer.
15 He who is not trusted with his own actions, his drift not being known to be evill, and standing to the hazard of law and
penalty, has no great argument to think himself reputed in
the Commonwealth wherin he was born, for other then a
fool or a foreiner. When a man writes to the world, he sum-
20 mons up all his reason and deliberation to assist him; he
searches, meditats, is industrious, and likely consults and
conferrs with his judicious friends; after all which done he
takes himself to be inform'd in what he writes, as well as any
that writ before him; if in this the most consummat act of his
25 fidelity and ripenesse, no years, no industry, no former proof
of his abilities can bring him to that state of maturity, as not
to be still mistrusted and suspected, unlesse he carry all his
considerat diligence, all his midnight watchings, and ex-

pence of *Palladian* oyl, to the hasty view of an unleasur'd
licencer, perhaps much his younger, perhaps far his inferiour
in judgement, perhaps one who never knew the labour of
book-writing, and if he be not repulst, or slighted, must ap-
5 pear in Print like a punie with his guardian, and his censors
hand on the back of his title to be his bayl and surety, that he
is no idiot, or seducer, it cannot be but a dishonor and dero-
gation to the author, to the book, to the priviledge and dignity
of Learning. And what if the author shall be one so copious
10 of fancie, as to have many things well worth the adding,
come into his mind after licencing, while the book is yet
under the Presse, which not seldom happ'ns to the best and
diligentest writers; and that perhaps a dozen times in one
book. The Printer dares not go beyond his licenc't copy; so
15 often then must the author trudge to his leav-giver, that those
his new insertions may be viewd; and many a jaunt will be
made, ere that licencer, for it must be the same man, can
either be found, or found at leisure; mean while either the
Presse must stand still, which is no small damage, or the
20 author loose his accuratest thoughts, & send the book forth
wors then he had made it, which to a diligent writer is the
greatest melancholy and vexation that can befall. And how
can a man teach with autority, which is the life of teaching,
how can he be a Doctor in his book as he ought to be, or else
25 had better be silent, whenas all he teaches, all he delivers, is
but under the tuition, under the correction of his patriarchal
licencer to blot or alter what precisely accords not with the
hidebound humor which he calls his judgement. When every

acute reader upon the first sight of a pedantick licence, will be ready with these like words to ding the book a coits distance from him, I hate a pupil teacher, I endure not an instructer that comes to me under the wardship of an oversee-
5 ing fist. I know nothing of the licencer, but that I have his own hand here for his arrogance; who shall warrant me his judgement? The State Sir, replies the Stationer, but has a quick return, The State shall be my governours, but not my criticks; they may be mistak'n in the choice of a licencer, as
10 easily as this licencer may be mistak'n in an author: This is some common stuffe; and he might adde from Sir *Francis Bacon,* That *such authoriz'd books are but the language of the times.* For though a licencer should happ'n to be judicious more then ordnary, which will be a great jeopardy of
15 the next succession, yet his very office, and his commission enjoyns him to let passe nothing but what is vulgarly receiv'd already. Nay, which is more lamentable, if the work of any deceased author, though never so famous in his life time, and even to this day, come to their hands for licence to be Printed,
20 or Reprinted, if there be found in his book one sentence of a ventrous edge, utter'd in the height of zeal, and who knows whether it might not be the dictat of a divine Spirit, yet not suiting with every low decrepit humor of their own, though it were *Knox* himself, the Reformer of a Kingdom that spake
25 it, they will not pardon him their dash: the sense of that great man shall to all posterity be lost, for the fearfulnesse, or the presumptuous rashnesse of a perfunctory licencer. And to what an author this violence hath bin lately done, and in

what book of greatest consequence to be faithfully publisht,
I could now instance, but shall forbear till a more convenient
season. Yet if these things be not resented seriously and
timely by them who have the remedy in their power, but that
5 such iron moulds as these shall have autority to knaw out the
choisest periods of exquisitest books, and to commit such a
treacherous fraud against the orphan remainders of worthiest men after death, the more sorrow will belong to that hap-
les race of men, whose misfortune it is to have understanding.
10 Henceforth let no man care to learn, or care to be more then
worldly wise; for certainly in higher matters to be ignorant
and slothfull, to be a common stedfast dunce will be the only
pleasant life, and only in request.

And as it is a particular disesteem of every knowing per-
15 son alive, and most injurious to the writt'n labours and mon-
uments of the dead, so to me it seems an undervaluing and
vilifying of the whole Nation. I cannot set so light by all the
invention, the art, the wit, the grave and solid judgement
which is in England, as that it can be comprehended in any
20 twenty capacities how good soever, much lesse that it should
not passe except their superintendence be over it, except it be
sifted and strain'd with their strainers, that it should be un-
currant without their manuall stamp. Truth and understanding are not such wares as to be monopoliz'd and traded in by
25 tickets and statutes, and standards. We must not think to
make a staple commodity of all the knowledge in the Land,
to mark and licence it like our broad cloath, and our wooll
packs. What is it but a servitude like that impos'd by the Phil-

istims, not to be allow'd the sharpning of our own axes and
coulters, but we must repair from all quarters to twenty
licencing forges. Had any one writt'n and divulg'd erroneous things & scandalous to honest life, misusing and forfeit-
5 ing the esteem had of his reason among men, if after conviction this only censure were adjudg'd him, that he should
never henceforth write, but what were first examin'd by an
appointed officer, whose hand should be annext to passe his
credit for him, that now he might be safely read, it could
10 not be apprehended lesse then a disgracefull punishment.
Whence to include the whole Nation, and those that never
yet thus offended, under such a diffident and suspectfull prohibition, may plainly be understood what a disparagement it
is. So much the more, when as dettors and delinquents may
15 walk abroad without a keeper, but unoffensive books must
not stirre forth without a visible jaylor in thir title. Nor is it
to the common people lesse then a reproach; for if we be so
jealous over them, as that we dare not trust them with an
English pamphlet, what doe we but censure them for a giddy,
20 vitious, and ungrounded people; in such a sick and weak
estate of faith and discretion, as to be able to take nothing
down but through the pipe of a licencer. That this is care or
love of them, we cannot pretend, whenas in those Popish
places where the Laity are most hated and dispis'd the same
25 strictnes is us'd over them. Wisdom we cannot call it, because it stops but one breach of licence, nor that neither;
whenas those corruptions which it seeks to prevent, break in
faster at other dores which cannot be shut.

And in conclusion it reflects to the disrepute of our Ministers also, of whose labours we should hope better, and of the
proficiencie which thir flock reaps by them, then that after
all this light of the Gospel which is, and is to be, and all this
5 continuall preaching, they should be still frequented with
such an unprincipl'd, unedify'd, and laick rabble, as that the
whiffe of every new pamphlet should stagger them out of
thir catechism, and Christian walking. This may have much
reason to discourage the Ministers when such a low conceit
10 is had of all their exhortations, and the benefiting of their
hearers, as that they are not thought fit to be turn'd loose to
three sheets of paper without a licencer, that all the Sermons,
all the Lectures preacht, printed, vented in such numbers,
and such volumes, as have now well-nigh made all other
15 books unsalable, should not be armor anough against one
single *enchiridion,* without the castle St. *Angelo* of an *Imprimatur.*

And lest som should perswade ye, Lords and Commons,
that these arguments of lerned mens discouragement at this
20 your order, are meer flourishes, and not reall, I could recount
what I have seen and heard in other Countries, where this
kind of inquisition tyrannizes; when I have sat among their
lerned men, for that honor I had, and bin counted happy to
be born in such a place of *Philosophic* freedom, as they sup-
25 pos'd England was, while themselvs did nothing but bemoan the servil condition into which lerning amongst them
was brought; that this was it which had dampt the glory of
Italian wits; that nothing had bin there writt'n now these

many years but flattery and fustian. There it was that I found
and visited the famous *Galileo* grown old, a prisner to the
Inquisition, for thinking in Astronomy otherwise then the
Franciscan and Dominican licencers thought. And though I
5 knew that England then was groaning loudest under the
Prelaticall yoak, neverthelesse I took it as a pledge of future
happines, that other Nations were so perswaded of her liberty. Yet was it beyond my hope that those Worthies were
then breathing in her air, who should be her leaders to such
10 a deliverance, as shall never be forgott'n by any revolution of
time that this world hath to finish. When that was once begun, it was as little in my fear, that what words of complaint
I heard among lerned men of other parts utter'd against the
Inquisition, the same I should hear by as lerned men at home
15 utterd in time of Parlament against an order of licencing;
and that so generally, that when I had disclos'd my self a
companion of their discontent, I might say, if without envy,
that he whom an honest *quæstorship* had indear'd to the
Sicilians, was not more by them importun'd against *Verres,*
20 then the favourable opinion which I had among many who
honour ye, and are known and respected by ye, loaded me
with entreaties and perswasions, that I would not despair to
lay together that which just reason should bring into my
mind, toward the removal of an undeserved thraldom upon
25 lerning. That this is not therefore the disburdning of a particular fancie, but the common grievance of all those who had
prepar'd their minds and studies above the vulgar pitch to
advance truth in others, and from others to entertain it, thus

much may satisfie. And in their name I shall for neither
friend nor foe conceal what the generall murmur is; that if
it come to inquisitioning again, and licencing, and that we
are so timorous of our selvs, and so suspicious of all men, as
5 to fear each book, and the shaking of every leaf, before we
know what the contents are, if some who but of late were
little better then silenc't from preaching, shall come now to
silence us from reading, except what they please, it cannot be
guest what is intended by som but a second tyranny over
10 learning: and will soon put it out of controversie that Bishops
and Presbyters are the same to us both name and thing. That
those evills of Prelaty which before from five or six and
twenty Sees were distributivly charg'd upon the whole
people, will now light wholly upon learning, is not obscure
15 to us: whenas now the Pastor of a small unlearned Parish, on
the sudden shall be exalted Archbishop over a large dioces
of books, and yet not remove, but keep his other cure too, a
mysticall pluralist. He who but of late cry'd down the sole
ordination of every novice Batchelor of Art, and deny'd sole
20 jurisdiction over the simplest Parishioner, shall now at home
in his privat chair assume both these over worthiest and ex-
cellentest books and ablest authors that write them. This is
not, Yee Covnants and Protestations that we have made, this
is not to put down Prelaty, this is but to chop an Episcopacy,
25 this is but to translate the Palace *Metropolitan* from one kind
of dominion into another, this is but an old canonicall slight
of *commuting* our penance. To startle thus betimes at a meer
unlicenc't pamphlet will after a while be afraid of every

conventicle, and a while after will make a conventicle of
every Christian meeting. But I am certain that a State govern'd by the rules of justice and fortitude, or a Church built
and founded upon the rock of faith and true knowledge,
5 cannot be so pusillanimous. While things are yet not constituted in Religion, that freedom of writing should be restrain'd by a discipline imitated from the Prelats, and learnt
by them from the Inquisition to shut us up all again into the
brest of a licencer, must needs give cause of doubt and dis-
10 couragement to all learned and religious men. Who cannot
but discern the finenes of this politic drift, and who are the
contrivers; that while Bishops were to be baited down, then
all Presses might be open; it was the peoples birthright and
priviledge in time of Parlament, it was the breaking forth of
15 light. But now the Bishops abrogated and voided out of the
Church, as if our Reformation sought no more, but to make
room for others into their seats under another name, the
Episcopall arts begin to bud again, the cruse of truth must
run no more oyle, liberty of Printing must be enthrall'd again
20 under a Prelaticall commission of twenty, the privilege of the
people nullify'd, and which is wors, the freedom of learning
must groan again, and to her old fetters; all this the Parlament yet sitting. Although their own late arguments and defences against the Prelats might remember them that this
25 obstructing violence meets for the most part with an event
utterly opposite to the end which it drives at: instead of suppressing sects and schisms, it raises them and invests them
with a reputation: *The punishing of wits enhaunces their au-*

tority, saith the Vicount St. *Albans, and a forbidd'n writing is thought to be a certain spark of truth that flies up in the faces of them who seeke to tread it out.* This order therefore may prove a nursing mother to sects, but I shall easily shew
5 how it will be a step-dame to Truth: and first by disinabling us to the maintenance of what is known already.

Well knows he who uses to consider, that our faith and knowledge thrives by exercise, as well as our limbs and complexion. Truth is compar'd in Scripture to a streaming foun-
10 tain; if her waters flow not in a perpetuall progression, they sick'n into a muddy pool of conformity and tradition. A man may be a heretick in the truth; and if he beleeve things only because his Pastor sayes so, or the Assembly so determins, without knowing other reason, though his belief be true, yet
15 the very truth he holds, becomes his heresie. There is not any burden that som would gladlier post off to another, then the charge and care of their Religion. There be, who knows not that there be of Protestants and professors who live and dye in as arrant an implicit faith, as any lay Papist of Loretto. A
20 wealthy man addicted to his pleasure and to his profits, finds Religion to be a traffick so entangl'd, and of so many piddling accounts, that of all mysteries he cannot skill to keep a stock going upon that trade. What should he doe? fain he would have the name to be religious, fain he would bear up
25 with his neighbours in that. What does he therefore, but resolvs to give over toyling, and to find himself out som factor, to whose care and credit he may commit the whole managing of his religious affairs; som Divine of note and estima-

tion that must be. To him he adheres, resigns the whole ware-
house of his religion, with all the locks and keyes into his
custody; and indeed makes the very person of that man his
religion; esteems his associating with him a sufficient evi-
5 dence and commendatory of his own piety. So that a man
may say his religion is now no more within himself, but is
becom a dividuall movable, and goes and comes neer him,
according as that good man frequents the house. He enter-
tains him, gives him gifts, feasts him, lodges him; his re-
10 ligion comes home at night, praies, is liberally supt, and
sumptuously laid to sleep, rises, is saluted, and after the
malmsey, or some well spic't bruage, and better breakfasted
then he whose morning appetite would have gladly fed on
green figs between *Bethany* and *Ierusalem,* his Religion
15 walks abroad at eight, and leavs his kind entertainer in the
shop trading all day without his religion.

Another sort there be who when they hear that all things
shall be order'd, all things regulated and setl'd; nothing
writt'n but what passes through the custom-house of certain
20 Publicans that have the tunaging and the poundaging of all
free spok'n truth, will strait give themselvs up into your
hands, mak'em & cut'em out what religion ye please; there
be delights, there be recreations and jolly pastimes that will
fetch the day about from sun to sun, and rock the tedious
25 year as in a delightfull dream. What need they torture their
heads with that which others have tak'n so strictly, and so
unalterably into their own pourveying. These are the fruits
which a dull ease and cessation of our knowledge will bring

forth among the people. How goodly, and how to be wisht
were such an obedient unanimity as this, what a fine conformity would it starch us all into? doubtles a stanch and
solid peece of frame-work, as any January could freeze to-
5 gether.

Nor much better will be the consequence ev'n among the
Clergy themselvs; it is no new thing never heard of before,
for a *parochiall* Minister, who has his reward, and is at his
Hercules pillars in a warm benefice, to be easily inclinable,
10 if he have nothing else that may rouse up his studies, to finish
his circuit in an English concordance and a *topic folio,* the
gatherings and savings of a sober graduatship, a *Harmony*
and a *Catena,* treading the constant round of certain common doctrinall heads, attended with their uses, motives,
15 marks and means, out of which as out of an alphabet or sol
fa by forming and transforming, joyning and dis-joyning
variously a little book-craft, and two hours meditation might
furnish him unspeakably to the performance of more then a
weekly charge of sermoning: not to reck'n up the infinit
20 helps of interlinearies, breviaries, *synopses,* and other loiter-
ing gear. But as for the multitude of Sermons ready printed
and pil'd up, on every text that is not difficult, our London
trading St. *Thomas* in his vestry, and adde to boot St. *Martin,*
and St. *Hugh,* have not within their hallow'd limits more
25 vendible ware of all sorts ready made: so that penury he
never need fear of Pulpit provision, having where so plente-
ously to refresh his magazin. But if his rear and flanks be
not impal'd, if his back dore be not secur'd by the rigid

licencer, but that a bold book may now and then issue forth,
and give the assault to some of his old collections in their
trenches, it will concern him then to keep waking, to stand
in watch, to set good guards and sentinells about his receiv'd
5 opinions, to walk the round and counter-round with his fellow inspectors, fearing lest any of his flock be seduc't, who
also then would be better instructed, better exercis'd and disciplin'd. And God send that the fear of this diligence which
must then be us'd, doe not make us affect the lazines of a
10 licencing Church.

For if we be sure we are in the right, and doe not hold the
truth guiltily, which becomes not, if we our selves condemn
not our own weak and frivolous teaching, and the people for
an untaught and irreligious gadding rout, what can be more
15 fair, then when a man judicious, learned, and of a conscience,
for ought we know, as good as theirs that taught us what we
know, shall not privily from house to house, which is more
dangerous, but openly by writing publish to the world what
his opinion is, what his reasons, and wherefore that which is
20 now thought cannot be sound. Christ urg'd it as wherewith
to justifie himself, that he preacht in publick; yet writing is
more publick then preaching; and more easie to refutation,
if need be, there being so many whose businesse and profession meerly it is, to be the champions of Truth; which if they
25 neglect, what can be imputed but their sloth, or unability?

Thus much we are hinder'd and dis-inur'd by this cours
of licencing toward the true knowledge of what we seem to
know. For how much it hurts and hinders the licencers them-

selves in the calling of their Ministery, more then any secular
employment, if they will discharge that office as they ought,
so that of necessity they must neglect either the one duty or
the other, I insist not, because it is a particular, but leave it to
5 their own conscience, how they will decide it there.

There is yet behind of what I purpos'd to lay open, the
incredible losse, and detriment that this plot of licencing puts
us to, more then if som enemy at sea should stop up all our
hav'ns and ports, and creeks, it hinders and retards the im-
10 portation of our richest Marchandize, Truth: nay it was first
establisht and put in practice by Antichristian malice and
mystery on set purpose to extinguish, if it were possible, the
light of Reformation, and to settle falshood; little differing
from that policie wherewith the Turk upholds his *Alcoran,*
15 by the prohibition of Printing. 'Tis not deny'd, but gladly
confest, we are to send our thanks and vows to heav'n, louder
then most of Nations, for that great measure of truth which
we enjoy, especially in those main points between us and the
Pope, with his appertinences the Prelats: but he who thinks
20 we are to pitch our tent here, and have attain'd the utmost
prospect of reformation, that the mortall glasse wherein we
contemplate, can shew us, till we come to *beatific* vision, that
man by this very opinion declares, that he is yet farre short
of Truth.

25 Truth indeed came once into the world with her divine
Master, and was a perfect shape most glorious to look on: but
when he ascended, and his Apostles after him were laid
asleep, then strait arose a wicked race of deceivers, who as

that story goes of the *Ægyptian Typhon* with his conspira-
tors, how they dealt with the good *Osiris,* took the virgin
Truth, hewd her lovely form into a thousand peeces, and
scatter'd them to the four winds. From that time ever since,
5 the sad friends of Truth, such as durst appear, imitating the
carefull search that *Isis* made for the mangl'd body of *Osiris,*
went up and down gathering up limb by limb still as they
could find them. We have not yet found them all, Lords and
Commons, nor ever shall doe, till her Masters second com-
10 ming; he shall bring together every joynt and member, and
shall mould them into an immortall feature of lovelines and
perfection. Suffer not these licencing prohibitions to stand at
every place of opportunity forbidding and disturbing them
that continue seeking, that continue to do our obsequies to
15 the torn body of our martyr'd Saint. We boast our light; but
if we look not wisely on the Sun it self, it smites us into darknes. Who can discern those planets that are oft *Combust,* and
those stars of brightest magnitude that rise and set with the
Sun, untill the opposite motion of their orbs bring them to
20 such a place in the firmament, where they may be seen evning
or morning. The light which we have gain'd, was giv'n us,
not to be ever staring on, but by it to discover onward things
more remote from our knowledge. It is not the unfrocking
of a Priest, the unmitring of a Bishop, and the removing him
25 from off the *Presbyterian* shoulders that will make us a happy
Nation, no, if other things as great in the Church, and in the
rule of life both economicall and politicall be not lookt into
and reform'd, we have lookt so long upon the blaze that

Zuinglius and *Calvin* hath beacon'd up to us, that we are
stark blind. There be who perpetually complain of schisms
and sects, and make it such a calamity that any man dissents
from their maxims.'Tis their own pride and ignorance which
5 causes the disturbing, who neither will hear with meeknes,
nor can convince, yet all must be supprest which is not found
in their *Syntagma*. They are the troublers, they are the di-
viders of unity, who neglect and permit not others to unite
those dissever'd peeces which are yet wanting to the body of
10 Truth. To be still searching what we know not, by what we
know, still closing up truth to truth as we find it (for all her
body is *homogeneal,* and proportionall) this is the golden
rule in *Theology* as well as in Arithmetick, and makes up the
best harmony in a Church; not the forc't and outward union
15 of cold, and neutrall, and inwardly divided minds.

Lords and Commons of England, consider what Nation it
is wherof ye are, and wherof ye are the governours: a Nation
not slow and dull, but of a quick, ingenious, and piercing
spirit, acute to invent, suttle and sinewy to discours, not be-
20 neath the reach of any point the highest that human capacity
can soar to. Therefore the studies of learning in her deepest
Sciences have bin so ancient, and so eminent among us, that
Writers of good antiquity, and ablest judgement have bin
perswaded that ev'n the school of *Pythagoras,* and the *Per-*
25 *sian* wisdom took beginning from the old Philosophy of this
Iland. And that wise and civill Roman, *Julius Agricola,* who
govern'd once here for *Cæsar,* preferr'd the naturall wits of
Britain, before the labour'd studies of the French. Nor is it

for nothing that the grave and frugal *Transilvanian* sends out yearly from as farre as the mountanous borders of *Russia,* and beyond the *Hercynian* wildernes, not their youth, but their stay'd men, to learn our language, and our *theologic*
5 arts. Yet that which is above all this, the favour and the love of heav'n we have great argument to think in a peculiar manner propitious and propending towards us. Why else was this Nation chos'n before any other, that out of her as out of *Sion* should be proclam'd and sounded forth the first tidings and
10 trumpet of Reformation to all *Europ*. And had it not bin the obstinat perversnes of our Prelats against the divine and admirable spirit of *Wicklef,* to suppresse him as a schismatic and *innovator,* perhaps neither the *Bohemian Husse* and *Jerom,* no nor the name of *Luther,* or of *Calvin* had bin ever
15 known: the glory of reforming all our neighbours had bin compleatly ours. But now, as our obdurat Clergy have with violence demean'd the matter, we are become hitherto the latest and the backwardest Schollers, of whom God offer'd to have made us the teachers. Now once again by all concur-
20 rence of signs, and by the generall instinct of holy and devout men, as they daily and solemnly expresse their thoughts, God is decreeing to begin some new and great period in his Church, ev'n to the reforming of Reformation it self: what does he then but reveal Himself to his servants, and as his
25 manner is, first to his English-men; I say as his manner is, first to us, though we mark not the method of his counsels, and are unworthy. Behold now this vast City; a City of refuge, the mansion house of liberty, encompast and surrounded

with his protection; the shop of warre hath not there more
anvils and hammers waking, to fashion out the plates and
instruments of armed Justice in defence of beleaguer'd Truth,
then there be pens and heads there, sitting by their studious
5 lamps, musing, searching, revolving new notions and idea's
wherewith to present, as with their homage and their fealty
the approaching Reformation: others as fast reading, trying
all things, assenting to the force of reason and convincement.
What could a man require more from a Nation so pliant and
10 so prone to seek after knowledge. What wants there to such
a towardly and pregnant soile, but wise and faithfull labour-
ers, to make a knowing people, a Nation of Prophets, of
Sages, and of Worthies. We reck'n more then five months
yet to harvest; there need not be five weeks, had we but eyes
15 to lift up, the fields are white already. Where there is much
desire to learn, there of necessity will be much arguing, much
writing, many opinions; for opinion in good men is but
knowledge in the making. Under these fantastic terrors of
sect and schism, we wrong the earnest and zealous thirst after
20 knowledge and understanding which God hath stirr'd up in
this City. What some lament of, we rather should rejoyce at,
should rather praise this pious forwardnes among men, to
reassume the ill deputed care of their Religion into their
own hands again. A little generous prudence, a little for-
25 bearance of one another, and som grain of charity might win
all these diligences to joyn, and unite into one generall and
brotherly search after Truth; could we but forgoe this Prelaticall tradition of crowding free consciences and Christian

liberties into canons and precepts of men. I doubt not, if some great and worthy stranger should come among us, wise to discern the mould and temper of a people, and how to govern it, observing the high hopes and aims, the diligent
5 alacrity of our extended thoughts and reasonings in the pursuance of truth and freedom, but that he would cry out as *Pirrhus* did, admiring the Roman docility and courage, if such were my *Epirots,* I would not despair the greatest design that could be attempted to make a Church or Kingdom
10 happy. Yet these are the men cry'd out against for schismaticks and sectaries; as if, while the Temple of the Lord was building, some cutting, some squaring the marble, others hewing the cedars, there should be a sort of irrationall men who could not consider there must be many schisms and
15 many dissections made in the quarry and in the timber, ere the house of God can be built. And when every stone is laid artfully together, it cannot be united into a continuity, it can but be contiguous in this world; neither can every peece of the building be of one form; nay rather the perfection con-
20 sists in this, that out of many moderat varieties and brotherly dissimilitudes that are not vastly disproportionall arises the goodly and the gracefull symmetry that commends the whole pile and structure. Let us therefore be more considerat builders, more wise in spirituall architecture, when great reforma-
25 tion is expected. For now the time seems come, wherein *Moses* the great Prophet may sit in heav'n rejoycing to see that memorable and glorious wish of his fulfill'd, when not only our sev'nty Elders, but all the Lords people are become

Prophets. No marvell then though some men, and some good
men too perhaps, but young in goodnesse, as *Joshua* then
was, envy them. They fret, and out of their own weaknes
are in agony, lest these divisions and subdivisions will undoe
5 us. The adversarie again applauds, and waits the hour, when
they have brancht themselves out, saith he, small anough
into parties and partitions, then will be our time. Fool! he
sees not the firm root, out of which we all grow, though into
branches: nor will beware untill he see our small divided
10 maniples cutting through at every angle of his ill united and
unweildy brigade. And that we are to hope better of all these
supposed sects and schisms, and that we shall not need that
solicitude honest perhaps though over timorous of them that
vex in this behalf, but shall laugh in the end, at those ma-
15 licious applauders of our differences, I have these reasons to
perswade me.

First, when a City shall be as it were besieg'd and blockt
about, her navigable river infested, inrodes and incursions
round, defiance and battell oft rumor'd to be marching up
20 ev'n to her walls, and suburb trenches, that then the people,
or the greater part, more then at other times, wholly tak'n up
with the study of highest and most important matters to be
reform'd, should be disputing, reasoning, reading, invent-
ing, discoursing, ev'n to a rarity, and admiration, things not
25 before discourst or writt'n of, argues first a singular good
will, contentednesse and confidence in your prudent fore-
sight, and safe government, Lords and Commons; and from
thence derives it self to a gallant bravery and well grounded

contempt of their enemies, as if there were no small number of as great spirits among us, as his was, who when Rome was nigh besieg'd by *Hanibal,* being in the City, bought that peece of ground at no cheap rate, whereon *Hanibal* himself
5 encampt his own regiment. Next it is a lively and cherfull presage of our happy successe and victory. For as in a body, when the blood is fresh, the spirits pure and vigorous, not only to vital, but to rationall faculties, and those in the acutest, and the pertest operations of wit and suttlety, it
10 argues in what good plight and constitution the body is, so when the cherfulnesse of the people is so sprightly up, as that it has, not only wherewith to guard well its own freedom and safety, but to spare, and to bestow upon the solidest and sub- limest points of controversie, and new invention, it betok'ns
15 us not degenerated, nor drooping to a fatall decay, but cast- ing off the old and wrincl'd skin of corruption to outlive these pangs and wax young again, entring the glorious waies of Truth and prosperous vertue destin'd to become great and honourable in these latter ages. Methinks I see in my mind
20 a noble and puissant Nation rousing herself like a strong man after sleep, and shaking her invincible locks: Methinks I see her as an Eagle muing her mighty youth, and kindling her undazl'd eyes at the full midday beam; purging and un- scaling her long abused sight at the fountain it self of heav'nly
25 radiance; while the whole noise of timorous and flocking birds, with those also that love the twilight, flutter about, amaz'd at what she means, and in their envious gabble would prognosticat a year of sects and schisms.

What should ye doe then, should ye suppresse all this flowry crop of knowledge and new light sprung up and yet springing daily in this City, should ye set an *Oligarchy* of twenty ingrossers over it, to bring a famin upon our minds again, when we shall know nothing but what is measur'd to us by their bushel? Beleeve it, Lords and Commons, they who counsell ye to such a suppressing, doe as good as bid ye suppresse your selves; and I will soon shew how. If it be desir'd to know the immediat cause of all this free writing and free speaking, there cannot be assign'd a truer then your own mild, and free, and human government; it is the liberty, Lords and Commons, which your own valorous and happy counsels have purchast us, liberty which is the nurse of all great wits; this is that which hath rarify'd and enlightn'd our spirits like the influence of heav'n; this is that which hath enfranchis'd, enlarg'd and lifted up our apprehensions degrees above themselves. Ye cannot make us now lesse capable, lesse knowing, lesse eagarly pursuing of the truth, unlesse ye first make your selves, that made us so, lesse the lovers, lesse the founders of our true liberty. We can grow ignorant again, brutish, formall, and slavish, as ye found us; but you then must first become that which ye cannot be, oppressive, arbitrary, and tyrannous, as they were from whom ye have free'd us. That our hearts are now more capacious, our thoughts more erected to the search and expectation of greatest and exactest things, is the issue of your owne vertu propagated in us; ye cannot suppresse that unlesse ye reinforce an abrogated and mercilesse law, that fathers may dis-

patch at will their own children. And who shall then stick closest to ye, and excite others? not he who takes up armes for cote and conduct, and his four nobles of Danegelt. Although I dispraise not the defence of just immunities, yet
5 love my peace better, if that were all. Give me the liberty to know, to utter, and to argue freely according to conscience, above all liberties.

What would be best advis'd then, if it be found so hurtfull and so unequall to suppresse opinions for the newnes, or
10 the unsutablenes to a customary acceptance, will not be my task to say; I only shall repeat what I have learnt from one of your own honourable number, a right noble and pious Lord, who had he not sacrific'd his life and fortunes to the Church and Commonwealth, we had not now mist and bewayl'd a
15 worthy and undoubted patron of this argument. Ye know him I am sure; yet I for honours sake, and may it be eternall to him, shall name him, the Lord *Brook*. He writing of Episcopacy, and by the way treating of sects and schisms, left Ye his vote, or rather now the last words of his dying charge,
20 which I know will ever be of dear and honour'd regard with Ye, so full of meeknes and breathing charity, that next to his last testament, who bequeath'd love and peace to his Disciples, I cannot call to mind where I have read or heard words more mild and peacefull. He there exhorts us to hear with
25 patience and humility those, however they be miscall'd, that desire to live purely, in such a use of Gods Ordinances, as the best guidance of their conscience gives them, and to tolerat them, though in some disconformity to our selves. The book

it self will tell us more at large being publisht to the world, and dedicated to the Parlament by him who both for his life and for his death deserves, that what advice he left be not laid by without perusall.

5 And now the time in speciall is, by priviledge to write and speak what may help to the furder discussing of matters in agitation. The Temple of *Janus* with his two *controversal* faces might now not unsignificantly be set open. And though all the windes of doctrin were let loose to play upon the earth, 10 so Truth be in the field, we do injuriously by licencing and prohibiting to misdoubt her strength. Let her and Falshood grapple; who ever knew Truth put to the wors, in a free and open encounter. Her confuting is the best and surest suppressing. He who hears what praying there is for light and 15 clearer knowledge to be sent down among us, would think of other matters to be constituted beyond the discipline of *Geneva,* fram'd and fabric't already to our hands. Yet when the new light which we beg for shines in upon us, there be who envy, and oppose, if it come not first in at their case- 20 ments. What a collusion is this, whenas we are exhorted by the wise man to use diligence, *to seek for wisdom as for hidd'n treasure*s early and late, that another order shall enjoyn us to know nothing but by statute. When a man hath bin labouring the hardest labour in the deep mines of knowl- 25 edge, hath furnisht out his findings in all their equipage, drawn forth his reasons as it were a battell raung'd, scatter'd and defeated all objections in his way, calls out his adversary into the plain, offers him the advantage of wind and sun, if

he please; only that he may try the matter by dint of argument, for his opponents then to sculk, to lay ambushments, to keep a narrow bridge of licencing where the challenger should passe, though it be valour anough in shouldiership, is
5 but weaknes and cowardise in the wars of Truth. For who knows not that Truth is strong next to the Almighty; she needs no policies, nor stratagems, nor licencings to make her victorious, those are the shifts and the defences that error uses against her power: give her but room, & do not bind her
10 when she sleeps, for then she speaks not true, as the old *Proteus* did, who spake oracles only when he was caught & bound, but then rather she turns herself into all shapes, except her own, and perhaps tunes her voice according to the time, as *Micaiah* did before *Ahab,* untill she be adjur'd into
15 her own likenes. Yet is it not impossible that she may have more shapes then one. What else is all that rank of things indifferent, wherein Truth may be on this side, or on the other, without being unlike her self. What but a vain shadow else is the abolition of *those ordinances, that hand writing*
20 *nayl'd to the crosse,* what great purchase is this Christian liberty which *Paul* so often boasts of. His doctrine is, that he who eats or eats not, regards a day, or regards it not, may doe either to the Lord. How many other things might be tolerated in peace, and left to conscience, had we but charity, and
25 were it not the chief strong hold of our hypocrisie to be ever judging one another. I fear yet this iron yoke of outward conformity hath left a slavish print upon our necks; the ghost of a linnen decency yet haunts us. We stumble and are im-

patient at the least dividing of one visible congregation from
another, though it be not in fundamentalls; and through our
forwardnes to suppresse, and our backwardnes to recover any
enthrall'd peece of truth out of the gripe of custom, we care not
5 to keep truth separated from truth, which is the fiercest rent and
disunion of all. We doe not see that while we still affect by all
means a rigid externall formality, we may as soon fall again
into a grosse conforming stupidity, a stark and dead congeal-
ment of *wood and hay and stubble* forc't and frozen together,
10 which is more to the sudden degenerating of a Church then
many *subdichotomies* of petty schisms. Not that I can think
well of every light separation, or that all in a Church is to be
expected *gold and silver and pretious stones:* it is not possible
for man to sever the wheat from the tares, the good fish from
15 the other frie; that must be the Angels Ministery at the end
of mortall things. Yet if all cannot be of one mind, as who
looks they should be? this doubtles is more wholsome, more
prudent, and more Christian that many be tolerated, rather
then all compell'd. I mean not tolerated Popery, and open
20 superstition, which as it extirpats all religions and civill su-
premacies, so it self should be extirpat, provided first that all
charitable and compassionat means be us'd to win and regain the weak and the misled: that also which is impious or
evil absolutely either against faith or maners no law can pos-
25 sibly permit, that intends not to unlaw it self: but those
neighboring differences, or rather indifferences, are what I
speak of, whether in some point of doctrine or of discipline,
which though they may be many, yet need not interrupt *the*

unity of Spirit, if we could but find among us *the bond of peace.* In the mean while if any one would write, and bring his helpfull hand to the slow-moving Reformation which we labour under, if Truth have spok'n to him before others, or
5 but seem'd at least to speak, who hath so bejesuited us that we should trouble that man with asking licence to doe so worthy a deed? and not consider this, that if it come to prohibiting, there is not ought more likely to be prohibited then truth it self; whose first appearance to our eyes blear'd and
10 dimm'd with prejudice and custom, is more unsightly and unplausible then many errors, ev'n as the person is of many a great man slight and contemptible to see to. And what doe they tell us vainly of new opinions, when this very opinion of theirs, that none must be heard, but whom they like, is the
15 worst and newest opinion of all others; and is the chief cause why sects and schisms doe so much abound, and true knowledge is kept at distance from us; besides yet a greater danger which is in it. For when God shakes a Kingdome with strong and healthfull commotions to a generall reforming,
20 'tis not untrue that many sectaries and false teachers are then busiest in seducing; but yet more true it is, that God then raises to his own work men of rare abilities, and more then common industry not only to look back and revise what hath bin taught heretofore, but to gain furder and goe on, some
25 new enlightn'd steps in the discovery of truth. For such is the order of Gods enlightning his Church, to dispense and deal out by degrees his beam, so as our earthly eyes may best sustain it. Neither is God appointed and confin'd, where and

out of what place these his chosen shall be first heard to
speak; for he sees not as man sees, chooses not as man chooses,
lest we should devote our selves again to set places, and as-
semblies, and outward callings of men; planting our faith one
5 while in the old Convocation house, and another while in the
Chappell at Westminster; when all the faith and religion
that shall be there canoniz'd, is not sufficient without plain
convincement, and the charity of patient instruction to supple
the least bruise of conscience, to edifie the meanest Christian,
10 who desires to walk in the Spirit, and not in the letter of
human trust, for all the number of voices that can be there
made; no though *Harry* the 7. himself there, with all his
leige tombs about him, should lend them voices from the
dead, to swell their number. And if the men be erroneous
15 who appear to be the leading schismaticks, what witholds
us but our sloth, our self-will, and distrust in the right
cause, that we doe not give them gentle meetings and gentle
dismissions, that we debate not and examin the matter
throughly with liberall and frequent audience; if not for their
20 sakes, yet for our own? seeing no man who hath tasted learning, but will confesse the many waies of profiting by those
who not contented with stale receits are able to manage, and
set forth new positions to the world. And were they but as
the dust and cinders of our feet, so long as in that notion they
25 may yet serve to polish and brighten the armoury of Truth,
ev'n for that respect they were not utterly to be cast away.
But if they be of those whom God hath fitted for the speciall
use of these times with eminent and ample gifts, and those

perhaps neither among the Priests, nor among the Pharisees, and we in the hast of a precipitant zeal shall make no distinction, but resolve to stop their mouths, because we fear they come with new and dangerous opinions, as we com-
5 monly forejudge them ere we understand them, no lesse then woe to us, while thinking thus to defend the Gospel, we are found the persecutors.

There have bin not a few since the beginning of this Parlament, both of the Presbytery and others who by their un-
10 licenc't books to the contempt of an *Imprimatur* first broke that triple ice clung about our hearts, and taught the people to see day: I hope that none of those were the perswaders to renew upon us this bondage which they themselves have wrought so much good by contemning. But if neither the
15 check that *Moses* gave to young *Joshua,* nor the countermand which our Saviour gave to young *John,* who was so ready to prohibit those whom he thought unlicenc't, be not anough to admonish our Elders how unacceptable to God their testy mood of prohibiting is, if neither their own remembrance
20 what evill hath abounded in the Church by this lett of licencing, and what good they themselves have begun by transgressing it, be not anough, but that they will perswade, and execute the most *Dominican* part of the Inquisition over us, and are already with one foot in the stirrup so active at sup-
25 pressing, it would be no unequall distribution in the first place to suppresse the suppressors themselves; whom the change of their condition hath puft up, more then their late experience of harder times hath made wise.

And as for regulating the Presse, let no man think to have
the honour of advising ye better then your selves have done
in that Order publisht next before this, that no book be
Printed, unlesse the Printers and the Authors name, or at
5 least the Printers be register'd. Those which otherwise come
forth, if they be found mischievous and libellous, the fire and
the executioner will be the timeliest and the most effectuall
remedy, that mans prevention can use. For this *authentic*
Spanish policy of licencing books, if I have said ought, will
10 prove the most unlicenc't book it self within a short while;
and was the immediat image of a Star-chamber decree to that
purpose made in those very times when that Court did the
rest of those her pious works, for which she is now fall'n
from the Starres with *Lucifer*. Whereby ye may guesse what
15 kinde of State prudence, what love of the people, what care
of Religion, or good manners there was at the contriving,
although with singular hypocrisie it pretended to bind books
to their good behaviour. And how it got the upper hand of
your precedent Order so well constituted before, if we may
20 beleeve those men whose profession gives them cause to
enquire most, it may be doubted there was in it the fraud of
some old *patentees* and *monopolizers* in the trade of book-
selling; who under pretence of the poor in their Company
not to be defrauded, and the just retaining of each man his
25 severall copy, which God forbid should be gainsaid, brought
divers glosing colours to the House, which were indeed but
colours, and serving to no end except it be to exercise a supe-
riority over their neighbours, men who doe not therefore

labour in an honest profession to which learning is indetted, that they should be made other mens vassalls. Another end is thought was aym'd at by some of them in procuring by petition this Order, that having power in their hands, malignant
5 books might the easier scape abroad, as the event shews. But of these *Sophisms* and *Elenchs* of marchandize I skill not: This I know, that errors in a good government and in a bad are equally almost incident; for what Magistrate may not be mis-inform'd, and much the sooner, if liberty of Printing be
10 reduc't into the power of a few; but to redresse willingly and speedily what hath bin err'd, and in highest autority to esteem a plain advertisement more then others have done a sumptuous bribe, is a vertue (honour'd Lords and Commons) answerable to Your highest actions, and whereof
15 none can participat but greatest and wisest men.

The End.

NOTES

THE JUDGEMENT OF MARTIN BUCER

T*HE Judgement of Martin Bucer concerning Divorce* was published in July, 1644; there was no other edition during Milton's lifetime. The present text is printed from a photostat of the first edition in the New York Public Library.

PAGE 3
—8 Mr.] M^r THE TITLES, Mr. AND Dr., APPEAR THUS IN THE ORIGINAL, AND HAVE BEEN SILENTLY CHANGED AS IN THE TEXT.
PAGE 4
—10 the] The
PAGE 5
—4 *Ibid.*] *Ibid,*   —18 *Martyr,*] *Martyr*
PAGE 10
—2 *the true*] *the the true*
PAGE 11
—13 *any man*] *anyman*   —15 *in the*] in the
PAGE 27
—22 *Authent.*] *Authent*
PAGE 31
—7 'Tis] T'is
PAGE 45
—9 female] famale

TETRACHORDON

The title-page of *Tetrachordon* bears the date 1645. Thomason, however, in his copy, now in the British Museum, has fixed the date more exactly by crossing out the 5 and writing the date "March 4, 1644." Books published near March 25 often bore the date of the year about to begin. No other edition appeared in Milton's lifetime. The present text is printed from a photostat of the first edition in the Columbia University Library.

PAGE 63
—19 *perswasion*] *perswaston*
PAGE 64
—18 *I*] I
PAGE 89
—20 without] withour
PAGE 100
—26 *&c.*] &c.   —28 thing.] thing,
PAGE 107
—26 divorce.] divorce,
PAGE 108
—19 in] *in*
PAGE 111
—1 *Mark*] *Mark.*
PAGE 112
—16 Chap. 26] *Chap.* 26
PAGE 113
—14 NO BRACKETS IN THE ORIGINAL.
PAGE 118
—1 Sabbath,] Sabbath
PAGE 123
—16 ransom,] ransom.
PAGE 133
—16 confus'd!] confus'd?
PAGE 138
—15 *It*] *It* PRECEDED BY A BRACKET.   he.] he
PAGE 140
—3 Ye] ye   —5 Judiciall] judiciall
PAGE 141
—8 in] *in*   —27 if] If
PAGE 144
—27 *wife.*] *wife*
PAGE 145
—6 madnesse,] madnesse.
PAGE 147
—1 (for)] (For)
PAGE 149
—21 forbidd] farbidd
PAGE 150
—13 notes,] notes.
PAGE 153
—14 explain'd.] explain'd

Page 156
—3 which] wich   —24 heart] heatt
Page 167
—4 them to] themt , o   corrected from the errata.
Page 168
—9 undiscoverably.] undiscoverably
Page 169
—26 *the*] *the the*
Page 170
—12 yet] yer
Page 171
—14 to either] toeeither
Page 172
—6 infirmity).] infirmity)
Page 177
—6 Matt. 5th.] no bracket.
Page 179
—21 *Divorce,*] *Divorce.*
Page 182
—23 *adultery.*] no bracket.
Page 189
—7 suffice.] suffice,   —25 endevor'd] endevo'rd
Page 190
—25 *away.*] no bracket.
Page 191
—7 reasons] rea- divided on the line; the last four letters are omitted in the next line.
Page 193
—3 *Infidels,*] *Infidels*
Page 194
—8 *I,*] *If*
Page 199
—6 commanded] conmanded
Page 206
—8 *determin'd*] *determi'nd*
Page 212
—4 *Cor.*] *Cor,*
Page 213
—20 *Agatha*] *Agatba*
Page 215
—25 successors] successor

PAGE 217
—8 *Basilius Macedo*] *Basilius, Macedo*   CORRECTED FROM THE
ERRATA.   —12 This] this
PAGE 222
—10 *Tolouse,*] *Tolouse*   —11 *Wicklef,*] *Wicklef.*
PAGE 224
—5 in] *in*
PAGE 231
—1 piety,] piety   —3 patient] pati-tient   DIVIDED ON THE
LINE.   —26 *usage;*] *usage?*

AT THE FOOT OF THE LAST PAGE, THE FIRST EDITION PRINTS THE
FOLLOWING
Errata.
Pag. 57. *lin.* 16 *and by them to prosecute, no comma between.*
Pag. 88. *lin.* 3. Basilius Macedo, *no comma between.*

COLASTERION

Colasterion was published on the same day as *Tetrachordon,* according to Thomason, who has written in the British
Museum copy "March 4, 1644." The title-page of the first,
and only edition published in Milton's lifetime, has the date
1645. The present text is printed from a photostat of the first
edition in the New York Public Library.

PAGE 237
—22 printed] Printed
PAGE 239
—13 Doctrine,] Doctrine.
PAGE 240
—14 then.] then,
PAGE 242
—8 Learn] learn
PAGE 243
—15 mischeif.] mischeif,
PAGE 250
—12 any.] any,
PAGE 251
—3 mariage.] mariage,

PAGE 252
—1 preaches] Preaches
PAGE 255
—20 and *John*] *and John*
PAGE 258
—24 *sake,*] *sake.*
PAGE 259
—16 *Beneficiis,*] *Beneficiis.*
PAGE 266
—6 occasion] oc-sion DIVIDED ON THE LINE.
PAGE 268
—17 it.] it,
PAGE 271
—7 maintains.] maintains?   —21 and] *and*

OF EDUCATION

The text is that of the second edition, being the last published in Milton's lifetime. It occupies pages 95 to 117 of "Poems, &c upon Several Occasions," 1673, of which the copy in the library of Columbia University has been collated with two copies in the New York Public Library. The three copies were identical, except for a difference in the address of the publisher, on the title-page, which reads "Printed for Tho. Dring at the White Lion next Xahncery Lane End, in Fleet-Street. 1673" in one of the New York Public Library copies, instead of "Printed for Tho. Dring at the Blew Anchor next Mitre Court over against Fetter Lane in Fleet-street. 1673" as in the other two. The present text was set from a photostat of the Columbia University Library copy.

The following notes refer to collation with the first edition, 1644, a pamphlet of eight pages, lacking title-page, date, and publisher, the copy used being in the New York Public Library.

OF EDUCATION

Written above twenty Years since.] NOT IN 1644.

—1 Mr. *Hartlib,*] *Master Hartlib,* —2 do] doe —3 memory] memory, —5 mankind] mankinde Nevertheless] Neverthelesse —6 designs] designes, —7 Nation] nation —10 mind] minde pursuance] persuance —14 laws] lawes —18 far] farre —19 Island] Iland —22 forreign] forreigne

—2 here] heer —4 think] thinke —6 over-ponderous] over ponderous —7 profess] professe —8 incidental] incidentall Discourses] discourses —9 and] & —13 try] trie —18 far] farre —20 Brief] Briefe —21 Nation] nation extream] extreame —22 spoken] spok'n —27 are, as it were,] are as it were —28 years] yeers

—3 ruines] ruins —4 Parents] parents —9 self] selfe clearly] cleerly —13 Nation] nation —14 enough] anough kind] kinde Learning] learning —15 Languages] languages —16 Language] language —17 Instrument] instrument —18 Linguist] linguist himself] himselfe —19 Tongues] tongues —20 Words & Lexicons] words and lexicons —22 Yeoman or Tradesman] yeoman or tradesman Mother] mother —23 Dialect] dialect —24 Learning] learning unsuccessful] unsuccessfull —25 amiss] amisse years] yeers —26 Latine] Latin, —27 year] yeer —28 behind] behinde

—2 Schools] schools —3 Children] children —4 Verses] verses, judgment] judgement —5 final] finall reading] reading, —8 Nose] nose —19 rational] rationall —20 Languages] languages —22 usual] usuall —23 Universities] universities —24 grossness] grossnesse —26 Novices] novices —28 Metaphysicks] 1673 Metapysicks 1644 metaphysicks

—1 and] & —3 climate] climat —4 turmoil'd] turmoild fadomless] fadomles —6 Learning] learning —7 Notions] notions Babblements] babblements —8 delightful] delightfull —9 years] yeers several] severall —13 prudent] prudent, —18 Court] court Aphorisms] aphorisms —24 unless] unlesse —25 undertaken] undertak'n And these

are the fruits] And these are the errours, these are the fruits   —27
meer] meere

PAGE 280

—1 you no longer] you now no longer   —2 do] doe   —6
Harp] harp   —10 Wits] wits   —13 compleat] compleate
—15 publick] publike   —16 Peace] peace   War] war
—17 less] lesse   —20 find] finde   —24 do] doe

PAGE 281

—1 general] generall   *Lilly*] Lilly   —3 Edifices] edifices
—4 needful] needfull   —5 Land] land   Learning] learning
—6 Civility] civility   less] lesse   —7 Company] company
—8 Troops] troops   Cavalry] cavalry   —9 Studies] studies
Exercise] exercise   —10 Diet] diet   —11 Studies] studies
—14 clear] cleer   near] neer   —15 Vowels] vowels
Englishmen] Englishmen   —16 far Northerly] farre northerly
do] doe   —17 Tongue] tongue   —18 Nations] nations
—19 Latine] Latin   —20 Law-French] law French   —21
Grammar] grammar   —24 delightful Book] delightfull book
—25 store,] store   —27 authority] authoritie   —28 Books]
books   pieces] peeces

PAGE 282

—2 Lectures and Explanations] lectures and explanations   —4
Learning] learning   Vertue] vertue   —6 Patriots] patriots
—7 ill-taught] ill taught   —8 liberal Exercises] liberall exercises
—9 Eloquence] eloquence   —10 effectual] effectuall   —15
matchless] matchlesse   —17 Elements] elements   —18 bed-
time] bed time   —23 difficulty] difficultie   years] yeers
—25 Country] country   —26 Soil] soil   waste] wast
—27 *Hercules*] Hercules   half] halfe   —28 read (which
. . . daily)] read, which . . . daily,

PAGE 283

—1 chuse] choose   —3 Maps; first] maps first   —4 names,
and] names; and   —5 natural] naturall   —9 Historical]
Historicall   —11 access] accesse   *Vitruvius*] Vitruvius
—12 *Seneca's* natural] *Senecas* naturall   —13 *Arithmetick*]
Arithmetic   —14 general] generall   —16 instrumental]
instrumentall   —17 Architecture] *Architecture*   Navigation]
navigation   —18 natural] naturall   leisurely] leisurly
—19 Meteors] *Meteors*   Minerals] minerals   Creatures]
creatures   far] farre   —21 Writer] writer   Institution]
institution   —22 humours] humors   —24 do] doe   only]
onely   Physitian] Physician   himself] himselfe   —26

frugal and expenseless means] frugall, and expencelesse meanes   —28
pity] pitty   less] lesse

PAGE 284

—1 Commander] commander   —2 Nature and Mathematicks]
nature & mathematicks   —3 shal] shall   needful] needfull
helpful] helpfull   —4 Fowlers] fowlers   Apothecaries]
Apothecaries   —5 Architects] *Architects*   —6 Anatomists]
Anatomists   doubtless] doubtlesse   —7 hopeful] hopefull
—8 natural] naturall   —9 daily] dayly   —13 rural] rurall
Virgil] Virgil   —14 years] yeers   general] generall
—17 contemplate] contemplat   moral] morall   evil] evill
—18 special] speciall   —20 Vertue] vertue   Vice] vice
—22 moral] morall   —25 determinate] determinat   *David*]
David,   Evanges] Evangels   —26 Apostolic Scriptures]
Apostolic scriptures   perfect] perfit   —27 personal] personall

PAGE 285

—1 odd] odde   Tongue] tongue   —2 wariness] warinesse,
—3 taste] tast   Comedies,] comedies   —4 Tragedies]
tragedies   treat] treate   Houshold] household   —5
Alcestis] Alcestis   —6 *Politicks*] *Politics*   —7 Political
Societies] politicall societies   —8 Common-wealth] common-
wealth   Reeds] reeds   —9 Conscience] conscience
Counsellers] counsellers   —11 Law] law   —12 legal Justice]
legall justice   —13 far] farre   —15 Tables] tables
—17 Laws] laws   *England*] England   —20 Tongue] tongue
—22 original] originall   add] adde   —23 Dialect] dialect
—25 *Heroic Poems*] *heroic poems*   Tragedies] tragedies   stateliest]
stateliest,   —26 Political Orations] Politicall orations

PAGE 286

—2 spirit] spirit,   —7 useful] usefull   —8 Heads] heads
—12 less] lesse   —15 Grammar] grammar   —16 Art] art
Poetics] *poetics*   —17 Commentaries] commentaries   —18
Poem] poem   —19 Decorum] decorum   —20 master-piece]
master-peece   —21 common] 1673 comm 1644 common
Rimers and Play-writers] rimers and play-writes   —22 religious]
Religious   —25 Writers and Composers] writers and composers
—27 universal] universall   —28 Counsel] counsell

PAGE 287

—2 Visages] visages   —2 stuff] stuffe   —3 trial] triall
—5 Studies] studies   Youth] youth   —7 unless] unlesse
—8 methodical] methodicall   —14 Roman Legion] Romane
legion   —15 Exercises] exercises,   Recreations] recreations

—18 Study] study   —19 guess] guesse   —20 Schools]
schools   —22 Orators] orators   —23 Studies] studies
—25 Common-wealth] common-wealth   —27 Youth] youth
War] warre

PAGE 288

—1 Gown] gown   —2 War] warre   —3 half] halfe
Noon] noon   —4 Exercise] exercise   —7 Weapon] weapon
—10 means] meanes   large and] large, and   —11 fearless]
fearlesse   —12 Lectures] lectures   Precepts] precepts
—13 Fortitude and Patience] fortitude, and patience   —15 Locks]
locks   —16 Gripes of Wrastling] gripes of wrastling   —17
tugg or grapple] tugg, to grapple   —18 enough] anough
—23 Musick] music   heard or] heard, or   —23 skilful]
skilfull   —25 artful] artfull   —26 chords] cords
choice Composer] choise composer   —27 Organ] organ   —28
Voices] voices   martial] martiall   civil Ditties] civill ditties

PAGE 289

—1 and Prophets] & prophets   —3 harshness] harshnesse
—4 Meat] meat   —5 Nature] nature   —6 minds] mindes
back] backe   —10 Roman] Romane   —11 Horseback] horse
back   —12 Art of Cavalry] art of cavalry   —13 exactness]
exactnesse   daily] dayly   —14 Embattelling] embatailing
Marching] marching   Encamping] encamping   —15
Fortifying, Besieging and Battering] fortifying, beseiging and battering
—16 *Tacticks*] Tactiks   —17 War] warre   —19 Country]
country   —20 hopeful] hopefull   —23 and] &   Colonels]
Colonells   —24 Company] company,   quaff] quaffe   convey]
convay   —26 over-masterd] overmaster'd   —27 souldery]
souldiery   —28 No] no

PAGE 290

—1 Governours] governours   —5 self] selfe   year] yeer
—6 sullenness] sullenesse   —8 Heaven] heaven   Earth]
earth   —10 year] yeer   —11 Companies] companies
Guides] guides   —12 Land] land   —13 Towns] towns
—14 Tillage, Harbours and Ports for Trade] tillage, harbours and
Ports for trade   Sometimes] Somtimes   —15 Sea] sea   far]
farre   —16 practical] practicall   Sea-fight] sea fight   —17
ways] wayes   try] trie   Nature] nature   —19] self] selfe
—20 Nation] nation   —21 Vertues] vertues   Excellencies]
excellencies   —22 far] farre   purity] puritie   —24 Youth]
youth   prodigal] prodigall   —26 Mimicks, Apes and] mimics,
apes &   —27 Countries] countries   years] yeers   —28

Principles but] principles, but   Experience] experience
PAGE 291
—2 pass] passe   —5 Breeding] breeding   —7 Diet] diet
—8 House] house   —10 healthful] healthfull   moderate]
moderat   —11 Mr.] Master   general] generall   —12
several] severall   —14 beginning as] beginning, as   —15
Cradle] cradle   —18 trial] triall   enough] anough   —19
Bow] bow   —20 himself a Teacher] himselfe a teacher   —21
equal] equall   *Homer*] Homer   *Ulysses*] Ulysses   —27
enough] anough

AREOPAGITICA

Areopagitica; a Speech of Mr. John Milton For the Liberty of Unlicenc'd Printing, To the Parliament of England was published in London in 1644 without indication of printer or book-seller and without licence. On the title-page of the copy in the Thomason Collection appear in Thomason's autograph the words, *"Ex dono Authoris,"* and the date, November 24. A copy presented by Milton to John Rous is preserved in the Bodleian Library at Oxford, and another presented by Milton to Patrick Young is preserved in the library of Trinity College, Dublin. The occasion of the work arose from the acrimonious discussion of toleration which followed the publication of *An Apologeticall Narration* on or before January 3, 1644, by the Independent members of the Westminster Assembly. This led to the attempt on the part of the Assembly to persuade Parliament to enforce against John Goodwin, Roger Williams, Milton and others the ordinance for licensing the press which had been adopted on June 14, 1643. On August 13, 1644, Herbert Palmer preached before Parliament a sermon against toleration in which Milton was condemned as the author of *The Doctrine and Discipline of*

Divorce. On August 24 The Stationers' Company petitioned Parliament for stricter enforcement of the licensing ordinance and cited Milton as one of the transgressors of the law. (Masson, *Life,* III, 161, 265.) *Areopagitica* was Milton's reply to these attacks, specific reference being made in his concluding pages to the Stationers' Company. In his *Second Defence* Milton says, "I wrote my Areopagitica, in order to deliver the press from the restraints with which it was encumbered."

The text of the present edition has been set up from a photostat of an original copy in the Yale University Library. This has been collated with a photostat of the Thomason copy. A copy in the New York Public Library and the Rous copy in the Bodleian have also been examined by the editor. All copies mentioned appear to be identical. In the text as here given a few obvious omissions and misprints have been corrected and recorded in the notes which follow.

PAGE 311

—8 wayfaring] THAT MILTON INTENDED warfaring SEEMS NOT IMPROBABLE. THERE ARE EXTANT THREE COPIES OF THE ORIGINAL EDITION WHICH IN ALL PROBABILITY PASSED THROUGH HIS HANDS (P. 366). IN EACH AS IN SEVERAL OTHER COPIES EXAMINED BY THE EDITOR y HAS HERE BEEN STRUCK OUT BY THE PEN AND r INSERTED ABOVE THE LINE. IN NONE OF THE THREE COPIES MENTIONED DOES ANY SIMILAR EMENDATION APPEAR ELSEWHERE IN THE TEXT. IN EACH CASE INK AND WRITING APPEAR CONTEMPORARY, AND THE EMENDATION IS MADE IN THE SAME WAY. THE FORM OF MILTON'S r IN EXTANT AUTOGRAPHS IS SUCH AS MIGHT EASILY HAVE BEEN MISTAKEN BY A PRINTER FOR y. THE INSERTED r IN THIS INSTANCE CLOSELY RESEMBLES HIS y. THAT THE INSERTION WAS MADE BY THE AUTHOR'S OWN HAND IS NOT UNLIKELY. COMPARE *Doctrine and Discipline of Divorce* (VOL. III, PT. 2, P. 373), what more suttle stratagem against our Christian warfare.

PAGE 314
  —28 judgement] judgemenr
PAGE 319
  —12 eyes;] eyes
PAGE 322
  —25 doubtlesse] doublesse
PAGE 345
  —12 Lords] Lord

COLUMBIA UNIVERSITY PRESS
Columbia University
New York

————

FOREIGN AGENT
OXFORD UNIVERSITY PRESS
Humphrey Milford
Amen House, London, E.C.

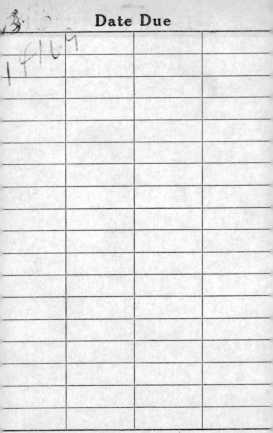

Date Due